Understanding Race, Class, Gender, and Sexuality

A Conceptual Framework

Lynn Weber

University of South Carolina

Boston Burr Ridge, IL Dubuque, IA Madison, WI New York
San Francisco St. Louis Bangkok Bogotá Caracas Kuala Lumpur
Lisbon London Madrid Mexico City Milan Montreal New Delhi
Santiago Seoul Singapore Sydney Taipei Toronto

McGraw-Hill Higher Education

*A Division of The **McGraw-Hill** Companies*

UNDERSTANDING RACE, CLASS, GENDER, AND SEXUALITY
A CONCEPTUAL FRAMEWORK

Published by McGraw-Hill, an imprint of The McGraw-Hill Companies, Inc. 1221 Avenue of the Americas, New York, NY, 10020.

This book is printed on acid-free paper.

1 2 3 4 5 6 7 8 9 0 FGR/FGR 0 9 8 7 6 5 4 3 2 1

ISBN 0-07-243461-9

Editorial director: *Phillip A. Butcher*
Sponsoring editor: *Sally Constable*
Developmental editor: *Katherine Blake*
Project manager: *Laura Griffin*
Manager, new book production: *Melonie Salvati*
Designer: *Matthew Baldwin*
Supplement coordinator: *Joyce J. Chappetto*
Cover design: *Adam Rooke*
Cover illustration: *Diana Ong/SuperStock*
Compositor: *Shepherd Incorporated*
Typeface: *10/12 Times Roman*
Printer: *Quebecor World Fairfield Inc.*

Library of Congress Cataloging-in-Publication Data

Weber, Lynn.
   Understanding race, class, gender, and sexuality : a conceptual framework / Lynn Weber.
     p. cm.
   Includes bibliographical references and index.
   ISBN 0-07-243461-9 (alk. paper)
   1. Social stratification. 2. Race discrimination. 3. Sex discrimination. I. Title.

HM821 .W44 2001
305--dc21

00-048679

www.mhhe.com

Brief Contents

Section Three
A RACE, CLASS, GENDER, AND SEXUALITY
ANALYSIS OF EDUCATION

Contents

Section Three
A RACE, CLASS, GENDER, AND SEXUALITY ANALYSIS
OF EDUCATION

About the Author

Lynn Weber has been the Director of Women's Studies and a Professor of Sociology at the University of South Carolina since 1996. She arrived at South Carolina after serving two years as Distinguished Professor in Race, Class, and Gender at the University of Delaware and having spent the previous 13 years co-founding and later directing the Center for Research on Women at the University of Memphis.

Founded in 1982 by Weber, Bonnie Thornton Dill, and Elizabeth Higginbotham, the Center for Research on Women was the first in the nation to focus on women of color and on the intersections of race, class, and gender. Over the years, Weber—in conjunction with many scholars associated with the Center—provided pioneering scholarship on race, class, and gender and served as a leader in innovative teaching and curriculum change focused on race, class, and gender. Many of today's leading race, class, and gender scholars have been deeply involved with the work of the Center, serving on the faculty, on the advisory board, as visiting scholars, and as curriculum workshop leaders and participants. These scholars include Patricia Hill Collins, Maxine Baca Zinn, Evelyn Nakano Glenn, Judith Rollins, Esther Chow, Elaine Bell Kaplan, Cheryl Gilkes, Kenneth Goings, Sharon Harley, Leith Mullings, Sandra Morgen, Kathy Ward, Denise Segura, Ruth Zambrana, Mary Romero, Bernice Barnett, Sheryl Ruzek, and many others. For the pioneering research of the center, Weber, Dill, and Higginbotham received the Jessie Bernard Award of the American Sociological Association in 1993, and for innovative pedagogical work, they received the ASA's Distinguished Contributions to Teaching Award in the same year—a dual honor never bestowed before or since.

Co-author of *The American Perception of Class,* Weber has published on the intersections of race, class, and gender—especially in the process of upward social mobility, in mental health, and in the lives of professional-managerial women. In addition, she has published articles on teaching race, class, and gender, including the lead article, "A Conceptual Framework for Understanding Race, Class, Gender, and Sexuality," in a recent special issue of *Psychology of Women Quarterly* devoted to teaching about gender and ethnicity.

Weber has consulted with many higher education institutions of all types on ways to integrate race, class, and gender into the curriculum. Her special focus has been on classroom dynamics and ways to convey difficult and potentially volatile material so that learning is enhanced.

Preface

By the time I reached the University of Delaware for my sabbatical in the fall of 1994, I was burned out. I had been administering the Center for Research on Women at the University of Memphis for the previous 12 years, a rewarding but continuous struggle.[1] I had been writing and running grants for which the time-tables were always too short, the money too little, and the deadlines too soon.

Because I always felt unprepared, it had been a while since I had walked into a classroom feeling excited. I fell behind in reading the latest works in the growing field of race, class, gender, and sexuality, and I felt that I hadn't revised my pedagogy enough. Despite receiving consistently good teaching evaluations from my students and being the recipient of an ASA teaching award, I had begun to think of myself as a bad teacher.

But, as the Distinguished Visiting Professor in Race, Class, and Gender at the University of Delaware, I was teaching only one course, a graduate seminar in race, class, and gender. I had few other responsibilities. I read, rested, exercised, thought, and taught. I loved teaching again. I went to class feeling prepared, a luxury in today's academy, and I began to see that I hadn't been a bad teacher after all—just an exhausted one. As I became energized in my teaching, I started to address a problem that had bothered me for some time—namely, the lack of a conceptual framework for evaluating the scholarship on, and for teaching about, the nature of race, class, gender, and sexuality as systems of oppression.

Those of us who had been teaching about the intersections of race, class, gender, and sexuality had relied on anthologies[2] or course packets of articles and books to demonstrate how these systems of social inequality operate simultaneously and are inextricably intertwined, and thus must be examined together. Yet, while the anthologies very clearly illustrate how truly interconnected these systems are—especially in our individual lives—they fail to provide us with a frame-

---

[1]For a history of the Center for Research on Women, see Weber, Higginbotham, and Dill (1998).
[2]For a list of some of these anthologies, see Weber and Dillaway (2001), *Understanding Race, Class, Gender, and Sexuality: Case Studies*. New York: McGraw-Hill.

work for conducting such analyses ourselves or for assessing the studies we read for their effectiveness and quality in revealing the intersecting dynamics and fundamental character of race, class, gender, and sexuality.

Even as I began this project, I had doubts that it should be done. The study of race, class, gender, and sexuality arose primarily from women of color, from working-class and lesbian scholars who critiqued feminist scholarship for its unstated and unproblematized White, middle-class, Eurocentric, and heterosexual bent. In their critiques, these scholars contended that, to be inclusive, feminist scholarship should be historically and geographically/globally situated—in time and place—and clear about the social locations or standpoints of the groups studied and the scholars themselves. Furthermore, the critiques implied that claiming to have uncovered universal or at least pervasive truths about women and gender from analyses that were based only on dominant-culture women's lives was as problematic as the universal claims of male-centered scholarship that White feminists had so vehemently and correctly contradicted.[3] So, I had to ask myself if it would be possible to construct a conceptual framework for understanding race, class, gender, and sexuality that would not be abstract and ahistorical and a replication of the very model it would be designed to replace.

As it turned out, I didn't have to ponder these possibilities for too long, for I was thrust into this book project by a request that made the need for such a framework even more clear to me. I was asked to be one of six scholars of race, class, gender, and sexuality to write a response to an article entitled "Doing Difference," by Candace West and Sarah Fenstermaker (1995), which *Gender & Society* was planning to publish in a forthcoming issue of the journal (see Collins et al. 1995). Earlier, West and Don Zimmerman (1987) had written an influential piece entitled "Doing Gender" that made a case for the social construction of gender but was subsequently criticized for omission of race and class. "Doing Difference" was written in response to the criticism. At the time, I thought writing my response to "Doing Difference" would give me a chance to clarify the common themes I had started to identify in the scholarship on race, class, gender, and sexuality. I even hoped that West and Fenstermaker would give us the framework that I was looking for.

However, as I read that piece, I became angry. Surprised at my own reaction, I began frantically writing about all the problems I had with the article. Most significantly, I felt their argument—that gender, race, and class are, foremost, patterns of behavior created in small-group, face-to-face interactions—minimized the ways that the macro-institutional, political, economic, and ideological power arrangements shape every interaction among individuals in our society. To fail to make the connection between these face-to-face interactions and the historically embedded political, economic, and ideological structures shaping the nation was to miss the point.

I wrote and wrote and quickly realized that my response had gone way beyond the couple of pages I would be allotted. More importantly, I came to see that

---

[3]For an example of these debates in which I participated, see Baca Zinn et al. (1986).

my reaction was so intense because West's and Fenstermaker's argument had run counter to several of the characteristic themes and common assumptions that ran through the scholarship on race, class, gender, and sexuality. At that point, I realized that I wanted and needed to write a book.

The book that I have written is in many ways a collaborative effort, which includes the feedback and understandings about curriculum transformation that I gained from faculty from across the nation in workshops beginning in the early 1980s at the Center for Research on Women. It reflects the perspective I developed from years of working with Bonnie Thornton Dill and Elizabeth Higginbotham. More directly, in the early stages of work on the book, I benefited from brainstorming sessions and the critical pedagogical, empirical, and theoretical insights of two good colleagues—Higginbotham and Tina Hancock. They were especially helpful in thinking about the use of case studies in the book. Over the next few years, as I continued to work on the conceptual framework, I was invited to publish it as the lead article in a special issue of *Psychology of Women Quarterly* devoted to teaching about gender and ethnicity. The feedback I received from Janet Hyde, Margaret Madden, and the anonymous reviewers greatly improved the manuscript.

But this book was primarily developed in the classroom. From 1994, when I began this project, until the spring of 2000, I incorporated the framework and the latest iteration of the text into my classes. My students, graduate and undergraduate, at the University of Delaware and the University of South Carolina, gave me honest and valuable feedback. They were my best critics. They took my seminar on race, class, gender, and sexuality, my seminar in women's studies, and my sociology of gender courses. They came from a wide array of disciplinary backgrounds. They pushed me to strive for greater clarity and to make my analysis better—to make it consistent with the ideals I claimed to be working towards and to make it useful for the purposes of social justice. Because there were no similar books to serve as models, I tried a number of different formats. My students helped me decide what worked and what didn't, and they always encouraged me to pursue the project even when I wasn't sure I would ever finish it or if it would ever be published. As they read it now in its final form, I'm sure they will see that I couldn't make it go all of the places or address all of the issues they had recommended. These are the limits of my vision. But I hope they recognize that the final product is so much a reflection of their prodding, insights, and input. I cannot name all of the students here, but I deeply appreciate their help.

Throughout the process of writing this book, I was aided by a group of incredibly hardworking and insightful graduate student research assistants. The historical time line in Chapter 2 was a major research project, begun by Enashea Kohler and finished (a task that included rechecking every reference) by Rebecca Shrum and Kerry McLoughlin. Shannon Hunnicutt worked for the last three years researching almost every topic covered. Shannon's, Rebecca's, and Kerry's persistent, steady, and meticulous work kept me on track, and their insights often helped me to reshape an argument. Heather Dillaway's co-authorship of the case studies book that accompanies this text reflects the collaboration involved in that project, but I also benefited greatly from her feedback on the text itself. I am also indebted to Rosa

Thorn, program coordinator, and Jackie McClary, administrative assistant, of the Women's Studies Program at the University of South Carolina. They have supported my work and the project in numerous ways, not the least of which was making sure I had the time and resources to get the job done.

Several colleagues read the manuscript and gave detailed and enormously helpful critiques—Judith Barker, Kathleen Blee, Craig Kridel, Mary Margaret Fonow, Joan Spade, Susan Spivey, Kathy Ward, and Bruce Williams. Bonnie Thornton Dill not only read the manuscript, but also used a draft in her women's studies seminar on power and conflict at the University of Maryland. I thank both Bonnie and her students for their critical vision and many good suggestions for improving the manuscript. My editors at McGraw-Hill, Sally Constable and Kathy Blake, and the project manager, Laura Griffin, were a pleasure to work with. Even when we ran into snags, they were always professional, supportive, and maintained a much appreciated sense of humor. I am also grateful to my friends Chris, Russ, Annie, and Kate Bohner, who have engaged in numerous discussions of the issues and themes contained in the book and who have always given me thoughtful and honest feedback.

Finally, in writing this book, I often had to confront my own doubts. How can any one person claim to write clearly and succinctly about such a massive and complex topic and to do it well? Even with all the encouragement I received from students, colleagues, and friends, this project would not have been completed without the unflagging confidence and support of Jean Astolfi Bohner, to whom I dedicate this book. She consistently encouraged me when I just didn't think I could possibly finish. She talked to me about every issue in the book, and she used her amazing editing skills to fine-tune the manuscript. Most importantly, she lives her life as a model for relating across differences, and in so doing helps me to see new ways of achieving justice.

Lynn Weber
University of South Carolina

INTRODUCTION

W hen the millennium began:

- Bill Gates was worth $90 billion, up from $6.4 billion in the seven years since 1992.
- The seven richest people in the world were heterosexual, White men from the United States, worth a total of $208 billion.
- The average full-time employed male college graduate over the age of 25 earned $49,982 while his female counterpart earned $35,408.
- For every dollar earned by full-time, year-round employed White men, Black men earned 74¢, White women earned 73¢, Black women earned 64¢, Hispanic[1] men earned 61¢, and Hispanic women earned 53¢.
- The U.S. minimum wage was $5.15 an hour, or $10,712 a year for a full-time worker.
- The 200 richest people in the world (4 women, 196 men) were worth $1 trillion—enough to pay 93.3 million people the U.S. minimum wage.
- About 10 million U.S. workers earned the minimum wage.
- Because many employers (e.g., some small businesses, restaurants, and bars—places that tip) are exempt from paying the minimum wage, and many others simply avoid it (e.g., domestic worker employers), 2.8 million workers earned less than the minimum wage.
- The majority of those earning the minimum wage or less are women and people of color.[2]

---

[1] Throughout the text you will see the words Hispanic and Latino/a used to refer to Spanish-speaking people of the United States. Although neither term is preferred by all Spanish-speaking people, the term Hispanic was initiated by the U.S. government while Latino/a is a self-designation preferred by many people of Latin American descent. Consequently, I have chosen to use Hispanic when quoting other sources or using government data and Latino/a otherwise.

[2] All data on wealth are from Kerry Dolan, ed., "200 Global Billionnaires," *Forbes,* July 5, 1999, pp. 153–228; see U.S. Census Bureau, *Statistical Abstract of the United States* (Washington, DC: U.S. Government Printing Office, 1999) for wage and earnings data. Data are for 1998 earnings. Minimum wage data are from Eric Schmitt, "Minimum Wage Rise of $1 Is Approved," *New York Times,* March 9, 2000, p. A1.

As we begin the next millennium in the United States, several trends foreshadow what we can expect in our social, political, and economic future as a nation:

- Both the power of economic elites and the concentration of the nation's wealth in the hands of fewer people will continue to increase while poverty persists.
- The racial and ethnic diversity of the population will increase as people of color become one-half of the population within the next 50 years.
- Gender relations will become more complex, and diverse family forms (e.g., single parents, gay and lesbian parents, older parents) will become more prevalent as women and men increasingly challenge restrictions on their work, family, and personal lives.
- Sexual politics will continue to generate controversy as the marketing of sexuality and individual desires for exploration and free expression of sexuality confront the reassertion of traditional heterosexual norms.
- International government and business relations will increasingly shape political, economic, and social processes in the United States.

It does not take a crystal ball or psychic powers to make these predictions and to be fairly confident that they will hold for the foreseeable future. These trends have characterized at least the last 50 years in the United States, and they represent some of the most significant processes for understanding what life will be like for most Americans in the 21st century.

Inequality in wealth and power permeates all areas of social life: We are continually confronted with these issues at work, in our homes, and even at play. In 1999, on the eve of the millennium, for example, the premier tennis tournament in the world, Wimbledon, was consumed with discussion of gender, race, sexuality, and class. Although the crowds for women's tennis were the same as or greater than those for men's tennis, the prize money was less for women. And Tim Henman, a British male player, stirred great controversy by stating that the women were "greedy" for wanting the same prize. Alexandra Stevenson, whose mother is White and a single parent, became the focus of attention when it was revealed that her biological father was –Julius Erving, one of the most famous African-American professional basketball players of all time. And her mother was criticized for the way Alexandra had been isolated from the other girls on the tour because, her mother stated, she needed to protect her daughter from the racism on the tour and the "lifestyles" of the players, meaning the presence of lesbians in the sport. Jelena Dokic, a working-class girl from Serbia but then living in Australia, was pilloried in the British press for staying in an inexpensive hotel it labeled a "bordelo," instead of in the expensive hotels where most of the players stayed.

While 1999 seemed to be a particularly interesting year at Wimbledon for highlighting the pervasiveness of inequalities of race, class, gender, and sexuality in our world, tennis always reminds me of the power of these social relationships in our lives. For I first began to learn about my own "place" in race, class, gender, and sexuality hierarchies when I entered the world of competitive tennis almost 40 years ago. In the early 1960s tennis was a "country club sport," played almost solely at racially, socially, and economically exclusive country clubs by White upper-middle-class and upper-class men and by growing numbers of women. In 1961, at the age of 11, I enrolled in free tennis lessons in the public parks in Nashville, Tennessee. Soon I began to enter local tournaments and to win. Over the next 12 summers, I became city and state champion and traveled across the South and to other regions playing—and ultimately teaching—tennis. I was the first person ever in Nashville who had learned to play tennis in the public parks to become a city or state champion, to become the fifth-ranked woman in the South.

What those years afforded me was the opportunity to see things that many White working-class people never see. I frequently stayed with upper-class families who had agreed to house tournament participants. I was in the world of competitive tennis, but it was always clear to me in subtle and not so subtle ways that I was not of it. It was not my world. My clothes were homemade, not designer made. My socks were cheaper, thinner. I had no personal coach. My parents rarely traveled with me to tournaments. In the country clubs, I could play in the tournaments but not eat in the restaurants as did most of the participants who were either members of the clubs or of similar clubs with reciprocal agreements. I could not afford to travel to all of the important tournaments needed to attain regional and national rankings.

Yet I was young, and I was determined. I also believed that tennis was a game—where the rules are known, where talent, skill, and effort pay off more than in any other place. Class doesn't matter. Race doesn't matter. Your clothes don't matter. The rules are in place. The ball is either in or out. You win or you lose.

But I came to see that it's not that simple. The better I got, the higher I was ranked; the farther I traveled, the clearer the differences became. Over a period of several years, for example, I played the same player nine different times in the finals of city, state, and regional tournaments. I won all but the last time we played. But often when we traveled to the next tournament, she and her parents would arrive a day or two ahead. They would meet tournament officials and she would play on the courts. Often, she would receive top seeding (a ranking that determines whom you play). And every time, she would be seeded first—and she played easier matches on the way to the finals. She had lessons, she had coaches, and somehow she had a power that I didn't. It was as if what I did didn't matter. When she finally beat me, I felt as if I had held off the inevitable for a very long time.

I also came to see myself associated with other people who were "outsiders" within the world of competitive tennis. The most elite state tournament was called—not ironically—the "closed" tournament. Regions of the state sent teams, by invitation only, to compete at the most exclusive country club in Nashville. The year that Chattanooga sent a Black woman on its team, I was slated to play her. And after much ado and a two-hour delay, we were sent to play at another club in the city—alone, the two of us. In 1970 Black people were not allowed to belong to the exclusive club nor even to play on its courts. Every servant in the club, however, was Black—allowed only in servant's, not tennis, whites. While I had faced great obstacles to success and certainly felt that I was an outsider, I had never been banished. Class and gender circumscribed my presence in the tennis world, but my racial privilege had protected me from the most insurmountable obstacle—complete exclusion.

I was aware of the obstacles that I faced in tennis because of my social class location and because of my gender—girls and women received smaller rewards for winning, got less press, played at less desirable times, and had fewer options to continue in tennis as a career either as a playing or teaching pro. I was also aware of how heterosexual norms and homophobia shaped my and other girls' presence in tennis. Leaders in the sport have always promoted it as a more genteel (i.e., upper-class) and more feminine sport for women—one that leaves players less vulnerable to homophobic accusations of being manly, dykes, lesbians—than basketball or softball often do. But I had been unaware of the ways that my race was simultaneously benefiting me—by allowing me on the court to begin with. And that is the nature of privilege: It obscures rather than illuminates the unequal power relationships on which the systems of oppression are built. In contrast, to lack power, to experience oppression, draws attention to those same relationships.

I began to understand how these complex, pervasive, and persistent systems operate in the same way that most people do. I experienced their negative and limiting effects in my own life at the same time that I occupied a social location—a "place" in social life—that tended to illuminate rather than obscure the impact of group membership on personal life chances. Patricia Hill Collins (1991b; 1998) has described social positions like the one I occupied as "outsiders within"; others have called it "border-crossing," or "migrating." Outsiders within occupy social positions that enable them to gain knowledge of a dominant group without gaining the full power accorded members of the group.

I use the tennis example from my life to explain the roots of my interest in race, class, gender, and sexuality and to illustrate several points: that the systems of race, class, gender, and sexuality are pervasive throughout the seemingly most unimportant aspects of our lives (such as whether or not we win a tennis match), that all the systems are operating at all times and in all places, and that they are interrelated and complex. But I do not intend by this example to equate tennis to other more significant arenas having a much wider impact on the life chances of oppressed groups—for example, work, school, family, and health.

Race, class, gender, and sexuality are powerful social systems that have structured individual private lives and collective social existence for the entire history of the United States. In this country, founded on the ideal that "all men are created equal," power and privilege, in fact, are distributed not only along individual but also along group lines so that some groups are privileged—Whites, heterosexuals, upper classes, men—while others are oppressed—people of color, gays, bisexuals, lesbians, the working classes, the poor, and women. This tension—between the ideal of individual equality and the reality of systematic group inequality—is a long-standing source of controversy and contest in U.S. society. Yet group inequality persists because the privilege and power of some is directly tied to the oppression of others: Powerful groups gain and maintain power by exploiting the labor and lives of others. Bill Gates, Michael Dell, the late Sam Walton's family, and others, for example, can amass billions of dollars *because* millions of people in the United States and across the globe earn the minimum wage or less. They earn those low wages in all sectors of the economy, including work in factories making and packaging Microsoft products and Dell computers and their parts, and in Wal-

Mart as cashiers and sales personnel. Exorbitant wealth is available to the few *only* because there are millions of workers whose low-wage labor makes, distributes, and sells products worth much more. And the political, economic, and social system in the United States supports—through tax, inheritance, minimum wage, welfare, and other business- and labor-related state policies and practices—the acceptance of this exploitation as a basis for the social order.

Yet the United States is also a nation where groups that face exploitation on the lines of race, class, gender, sexuality, ethnicity, and others have always challenged oppression in myriad ways. As a consequence of those challenges, significant shifts in power and privilege across group lines have also taken place:

- African Americans, initially brought to this country as slaves—one of the most extreme forms of exploitation known to our nation—have struggled and gained full citizenship rights, significant entry into middle- and upper-class social and economic positions, and a major political voice.
- Chinese Americans, initially denied families and citizenship and exploited as low-wage laborers in the building of railroads, have built communities, attained high levels of education, and gained considerable political and economic power, especially in California and New York.
- Native Americans, suffering conquest and removal from their own lands, have struggled successfully to gain political rights, to regain stolen lands, to raise their economic status—the lowest of all racial ethnic[3] groups in the United States—and to assert principles of dignity and respect for all peoples and the lands on which they live.
- Mexican Americans and other Latinos/as, both immigrants and native born, have maintained culture and family life despite the strains put on them by low wages and seasonal work in agriculture and mining. They have become such a strong political force in American life that Anglo candidates now target policies (e.g., on bilingualism in schools and immigration law) and speak Spanish to attract the rapidly growing Latino/a vote.
- Gays and lesbians, not long ago, had no legal protection against hate and harassment on the job or in their personal lives. Now many municipalities and states have enacted antidiscrimination measures, and through the campaign for civil rights, gays and lesbians have become a major political, social, and economic force in the United States today.

The interplay of exploitation and the struggle against it have always characterized the relations of dominant and subordinate groups in this country. Yet despite major changes in these social relations over time, the same groups who seized power and established this nation-state in 1776—married (heterosexual), upper-class, White men—continue to dominate it politically, economically, and socially.

---

[3]*Racial ethnic* is a term scholars have used in recent years to refer to ethnic groups that are also members of racially subordinate groups. This designation highlights their similarities with White ethnic groups (e.g., common culture) and an important difference—that racially designated groups have different experiences and social locations in the systems of oppression in the United States.

Despite significant resistance, how do such unequal and unfair power relationships as those between billionaire White men and impoverished women and children of color persist in a democracy founded on principles of equality? How do people view and deal with social and economic injustice in their own lives? What knowledge would empower oppressed groups to challenge injustice in effective ways—so that group membership no longer determines life's options and outcomes?

These are the types of questions that have concerned me—in one form or another—for most of my adult life and that have driven me to write this book. I began to see these inequalities as a working-class girl playing tennis at the same time that I experienced the desegregation of my all-White Catholic girls' high school in 1964. I pursued answers to these questions as a student, teacher, and scholar studying race, class, gender, and sexuality for the last 25 years—as a student in the tumultuous 1960s, as a professor of sociology since the mid-1970s, as a researcher and cofounder in the early 1980s of a center for research on women that focused on women of color and Southern women, and as the director of a women's studies program at the beginning of a new millennium.

What I learned in that time has led me to join others in seeking ways to analyze social life that

- are complex—not superficial and simplistic—and incorporate multiple dimensions of inequality in the same analysis
- do not seek to rank the dimensions of inequality according to which one represents the greatest oppression, which group has suffered the most
- empower—further the cause of social and economic justice by providing understanding and insights that lead to effective action to challenge injustice.

Many scholars have looked at social life by focusing attention on a single dimension of inequality, but increasingly I and other scholars have become dissatisfied with the resulting analyses that were not complex enough to capture the major social relations involved and consequently were not particularly effective when used as a basis for challenging social and economic injustice. When analyses have a singular focus in a world that is far more complex, the conclusions generated and the resulting change strategies are incomplete.

Often they have the unintended consequence of making it appear that one form of oppression (e.g., race or class, gender or ethnicity, sexuality or nation) is the most important, most serious, and that one group is most victimized. When one group is singled out in this way, the focus of attention moves away from relations of power among dominant and multiply oppressed groups. And oppressed groups often end up vying with each other for attention and for the status of "most victimized" so that they can be seen as most deserving of whatever resources might get shifted their way to redress inequality.

Instead, scholars focusing on the intersections of race, class, gender, and sexuality have begun to analyze social life by taking into account all dimensions simultaneously and through these complex analyses to empower people to challenge and overcome injustice centered in race, class, gender, and sexuality. In this book, I attempt to present a conceptual framework for the analysis of race, class, gender, and sexuality in the United States that will help to improve our understanding of the workings of these systems and to further the cause of social and economic justice. I derived this framework by identifying the common themes in the growing scholarship that takes account of all four dimensions in a complex way, that doesn't give priority to a single dimension, and that provides insights likely to move us toward greater social and economic justice because it deals with broad power relations among groups.

In thinking about the most effective way to communicate the framework, I made several decisions about the style, form, and structure of this book.

STYLE, FORM, AND STRUCTURE OF THE BOOK

Style—Simple but Not Simplistic

To reach the widest possible audience—not only scholars in the academic community but also students and people outside it, including those working for social justice—I have tried to make the writing accessible, to eliminate or to define when necessary disciplinary language. Using straightforward language to convey the subject clearly makes the work more powerful without being simplistic and enables it to reach a larger audience. The ideas are no less complex and difficult to comprehend when written in clear and concise language than when written in the more opaque language specific to academic disciplines. Such a style is far more useful in the struggle for justice. As Patricia Hill Collins (1998: xxiii) states, "Privatizing and hoarding ideas upholds inequality. Sharing ideas through translation and teaching supports democracy."

Form

Liberal Use of Examples and Case Studies

I have used numerous examples to illustrate the ideas in the work. Because race, class, gender, and sexuality must be understood within a social context, examples help to convey the meaning of these systems in the contexts within which they actually take their meaning. I use examples from my own life to foreground the way that my understanding of these systems is shaped by my own location in these hierarchies and by my own history. I also use several extensive case studies to enable the reader to follow an analysis of the race, class, gender, and sexuality dynamics in a particular case.

Emphasis on Micro and Macro Systems

The examples and the case studies were chosen to emphasize the simultaneous expression of race, class, gender, and sexuality in individual lives and in broad social patterns. To see these often hidden broader patterns, it is sometimes helpful to start from individual lives—from stories of people's personal, face-to-face, micro experiences. But because race, class, gender, and sexuality are fundamentally systems of group relationships, we must learn to investigate and understand larger group patterns of relations—the macro systems—to comprehend even our own individual experiences. Research by Faye Crosby (1989), for example, has demonstrated that only when members of powerful groups see the aggregate (overall, systemwide) patterns of discrimination against race and gender groups in an organization are they likely to believe that discrimination actually exists. In the absence of systemwide data (e.g., the average salaries or distribution among upper ranks of women and men and of people of color and Whites), individual stories of discrimination tend to be seen by those in power as problems that stem from individual traits, such as personality, and not from problems facing the group as a whole.

Emphasis on Both Dominant/Privileged and Subordinate/Oppressed Group Experiences

Because race, class, gender, and sexuality are interrelated systems of inequality based in social relationships of power and control, I use examples and case studies that focus on the lives of people in dominant as well as in subordinate groups. Because the privilege—advantages, benefits, options—of one group is dependent upon the oppression—disadvantages, harms, restrictions—of others, privilege and oppression cannot be understood in isolation from one another. Everyone is situated in race, class, gender, and sexuality hierarchies—not just people of color, working-class and poor people, women, and gays, bisexuals, and lesbians. The lives of Whites, the middle and upper classes, men, and heterosexuals are equally shaped by their social location along these dimensions. For example, my experiences in tennis were equally shaped by the fact that I was White and playing a "feminine" sport—and thus was both allowed on the courts to play and not subjected to homophobic attacks—and by the fact that I was working-class and female—realities that posed obstacles to my success. The fact that dominant groups are often ignored in public discussions of race, class, gender, and sexuality has to do with the processes of dominance itself. One way that dominant groups justify their existence and privilege is by promoting beliefs that race, class, gender, and sexuality are not important in determining group location and should not be taken into account when attempting to understand events or processes. This denial is represented in the familiar notions of society as "gender blind" or "race blind" and in parallel belief systems about class and sexuality—systems that are discussed in some detail in this book.

Women, people of color, working class and poor people, gays, bisexuals, and lesbians have a special role to play in alerting all of us to the workings and consequences of these harmful systems of inequality. So although the experiences of dominant groups will be included, those of oppressed groups will appear more frequently and more centrally in the text.

Organization

The book is organized into three sections. Section One introduces key concepts, identifies and defines the domains and structures of oppression, and provides historical and contemporary evidence of the contests over and consequences of oppression. Section Two presents a conceptual framework for the analysis of race, class, gender, and sexuality systems. The final section provides a detailed example of the application of this framework to the institution of education.

Education as an Example

Although the conceptual framework is intended to facilitate a race, class, gender, and sexuality analysis in any societal domain, I chose to focus the detailed example on the institution of education for several reasons.

Characteristics of the Educational System

- Education is the first major social institution that most people encounter fully outside the family.
- Through processes that include ability group tracking, school ranking, standardized testing, and different curricula, education plays a major role in sorting and preparing people for different social locations as adults—their occupations, social classes, earnings, political power.
- Education is the formal institution whose central purpose is to promote dominant culture beliefs about how and why society is the way it is, including the rationale for our systems of race, class, gender, and sexuality. The American Dream ideology—the belief that hard work and talent are rewarded and that anyone can succeed—is perhaps the primary rationale employed in the United States to explain and justify our system of inequality. The presence of educational opportunity for all is the cornerstone on which the American Dream rests.
- Education has been a central site of conflict over the gap between its egalitarian mission and its unequal structure, process, and outcomes. It is also a primary institution where groups seeking to challenge race, class, gender, and sexuality hierarchies have focused their efforts.

Researching, Teaching, and Learning in the Educational Environment

- Despite its central role in promoting and preserving race, class, gender, and sexuality systems, education—particularly kindergarten through grade 12— has received less attention in the scholarship that addresses the intersections of all four of these dimensions than have other areas, including family, work, economy, politics, social movements, health, and identity development.[4]
- For those of us who are teaching and learning in the educational system, it is important to develop a critical vision of the ways that race, class, gender, and sexuality shape our place and our interactions in this system. Teachers, for example, have power over students because of their location in the social class system, yet race, gender, and sexual orientation affect the extent of the power and the ways that power is played out in classroom environments.
- Almost everyone has extensive firsthand experiences in educational institutions from an early age. Except in the family, a person's experiences in most other institutions—work and the economy, politics, law and criminal justice, health care—are more intensively experienced as an adult. So education is a

---

[4]There is extensive literature that addresses race, class, gender, and increasingly sexuality as they separately manifest in the institution of education. Some combinations, particularly race and class, have also received extensive attention but less literature explores gender and/or sexuality in combination with race and class than in some other areas.

fruitful domain in which to explore the nature of diversity while having a common institutional referent for the largest number of people.

- Education is currently a major site of struggle over race, class, gender, and sexuality equity in multicultural curricula, affirmative action in admissions, bias in standardized tests, performance-based funding, single-gender schools, school desegregation, bilingual or multilingual instruction, and sex education curricula.

Although I illustrate the framework presented here by applying it to the specific case of American education, the focus of the book is to illuminate the framework, not to cover all the scholarship that has addressed race, class, gender, and sexuality in education. Many educators have provided theoretical treatments and in-depth analyses of the workings of educational inequality in particular locales, time periods, types of schools, and with various race, class, gender, and sexuality groups. Although I could not cover all their works here, I hope this analysis will encourage you to explore the works of James Anderson, Jean Anyon, Michael Apple, William Ayers, James Banks, Samuel Bowles, Dennis Carlson, Elizabeth Ellsworth, Michelle Fine, Michelle Foster, Paulo Friere, Herbert Gintis, Henry Giroux, Gloria Ladsen-Billings, Cameron McCarthy, Jeannie Oakes, Mike Rose, and many others.

WHAT'S IN IT FOR YOU? THE PERSONAL BENEFITS OF DEVELOPING A RACE, CLASS, GENDER, AND SEXUALITY ANALYSIS

Race, class, gender, and sexuality scholars study these hierarchies to further the course of social justice. But everyone can contribute to the course of social justice and gain personally from pursuing knowledge about these systems.

The study of race, class, gender, and sexuality is not simply about dichotomies such as good and bad, winners and losers, abusers and victims. Race, class, gender, and sexuality systems encompass a vast and complex array of human interactions and human responses that defy simple dichotomies. Awareness of these complexities is critical to understanding the ramifications of race, class, gender, and sexuality in our lives.

Recognizing Limiting Views of Others

Through our participation in a social system that devalues and denies resources and privileges to some people while elevating and rewarding others, each of us in all likelihood has contributed to the oppression of others—whether we are in dominant or subordinate groups or whether we occupy dominant and subordinate group locations simultaneously (e.g., working-class, heterosexual, White males or middle-class, Asian-American, heterosexual women). When we accept stereotypes—images that are meant to limit and control the lives of a group of people—we contribute to a system that in fact restricts the lives of others. If we accept, for example, controlling images of Asians as unscrupulous, are we likely to oppose legislation that would impose special tariffs or restrictions on Asian trade in this country?

Even if our own lives have been restricted by controlling images, we can unwittingly contribute to the oppression of others through the same process. For example, working-class people of color contribute to the social environment that oppresses others when they accept stereotypic images of poor and working-class White Appalachians as "White trash." When they challenge and reject these stereotypes, they confront the "oppressor within" themselves. In sum, when we allow controlling images to shape our thinking and behavior, we contribute to the oppression of others and of ourselves. When we confront and resist these destructive images, we liberate ourselves.

Recognizing the Oppressor Within—Internalized Oppression

Another benefit of studying these social structures is our increased ability to recognize negative or limiting views of ourselves associated with our own multiple social locations. These negative or limiting self-definitions—internalized oppression—come from subtle and not-so-subtle societal messages about what groups of people are like, what they should be like, and what material rewards and psychosocial resources such as respect and admiration or devaluation they should receive. The forces of internalized oppression are most often played out unwittingly in a person's life and may take the shape of many kinds of limitations. A person may deny his or her membership in a subordinate group (e.g., a gay's refusal to acknowledge even to himself his same-sex preference or a working-class person's pretending a middle-class upbringing). At the least, these compromises of identity and self-definition may lead to a self-image that is defined by the views of others and therefore may obstruct the process of valuing oneself and one's roots. In the extreme, internalized oppression may lead to severe identity and self-esteem problems and to self-destructive behaviors such as substance abuse or risky sexual practices.

Recognizing the Costs of Dominance

People in dominant groups reap many benefits but also pay a price to maintain their position of power and control. Growing attention is being given, for example, to the consequences that men—particularly White, middle-class, heterosexual men—may pay for a socialization process aimed at maintaining their dominance in U.S. society.

- In part because strength is associated with dominant masculinity and illness with weakness and femininity, men have a tendency to ignore their health and their need for medical attention. Both White men and men of color have a shorter life expectancy than women. In 1997 the life expectancy of men at birth was 73.6 years while women's expectancy was 79.4 years (National Center for Health Statistics 2000).

- Because expressing emotions, needs, and possibilities such as fear, sadness, nurturing, and compassion are associated with femininity, with weakness, dominant-culture men are socialized to bury or deny their own emotions and needs as well as those of others. Emotional numbness makes being expressive or intimate difficult and restricts the full experience of life, even though it also enables heterosexual, middle-class, White men to remain emotionally distant from those whose lives their economic, political, and ideological privilege restricts—people of color, the working class, women, gays (Brod and Kaufman 1994; Kaufman 1994).
- White men commit suicide four times as often as White women (21.5 vs. 5.3 per 100,000 deaths), almost twice as often as Black men (11.3) and 10 times as often as Black women (2.0) (Center for Disease Control and Prevention 1997). Because manhood, particularly for White men, is so tied to expectations for success in the world of work, as psychiatrist Willard Gaylin explains, suicide occurs often because of perceived social humiliation tied to failure in business:

  > Men become depressed because of loss of status and power in the world of men. It is not the loss of money, or the material advantages that money could buy, which produces the despair that leads to self-destruction. It is the "shame," the humiliation, the sense of personal failure. . . A man despairs when he has ceased being a man among men (Gaylin 1992:32).

Gaining a Realistic Assessment of Our Environment

Another benefit that comes from understanding the forces of social location in our own lives is the opportunity to examine unrealistic personal expectations that may accompany our social location. These expectations distort reality and serve to maintain personal oppression. People in subordinate groups, for example, may come to believe that socially unjust outcomes are an unchangeable reality and may withdraw from efforts to protest injustices through avenues that have at times worked, such as public demonstration. This withdrawal in turn serves to reinforce the political, ideological, and economic status quo. In this way oppressed group members contribute to the reproduction of the oppressive system and of the limits on their own lives by internalizing—believing and acting on—the negative and restricted views of their lives.

People in dominant groups may expect a disproportionate share of material rewards, or they may believe that their location in a dominant group will protect them from events such as unemployment that many subordinate groups have historically had to contend with. When these expectations are not realized, anger, bitterness, depression, guilt, and an overwhelming sense of abandonment may result. Unmet expectations for job security in an environment of corporate downsizing and shrinking wages, for example, may help to explain why some White middle- and working-class men have scapegoated—blamed—relatively powerless women and people of color and have opposed affirmative action programs and, in extreme cases, have targeted people of color for violence.

More realistic expectations serve to reduce negative behavior or attempts to scapegoat subordinate groups during times of economic insecurity. Realistic expectations also foster our ability to interact with a diverse range of people, to see their economic and social needs as being as legitimate as our own, and to work together to redress the injustices we face.

Achieving Good Mental Health

Studying race, class, gender, and sexuality also helps us understand how important it is to individual and group mental health that we resist negative images resulting from our locations in these social structures. Gay Pride marches are examples of resisting negative images by affirming and valuing self and asserting a positive group definition. These public displays of pride are especially critical because they counter the feeling that people are alone in their struggle to value themselves. Isolation renders people vulnerable to the powerful forces of negative controlling structures and images that pervade every institution of society, from families to schools to workplaces. Individuals and groups also affirm themselves every day in less public ways. When people speak up against negative treatment of themselves or of others on the job, they resist internalizing oppression and work toward positive mental health.

When Society Improves, We All Gain

The African-American phrase "Lifting as We Climb" refers to the belief that no individual can be truly free in a system that oppresses others. Individual liberation requires that we lift everyone as we seek to improve our own lives. When prosperity is not the result of restrictions on and harm to others, society becomes a more humane place for all. It is difficult to imagine how anyone can be free in a system where one's health and welfare depend on limiting and restricting the health of others. And yet our system currently does just that. The United States, for example, has the highest infant mortality rate of any industrialized country in the world and also spends more money per capita for health care than any nation in the world. Why? In part because we spend our health care money in grossly unequal ways—we have more highly paid medical specialists and more expensive technologies than any other country. If the wealthy are sick here, they can receive the best treatment in the world. But the poor, the near poor, and many working-class families, more likely families of color, have little or no access to basic preventive health care for routine life events such as pregnancy and childbirth, and many infants die unnecessarily as a consequence.

Think also of the ways that even the wealthiest and most successful Americans are not free to live and be as they please. Bill Gates, the wealthiest man in the world—his net worth was recently estimated at $90 billion dollars (up from $18 billion in 1996)—is certainly financially capable of buying anything he desires, including some small countries (Dolan 1999). So what is he doing with his money? Building a fortress to live in that has many of the characteristics of a prison. He is apparently trying to create a self-contained social world so that he can be "free" to live in comfort and happiness without fear of physical harm or loss of property. What does he have to fear? In part, he may fear the wrath of the desperate populations—the poor, the uneducated, the disenfranchised—whose exclusion from the system of opportunity made his excessive wealth possible. He also may fear the wrath of other business people—professionals, owners, and executives—who may seek even greater wealth by stealing his products, ideas, and plans. Is he free?

By referring to the constraints on Bill Gates' life I do not intend to equate them with the restricted options and life chances of, for example, a poor Puerto Rican family struggling to pay the rent and feed and educate their children in New York City. Instead, I wish to point out that the unfairness of the system that privileges Bill Gates by impoverishing Puerto Rican and other families will always produce some kinds of constraints—even in the lives of the privileged—because their place of dominance will always be threatened by those unfairly treated.

When all members of society, particularly of a society as diverse as the United States, have the opportunity to contribute to their fullest potential, more efficient, more effective, more creative solutions to problems can be found. When everyone has an excellent education, basic health care, quality housing, and rewarding work for decent wages, people are prepared to contribute to society. Then multiple cultures can bring diverse knowledge and perspectives to bear effectively on the complex issues facing modern societies in an increasingly interdependent world system.

Understanding race, class, gender, and sexuality offers many benefits. When we are involved in the pursuit of social justice, we gain a sense of purpose that makes our lives more fulfilling, more satisfying. Our work in turn makes society more humane and further enhances our sense of purpose.

Laying the Foundation

One of the greatest obstacles to understanding the system of race, class, gender, and sexuality oppression is that its continuation *depends* on ensuring that it is not clearly seen or understood. Just as cable television companies could not continue to sell access to specific channels for movies or sports unless they could scramble and make incomprehensible the signal to those homes that did not subscribe, so systems of oppression, which benefit some at the expense of others, could not possibly survive unless they were able to scramble and obscure the ways that they accomplish creating and perpetuating that oppression. Consequently, a first step toward understanding oppression is to make visible the processes that obscure and deny its existence—the signal scramblers—so that the underlying processes can be seen, the signal can be clearly received.

In Chapter 1 of this section, I define key concepts, including race, class, gender, sexuality, oppression, and social location and describe in detail some of the processes that make it difficult to see and to comprehend—even to define—race, class, gender, and sexuality oppression. Since these processes of oppression manifest themselves differently in different social arenas, the major social domains—ideological, political, and economic—in which race, class, gender, and sexuality systems are generated and maintained are also discussed.

Were it not for the success of processes that obscure their existence, we would all be clear on the workings of these systems of race, class, gender, and sexuality in part because so many current and historical indicators document the privilege of some groups and the harsh treatment and difficult existence of others. To give some general

15

markers that signal the extent of oppression for specific groups, Chapter 2 includes (1) a historical time line marking when basic rights were secured, gains made, and setbacks experienced by groups and (2) recent data indicating the current status of various groups on wealth, poverty, education, and political representation.

CHAPTER 1

Defining Contested Concepts

To analyze race, class, gender, and sexuality, it is necessary to characterize what we mean by the terms. This is not a simple task since their meanings are in fact contested and often obscured. This chapter offers working definitions of key terms, discusses some of the processes that operate to obscure these systems, and describes social arenas where they are manifested differently—in political, economic, and ideological institutions.

RACE, CLASS, GENDER, AND SEXUALITY AS COMPLEX SOCIAL SYSTEMS

Race, class, gender, and sexuality are social systems—patterns of social relationships among people—that are

- *Complex*   Intricate and interconnected
- *Pervasive*   Widespread throughout all societal domains (e.g., in families and communities, religion, education, the economy, government, the law and criminal justice, the media)
- *Variable*   Changing, always transforming
- *Persistent*   Prevailing over time and across places
- *Severe*   Serious in their consequences for social life
- *Hierarchical*   Unequal, stratified (ranked), benefiting and providing options and resources for some by harming and restricting options and resources for others

Stated otherwise, race, class, gender, and sexuality are systems of oppression. *Oppression* exists when one group has historically gained power and control over societally valued assets by exploiting the labor and lives of other groups and using those assets to secure its position of power into the future. In exploitative relationships, the welfare of one group of people—the exploiters, the dominant group—depends on the poverty and efforts of another—the exploited, the subordinate group. Exploitation is the result of the unequal distribution of the productive assets (i.e., wealth, property, information, and political power) in society (Van den Berg 1993). The unequal distribution of society's valued opportunities and resources is repeatedly reinforced in daily life, and its fundamental unfairness is masked in a pervasive belief system—an ideology, a set of stereotypes—that interprets the in-equalities as a "natural" outcome of a group's presumed superior or inferior traits.

When we first meet people, we often try to get an idea of who they are by ask-ing questions that situate them in time and place as well as in meaningful social categories. We ask "Where are you from?"—often meaning geographic location—and "What do you do?"—often meaning your work or occupation. But we actually use these questions as indicators of more important social and cultural experiences and backgrounds that we associate with time, place, and work. When we meet people, we also situate them in other critical social locations—race, class, gender, and sexuality—that are powerfully embedded in all our institutions, touch every aspect of our lives, and suggest other commonalities of experience and back-ground. *Social location* refers to the social "place" of an individual or group in the race, class, gender, and sexuality hierarchies as well as other critical social hierar-chies such as age, ethnicity, and nation.

Although many texts and scholars have argued that race, class, and gender are the primary systems of inequality operating today in the United States, the inclu-sion of sexuality is increasingly common. I include sexuality because it—like race, class, and gender—is a structure of inequality that is intricately intertwined with and mutually reinforces the other systems. The meanings of race, class, gen-der, *and* sexuality are not fixed, immutable, or universal but arise instead out of historically and geographically specific group struggles over socially valued re-sources, self-determination, and self-valuation. In recent years, the mass public movement of gays, lesbians, bisexuals, and transgender people for social power and self-determination has precipitated significant political, as well as scholarly, attention on sexuality (cf. Button, Rienzo, and Wald 1997; Cook 1999). Our grow-ing awareness and understanding of the pervasiveness, persistence, and severity of the system of sexual oppression and its intersections with race, class, and gender oppression has led many to conclude that a comprehensive understanding of con-temporary social relationships and psychological processes must include the analysis of sexuality.

By focusing on these four dimensions, however, I do not intend to suggest that these are the only hierarchical dimensions of inequality that matter in social life. People face oppression along many other dimensions—age, disability, region, na-tion, ethnicity—and those patterns of relationships are also hierarchical and inter-sect with race, class, gender, and sexuality. In different times and places, and with regard to particular issues, they may carry more significance than the four dimen-sions examined here. Furthermore, they will often also intersect with these four di-mensions. Although I cannot examine all of these dimensions in the present text, I hope that the framework provided here proves useful in understanding those sys-tems as well.

PROCESSES THAT OBSCURE RACE, CLASS, GENDER, AND SEXUALITY

Race, class, gender, and sexuality shape everyone's life every day. Yet these sys-tems are often hard to see, to understand, even to define. In U.S. society, these constructs are typically defined by referring to social groups selected for unequal treatment and ranked according to

- *Race*   Ancestry and selected physical characteristics such as skin color, hair texture, and eye shape
- *Class*   Position in the economy—in the distribution of wealth, income, and poverty; in the distribution of power and authority in the workforce
- *Sex/Gender*   Biological and anatomical characteristics attributed to males and females (sex); culturally and socially structured relationships between women and men (gender)
- *Sexual orientation*   Sex of partners in emotional-sexual relationships

Yet these definitions tend to reify the categories—to make them seem universal, tied to a presumably stable biology, rigid, and unchanging—characteristics quite the opposite of how the framework in this text presents them to be. One of the challenges of this text will be to present a more complex picture of these systems and their intersections so that we can see their persistence and significance in shaping social life and their shifting nature over time and space. Indeed, the reasons that these intersecting systems of oppression are so difficult to understand and to define are contained in the very nature of the systems themselves.

1. **Every social situation is affected by societywide historical patterns of race, class, gender, and sexuality that are not necessarily apparent to the participants and are experienced differently depending upon the race, class, gender, and sexuality of the people involved.**

Typically the beneficiaries of long-standing patently unfair practices that routinely reinforce social injustice (e.g., giving special preference in college and law school admissions to the sons and daughters of wealthy alumni) don't come away viewing the practices as unfair, don't associate them with affirmative action, and may in fact view them as fair and even desirable practices (Sturm and Guinier 1996). To those who occupy positions of privilege—that is, who benefit from the existing social arrangements—the fact that their privilege is dependent on the unfair exclusion of or direct harm to others is obscured, unimportant, practically invisible.

While I remember when my all-White girls' high school desegregated in the 1960s, the event meant very little to me at the time. I had never even seen the segregated African-American schools whose inferior conditions had made school desegregation such an important goal in the African-American community. But for my new African-American schoolmates, the unfairness of racial segregation was painfully apparent, and being the first African Americans to attend my school was most certainly a critical life event for them.

Systemic patterns of inequality can also be obscure to those disadvantaged by them because they lack access to information and resources that dominant groups control. For example, at the same time that, because of my racial privilege, I experienced my high school's integration as a nonevent, I became aware of the significant restrictions on my life imposed by the system of male gender privilege.

I rode to school on a bus with other students from my end of town who had gone to elementary school with me. The bus stopped at the three small Catholic girls' high schools and the single large Catholic boys' high school. Every day on the bus, my good friend Mickey O'Hara and I, who had competed with each other academically in elementary school, compared notes about what we were learning in high school. As the days, weeks, and years went on, it became clear that Mickey was being taught much more than I. The boys in college prep courses went further in math, read more in English, had more science. They scored better on standardized tests. They had better facilities, books, and teachers. Why? In large part because each parish was required to contribute money to the boys' high school for each boy in the parish who attended the school. And for the girls? Nothing. So the girls' schools ran on tuition alone; the boys,' on subsidies from the parishes—a fact I didn't learn until years later. My brother's education cost my parents far less and provided him much more—a discrepancy that few at the time saw as troublesome because the school system was organized to prepare boys to provide materially for their families and to prepare girls to have children and to raise them in two-parent, heterosexual nuclear families.

These assumptions about the fundamental aims of our education—to learn to enact gender-specific roles in heterosexual marriages and in the labor market—were profound. They shaped every aspect of our lives—from proms to course content, from sports to labs. The girls' schools provided the homecoming queens and the cheerleaders; the boys' school, the athletes. The girls' schools provided the home economics and typing labs; the boys' school, the physics course.

So in my position as a girl in a gender-stratified school system, I had been aware of many of the differences in education between the boys' and the girls' schools but was unaware of the funding practices that supported them and would have been unable to do much about the practices even if I had known. Likewise, law school applicants who lack class and family privilege may never know or may be unable to change the fact that their chances for admission were reduced by the preferences given to the children of alumni. People often come away from a discriminatory practice not knowing whether or how the discrimination took place—even when they are the victims of the injustice. While those who suffer the unfairness are more likely to see it, we all participate in discriminatory systems *with and without* knowing that or how we have done so.

2. The dominant ideologies of a color-blind, gender-blind, classless, and sexually restrained society obscure oppression and history.

The dominant ideology (belief system), particularly about race and gender but also about social class and sexuality, that pervades the media and dominates public policy is that the United States is or should be a gender-blind, race-blind, classless, and sexually restrained society. These ideologies are presented as "neutral" perspectives, suggesting that a gender-blind or race-blind society is the preferred outcome of any social policy that seeks to address pervasive inequalities—the goal to strive for—as well as the way that policies designed to achieve equity should operate.

We do not hear the term *class blind* used in public discourse because the dominant ideology of class differs from the ideology of race and gender. The classless ideology doesn't assert—as it does with race and gender—that even though classes are biologically determined, we should strive not to attend to them. While great differences in income, wealth, and other valuable resources are acknowledged, the classless ideology asserts that classes—either as biological groups or as social groups in a relation of oppression and conflict with one another—simply don't exist. Instead, the United States is presumed to be a free and open society where hard work and talent pay off—the land of the American Dream—and oppression is not implicated in the obvious, extreme economic differences present in the population.

The dominant ideology of sexuality is one of restraint, with the alleged sexual practices of the heterosexual majority taken as the moral norm against which the sexual orientation and practices of people who are gay, bisexual, lesbian, and transgendered[1] are seen as deviant and dangerous. The dominant ideology of sexuality is not that we should be blind to differences, that they shouldn't matter or don't exist, but rather that they should be denied or ignored—neither discussed in public nor condoned. The military's policy toward homosexuals of "Don't ask, don't tell" captures the dominant ideology of sexual restraint: "We won't ask and you shouldn't tell, because if you tell you will be punished."

Think about these ideologies. Why would we use *denial* and *blindness* as bases for social policy and the assessment of moral rightness? To do so implies that we seek not to see and therefore not to know. It suggests that ignorance is a preferred foundation for social policy—an anti-intellectual stance that has no valid place in the modern academy, where we use our senses to seek knowledge, truth, and wisdom.

Yet these stances to race, class, gender, and sexuality prevail for at least two basic reasons:

1. Because members of privileged groups are not disadvantaged and in fact benefit from these systems, people in these groups find it relatively easy to dismiss the claims of oppressed groups as unreal.
2. In our education and in mass media we do not systematically learn about the totality of the experiences of subordinate groups.

The experiences of oppressed groups are either excluded or distorted in our society by being presented in limited and stereotyped ways: gays, bisexuals, and lesbians solely as people who engage in particular sexual acts; African Americans as slaves, protesters in the 1960s civil rights movement, sports heroes and music stars, and welfare moms and criminals; Latinos/as as illegal aliens swelling the schools and welfare rolls in Texas, Florida, and California; Native Americans as unassimilable, alcoholic reservation dwellers benefiting from gambling-driven windfalls; and Asian Americans as hard workers who live clannishly in Chinatowns and Koreatowns, overcoming all obstacles to rise to educational and employment heights, especially in math and science. In short, we typically learn of

---

[1]Transgender is a term increasingly used by people whose gender expression (e.g., masculine, feminine) is deemed inappropriate for their biological sex (e.g., male, female). As Leslie Feinberg (1996:xi) states: "Because it is our entire spirit—the essence of who we are—that doesn't conform to narrow gender stereotypes many people who in the past have been referred to as cross-dressers, transvestites, drag queens, and drag kings today define themselves as trans*gender*."

these groups only as they can be seen to present "problems" or threats to the dominant group or as exceptions to the "normal" way of life.

We rarely learn of the common ground in our experiences or of the ways that the lives and struggles of oppressed groups can and have benefited the entire society. For example, the Civil Rights Act of 1964, although fought for and won primarily by African Americans, expanded protection against discrimination to women, religious minorities, and all racial groups. In a similar vein, Lani Guinier (1998b) compares the experiences of women and people of color to the miner's canary. Miners used to take a canary into the mines to signal whether or not the air was safe to breathe. If the canary thrived, the atmosphere was safe. If the canary became sick or died, the atmosphere was toxic. Members of oppressed groups—people of color, poor and working classes, women, gays, bisexuals, and lesbians—are like the canary: They signal when the atmosphere is not healthy. When oppressed groups experience high death rates from lack of access to medical care; high infant mortality rates; increasing high school dropout rates; declining college, graduate, and professional school attendance rates; high unemployment and poverty rates; and declining standardized test scores, something is wrong with the atmosphere—not with the canary. Trying to "fix" the canary or blaming the toxic atmosphere on the canary makes the atmosphere no less toxic to everyone in it. By learning about the atmosphere from the experience of the canary, we can develop a broader and healthier assessment of societal processes that affect us all—international relations, family life, the workings of the economy, education, and religion.

3. **These systems are never perfectly patterned—some people have experiences that defy the overall patterns.**

In my high school, some students in the college prep track never went to college; some home economics students did. However, the rags-to-riches stories so popular in the United States are always more complex than we are led to believe. For example, in *A Darker Shade of Crimson: Odyssey of a Harvard Chicano,* Ruben Navarrette, Jr., a 24-year-old Mexican-American man, went from valedictorian of his class in a school system with a 50 percent dropout rate for Latinos/as to Harvard University and then to graduate school in education at the University of California at Los Angeles. He describes the guilt, pain, and isolation he felt in graduate school:

> White student colleagues smile at me as they tell me, implicitly, that people like my parents, like my old friends, like the new girlfriend back home whose immeasurable love is sustaining me, are incompetent and unintelligent and unmotivated and hopeless. They wink and nod at me, perhaps taking comfort that I am different from the cultural caricature that they envision when they hear the word "Chicano."(Navarrette 1997:278).

So even though a pervasive pattern of oppression exists, there are always individual exceptions. And these exceptions tend to reinforce the views of dominant groups that the system is not oppressive but is indeed open and fair, because those who have benefited from the current arrangements are not inclined to see the ways that the exclusion of others has made their inclusion in the successful mainstream possible.

4. **These systems are not immutable—they change over time and vary across different regional locations, different cultural milieus.**

Race, class, gender, and sexuality are not fixed systems or traits of individuals. Because they are negotiated and contested every day in social relationships, they change over time and in different places. Many of the working-class White girls who were my high school classmates, for example, didn't attend college immediately after high school, but did so only years later, after marrying and having children. Changing economic conditions no longer allowed their husbands to be the sole support of the family; changing family conditions meant that many of their marriages ended in divorce; and changing education and labor market conditions meant that there were significantly increased opportunities for women. Thus, what race, class, gender, and sexuality meant for the lives of White, heterosexual, working-class women had changed considerably from the 1960s to the 1980s.

5. **Because of the pervasive, persistent, and severe nature of oppressive systems, people resist subordination. And in their resistance, they can develop positive skills, talents, and abilities. These skills will fortify them to survive and to challenge more effectively the very system designed to limit their opportunities to use their skills, talents, and abilities.**

Because no parish resources were sent to the all-girl schools in my community, the parishes could funnel all their resources into the education of the boys—to fortify their ability to succeed and to bolster the economic base of the patriarchal nuclear family. Yet because girls were segregated from boys in parochial schools, I was able to play leadership roles and participate in activities that were largely not open to girls in coed schools. In much the same way, segregated African-American schools, Native-American reservation schools, and Spanish-speaking barrio schools—typically inferior in resources, per pupil expenditures, physical facilities, and teacher preparation—have nevertheless become fertile ground for the development of future leaders and activists who effectively challenge the systems themselves.

Since members of oppressed groups can withstand and even succeed while facing oppression, dominant group members often consider that success to mean that the oppression either does not exist or is not severe. But it is not the oppression itself that creates the success that some people experience: It is the human will to resist oppression and overcome obstacles that makes this success possible. Resistance in individual and collective forms pressures the dominant system to change and transform over time.

DOMAINS AND STRUCTURES OF OPPRESSION

Race, class, gender, and sexuality are systems of oppression among dominant and subordinate groups in society. As Table 1.1 summarizes, dominant race, class, gender, and sexuality groups exploit subordinate groups in each of three major domains of society:

TABLE 1.1. Domains and Structures of Oppression

Domains of oppression	Ideology		Polity		Economy	
Associated institutions	Education Media Religion		The State (all levels of government) Law (civil and criminal justice, police, military)		Industry (agriculture, communication, finance, health care, manufacturing, mining, transportation, etc.) Work	
Power base	Control of ideas and knowledge		Legitimized direct control over others		Control of material goods and resources	
Structures of oppression: race, class, gender, and sexuality	Dominant[2] Group Activity	Subordinate Group Activity	Dominant Group Activity	Subordinate Group Activity	Dominant Group Activity	Subordinate Group Activity
Macro-social structure Society Community	Production and control of ideology that justifies, supports, and rationalizes interests of dominant group—e.g., • Negative stereotypes/ controlling images of subordinate groups • Positive/"normal" images of dominant group →	← Collective affirmation of group value, self-definition, positive identity: • Gay, race/ethnic pride • Women's "consciousness raising" • Alternative ideologies—e.g., multicultural education, liberation theologies	Production and control of laws, policies over participation as citizens—e.g., • Biased treatment in criminal justice system • Biased social policies—e.g., welfare policy • Denial of full participation in political system—e.g., high cost of participating →	← Resistance through—e.g., • Equal rights movements • Alternative organizations— e.g., grassroots organizations, Welfare Rights Organization • Demonstrations, riots, block voting	Production and control over good jobs, income, wealth, health care, housing, education—e.g., • Passage of favorable tax legislation • Exploitation of subordinate group members in labor market →	← Movements for— e.g., affirmative action, antidiscrimination measures, economic self-sufficiency—e.g., • Worker-owned companies • Minority businesses • Women's businesses • Strikes, slowdowns

TABLE 1.1. Domains and Structures of Oppression (*continued*)

Domains of oppression	Ideology		Polity		Economy	
Associated institutions	Education Media Religion		The State (all levels of government) Law (civil and criminal justice, police, military)		Industry (agriculture, communication, finance, health care, manufacturing, mining, transportation, etc.) Work	
Power base	Control of ideas and knowledge		Legitimized direct control over others		Control of material goods and resources	
Structures of oppression: race, class, gender, and sexuality	Dominant Group Activity	Subordinate Group Activity	Dominant Group Activity	Subordinate Group Activity	Dominant Group Activity	Subordinate Group Activity
Micro-social psychology Small Groups Individual	Ideological power → brings sense of privilege, superiority	← Empowered:[3] Self-definition, self-valuation, personal empowerment Not empowered: Internalized oppression, self-hatred, self-destructive behaviors	Legal authority → in public arena brings control over others in everyday life and reinforces personal power	← Empowered: Assertion of political/collective consciousness and identity Not empowered: Lack of political power, no sense of control over environment	Economic → power brings control over others in everyday life and reinforces personal power	← Empowered: Many forms of resistance—e.g., union organizing, extended kin networks for sharing economic resources Not empowered: job absenteeism, quitting, theft

[2] The activities listed here are not intended to be an exhaustive list but rather suggestive of the kinds of activities that take place in each domain.

[3] Some actions of subordinated groups reinforce the negative impact of oppression, while other actions are more effective in challenging the oppression and reflect a more empowered stance. While the difference will certainly depend on the context, history, and other social conditions like the relative power of the groups, the examples here are intended to remind us that not all activities have the same effect.

- *Ideological.* Control over such belief-shaping institutions as schools, the legal system, and the media enables dominant groups to shape public images and cultural beliefs about both dominant and subordinate groups.
- *Political.* Control over political decision-making processes enables dominant groups to shape public agendas and social institutions in a variety of ways, such as through political platforms, government operations, and public policy.
- *Economic.* Control over such material resources as good jobs, wages and benefits, quality housing, health care, quality day care, and education makes dominant groups more competitive in the workplace and in community life.

Social Institutions

Social institutions such as work, the state, or education represent patterns of social relations that are intended to meet particular societal needs and are often associated primarily with a single domain:

- *Ideological.* The media, religion, and education represent institutions whose primary purpose is *ideological*—producing and distributing ideas and knowledge about society, why it is organized the way it is, what people need to know in order to function in society.
- *Political.* The government, law, civil and criminal justice, the police, and the military represent institutions whose primary purpose is *political*—creating and enforcing the laws and government structures that define citizens' rights, responsibilities, and privileges.
- *Economic.* The major industries (e.g., finance, health care, manufacturing, housing, transportation, communication) and work represent institutions whose primary emphasis is *economic*—producing and distributing society's valued goods and services.

Each of these domains and the institutions within them is organized to reinforce and reproduce the prevailing social hierarchies of race, class, gender, and sexuality. They do so by producing and disseminating ideas that justify these inequalities, by concentrating government power and social control mechanisms among dominant groups, and by distributing society's valued material and social resources unequally to Whites, the middle and upper classes, men, and heterosexuals.

Although most institutions have a primary purpose, none of the major social institutions relates solely to any single domain of oppression—ideological, political, or economic. Just as race, class, gender, and sexuality are interconnected dimensions of oppression, so are social institutions intertwined with one another. Because the educational system certifies people for different social locations in the economic and political domains, for example, education is deeply implicated in economic and political institutions. Society's expenditures on schooling are justified on economic grounds as preparing and sorting people for different positions in the capitalist economic system as owners, managers, professionals, laborers, and—for those who drop out or otherwise fail—as society's underclass. Within higher education today, students are increasingly viewed as consumers who must be "sold" on the "product" that any given institution offers and who must be "satisfied" in order to keep their "business." Lawsuits brought by students against educational institutions for failure to educate them, unheard of 20 years ago, are becoming increasingly common. And because of the ideological and economic importance of education, the state is deeply involved in legislating the structure of education. Social movements seeking to challenge the fundamental basis of the social order often begin with and emanate from schools. Take, for example, the equity movements surrounding school desegregation, students with disabilities, Title IX of the Education Amendments of 1972 (gender equity), and affirmative action.

Furthermore, some institutions have no single focus and uniformly crosscut all dimensions—for example, the *family*. The family is a social institution whose purpose is to meet people's basic psychological, emotional, and physical needs. Even though emotional support, love, and nurturance take place in families, families also serve as sites where inequality is reproduced in the ideological, political, and economic realms.

Ideological. Families are institutions where the ideas that bolster and justify the dominant power structure are reinforced daily in an intimate setting. Conservative politicians and political interest groups in the 1990s, for example, used the term "family values" to refer to the political values that serve the interests of nuclear, heterosexual, White, middle- and upper-class, Christian families—that is, those values that serve to reinforce the dominant power structure.

Political. Families are institutions where the public authority and power of middle- and upper-class White, male heterosexuals are reinforced daily in a variety of ways. When a man rapes or otherwise sexually assaults the child of a neighbor, for example, the violation is typically seen as a crime and is often pursued in the criminal justice system. When, however, the same man rapes or otherwise sexually assaults his own daughter, the rape is more often either not challenged at all, treated as an issue for social services, or dealt with in therapy. The public power of men (including their greater economic power) gives them power in the family, making it especially difficult for women and children to successfully challenge the abuse of that power either within the family or in the criminal justice system (cf. Herman 1992).

Economic. Families are institutions where goods and services are distributed to reinforce the economic power of dominant groups. The family wage—a wage large enough to enable a man to provide for his entire family—was extended at the end of the nineteenth century to White men to lure them away from family farms and into factory work but was never extended to men of color. It also served as a mechanism for exerting control over women by both denying them access to wage work and by justifying lower wages for women (Hartmann 1997). Current tax laws determining what part of income earned by individual workers will be retained by the state are set by family status. Married, heterosexual couples pay one rate, unmarried individuals pay another rate, and deductions and tax credits accrue to parents with dependent children.

Social Relations of Control

A primary task for dominant groups is to maintain their control over subordinate groups. To do so, they must (1) structure ideology so that exploitation is explained, justified, and rationalized and is seen as a natural, normal, and acceptable part of social life; (2) structure the polity so that the state supports and enforces the exploitative relations; and (3) structure the economy so that the exploitative relations continue—that is, the poverty and labor of the exploited enhances the welfare of the exploiters.

Internalized Oppression

That society functions without major disruption every day serves as a testimony not only to the power of dominant groups to effectively control the ideological, political, and material resources that subordinate groups would need to shift the balance of power but also to the persuasive power of dominant ideologies to convince subordinate group members that the current social hierarchies are acceptable and/or cannot be changed (cf. Greene 1979). Two processes of *internalized oppression* are at work:

Self-Negation. Subordinate group members sometimes restrict their own lives out of a belief in the negative views and limits imposed on their group by the dominant ideology. When subordinate group members internalize oppression, they do not challenge the social order and may even exhibit self-destructive patterns such as drug abuse, family violence, or depression. In more subtle ways, for example, a woman who fails to put herself up for consideration for a promotion at work because she believes that she is less capable or less suited for management than her male counterparts has internalized the limits that society places on women.

Negation of Others. Subordinate group members sometimes restrict the lives of other members of oppressed groups or of their own group out of a belief in the negative views of and limits imposed on another subordinate group or on their own group. When working-class Latinos, for example, accept negative images of Latinas as sexually promiscuous and treat them as sexual objects, the Latinos reinforce the larger structural patterns of race, class, gender, and sexuality dominance. When women managers fail to promote other women because they believe that women are less capable than men, they also reinforce structures of race, class, gender, and sexuality dominance—the same structures that have restricted their own lives.

Resistance

Even though each of these social institutions is organized to reproduce the current social hierarchy and is thus a structure of oppression, strong forces of resistance occur within each. People resist oppression. The resistance occurs at both the *macro social structural level* of community and society and at the *micro social psychological level* of the individual and the family. Ever since the beginning of the U.S. public education system, for example, various groups have established alternative schools—religious schools, other private schools, African-American schools, bilingual schools, and home schools, to name a few—to resist the dominant culture's organization of education and to produce students who have different ideas about the social order. And because education is a primary institution charged with the socialization of the young, it holds a key to the future stability of the social order. Education is thus a critical site for resistance to all forms of oppression: racism, sexism, classism, and heterosexism, as well as religious, ethnic, national, political, age, and disability status.

A major focus of the civil rights, women's rights, gay and lesbian rights, and poor peoples' movements has been reform of the educational system through, for example, school desegregation; through battles over the gender, race, and sexuality content of school textbooks; through struggles for access for students with disabilities; through bilingual education; and through poor (mostly rural and inner-city) school districts' recent challenges to school district funding formulas based on property values.

Resistance also occurs at the micro level of the individual and the family when individuals develop an alternative consciousness, insist on self-definition and self-valuation, and refuse to incorporate negative images of their groups. An alternative consciousness is often nurtured in a community of resistance, such as a racial ethnic community, a community of workers, a gay and lesbian community, or a women's community. When groups publicly resist oppression, the individuals within them can participate in the development of a positive definition of self in the face of dominant culture oppression. For example, when gay, lesbian, transgender, and bisexual people acknowledge their sexual orientation on the job, they often face ostracism, hostility, lost opportunities for promotions, and even loss of their jobs. At the same time, however, by living their lives openly—something heterosexuals take for granted—they also contradict the denial and silence that enables dominant culture distortions about their lives to persist and to operate against them. In valuing themselves in this way, gay, bisexual, lesbian, and transgendered people contribute to an environment where others are better able to do the same. This process is one of *empowerment,* "a process aimed at consolidating, maintaining, or changing the nature and distribution of power in a particular social context" (Morgen and Bookman 1988:4).

Processes of oppression and resistance/empowerment exist in a dynamic relation to one another—each is in a continuous process of changing to adapt to the shifts in the other. By the early 1990s, for example, the mostly women workers in the U.S. athletic shoe industry had been successful in attaining wages approximately 1 1/2 times the minimum wage, which was $4.25 an hour in 1991. As Cynthia Enloe (1998) reports, the response of Nike and Reebok was quick and profound. Subcontracting production so they would no longer have to provide the wages, benefits, and health and safety protections that U.S. workers expect, the companies moved production overseas, first to South Korea and, after South Korean women successfully organized for higher wages, to China and Thailand. Hourly wages in athletic footwear factories in 1993 tell the story:

- China .... $ .10–$.14
- Indonesia .... .16– .20
- Thailand............................ .65– .74
- South Korea....................... 2.02–2.27
- United States 7.38–7.94

So when you bought a $70 pair of Nike Pegasus, here's where the money went:

- Labor (total for all 45 workers).. $ 1.66
- Materials 9.18
- Subcontractor's profit................. 1.19
- Administration/overhead............ 2.82
- Nike markup (costs/profits) .... <u>22.95</u>
- Shoe sold to retailer for............. 37.80

Nike's profits nearly tripled to $298 million in the five-year period ending in 1993, and Reebok experienced similarly large profits. Nevertheless, oppression invites resistance, so women in each of these countries have begun to wage successful campaigns against their exploitation. Allied through networks such as the Hong Kong–based Committee for Asian Women, women across Asia are developing their own "foreign policy" to address women's needs:

> How to convince fathers and husbands that a woman going out to organizing meetings at night is not sexually promiscuous; how to develop workplace agendas that respond to family needs; how to work with male unionists who push women's demands to the bottom of their lists; how to build a global movement (Enloe 1998:205).

American women and men workers are increasingly coming to connect their own plights with the oppression of workers in other countries, as the mass protests against the World Trade Organization in Seattle, Washington, in December 1999 so visibly and violently demonstrated (Brunner 2000; Postman, Broom, and King 1999). Such actions remind us that even though the focus of this text is on the United States, oppression, resistance, and empowerment take place in a global community.

SUMMARY

The meaning of race, class, gender, and sexuality is contested in struggles for ideological, political, and economic power and is constructed simultaneously at the macro social structural (society and community) and micro social psychological (family and individual) levels. Each of these domains of oppression, while primarily reflecting different societal functions and institutions, is integrally interdependent with the others, just as race, class, gender, and sexuality are interdependent systems of oppression.

CHAPTER 2

A Historical Time Line of Indicators of Oppression

Race, class, gender, and sexuality are systems of oppression that are continuously contested and that have severe and unequal impacts on different groups. To highlight the struggles of subordinate groups to secure the basic rights, privileges, and opportunities that dominant groups take for granted, the following time line presents a sample of significant stages and events in these struggles. Since social changes that represent significant shifts in the relations between dominant and subordinate groups do not take place overnight, a time line that allows us to scan a broad sweep of history can help us see patterns in the ways that dominant and subordinate group struggles have been waged, especially in the public arena.

LIMITS OF THE TIME LINE

As we read and think about them, time lines also require caution. They are superficial—they do not represent a comprehensive history of U.S. oppression and resistance, and they cannot convey the vast and complex social processes undergirding each "fact" on the line. The facts most easily conveyed on a time line tend to be policy changes, such as when laws were passed or Supreme Court decisions handed down. These indicators of change, however, tend to represent a view of history by the dominant culture: State policy changes typically mark the dominant culture's accommodation to social, political, and economic pressures for change that have emerged in struggles with oppressed groups over a long period of time. The indicators are much less accurate as representations of the most significant markers in the history of struggles by oppressed groups as seen from the groups' own vantage points.

The time line refers, for example, to passage of the Voting Rights Act of 1964—an event that culminated a century of struggle by African Americans to secure the right to vote unimpeded by the numerous legal and extralegal mechanisms designed to deny them that right (e.g., dual registration, poll taxes, literacy tests, and harassment at the polls). Few would deny that the Voting Rights Act of 1964 was one of the most significant events in group struggles for rights in this century. However, as Lani Guinier (1998a:303) relates, it was not all:

As one local sharecropper told SNCC (Student Non-Violent Coordinating Committee) organizer Bob Moses, the most important accomplishment of the civil rights movement, as far as blacks in Mississippi were concerned, was not the vote. It was the opportunity to meet. Coming together in small groups at citizenship schools or attending large mass meetings in black churches gave people a way to speak their stories and amplify their voices. Voting, which was a means of expressing that voice, could never substitute for the process of formulating, articulating, or pursuing a citizen-oriented, community-based agenda. The vote was crucial, but it wasn't all. In retrospect, maybe not even the most.

Even though it is more difficult to convey the significance of thousands of group meetings in this time line, they are no less important in understanding and historically situating the meaning of race, class, gender, and sexuality systems. Furthermore, it is worthwhile to remember that changes in national laws often reflect changes that have already taken place in people's behavior and that are already law in some states. Seventeen states, for example, had already extended women the right to vote by the time the U.S. Constitution was amended in 1920.

Every transformation of the race, class, gender, and sexuality order—the ways that society is organized to reinforce the existing hierarchies—is socially created through a process of conflict and compromise that takes place over time between resistance movements and the dominant culture as embodied in the state. Gramsci (1971) and Omi and Winant (1994) categorized these processes as taking place in different ways depending upon the place and power of the subordinate groups in the social hierarchy at any given time. They describe two general kinds of conflict: a "war of maneuvers" and a "war of position."

War of Maneuvers

A war of maneuvers takes place when subordinate groups lack democratic rights (e.g., the vote, representation in legislative and other government bodies), property, and any substantial basis on which to challenge the dominant social order. So challenges to dominant groups have to take place outside—in the margins of society. In a war of maneuvers, groups develop an alternative internal society as a counter to the repressive social system. Many racial ethnic communities before the racial liberation movements of the 1960s and 1970s, and gays and lesbians before the Stonewall riot in 1969, resisted oppression in the margins of society by managing to survive despite severe repression and particularly by developing internal communities that countered that repression. When you look at the time line, you will notice that during a war of maneuvers, there are significantly fewer indicators of positive progress in dominant culture arenas—congressional representation, educational and occupational attainment, representation in the military.

War of Position

More recent history suggests that oppressed racial ethnic groups and sexuality groups are moving from the *war of maneuvers* to the *war of position,* where subordinate groups have access to diverse institutional and cultural terrains on which to develop strategies to challenge oppression. In a war of position, subordinate group members, strengthened by the sense of community and political power developed in the war of maneuvers, are strategically positioned to challenge the state's race, class, gender, or sexuality hierarchies. This shift can be seen in the time line as the much more rapid pace of change evidenced in the last 40 or 50 years. Also, the White working classes and White heterosexual women have had legitimized access to some forms of democratic participation much longer than people of color or gays, bisexuals, and lesbians. Yet it is also clear that the recent period of increased democratization and cultural change has significantly improved the strategic position of White women, in particular, to resist oppression.

Just as during wars of maneuvers, group process and progress are more obscured in the time line, other processes obscure the actual histories of oppressed groups—for example, the ways the state gathers and reports data on the population. Since government allocations of resources for schools, welfare, roads, and health care are dependent upon accurate and up-to-date information about the size, composition, and distribution of groups, one of the struggles that oppressed groups face is simply the struggle to be counted. This is a struggle that racial ethnic groups, especially small groups and those with large, poor, transient, and rapidly growing populations, still face. Only since 1980, for example, has it been possible to more accurately identify Hispanics in government statistical reports of the population, and Asian and Pacific Islanders and Native Americans are still not included in the annual statistical summaries of major indicators. Thus, the most recent information on Asian and Pacific Islanders and Native Americans for these indicators is 1990. Table 2.1 shows the racial composition of the U.S. population since 1980 and the growing diversity of the population, which is projected until 2100, especially the rapid growth of Asians and Hispanics.

Still, racial groups have more accurate representation in government records than do gays, bisexuals, and lesbians, who have never been officially counted and who have been reluctant to self-identify in no small part because the government itself has a continuing history of oppression of gay people (Duberman, Vicinus, and Chauncey 1989). For example, since the implementation in 1994 of the military policy "Don't ask, don't tell, don't pursue," the intent of which was purportedly to protect gays and lesbians from harassment and expulsion, expulsions of gays and lesbians have increased by 73 percent, leading President Clinton to label his policy a failure (Sobel et al. 2000; Office of the Under Secretary of Defense 1999).

Another problem is that time lines are brief representations of broad sweeps of history and are necessarily selective. The data for this time line, for example, highlight the three domains of oppression and present separate time lines for significant markers in education (ideological); citizenship rights, representation in the federal government and the military (political); and work and income (economic). Crosscutting all three of these dimensions is the family, here marked by data on marriage and reproduction. Also, because the time line depicts events significant for a variety of groups, no single group is likely to see its historical line presented in a complete progression. Finally, the time line may be more useful as a set of markers or guides to changing patterns of relations that might point us toward the search for deeper understandings—to ask more questions.

TABLE 2.1. Percentage of the Population by Race, 1980 to 2000 and Projections

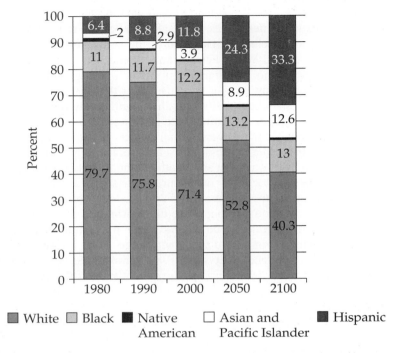

Source: U.S. Bureau of the Census. *National Estimates Quarterly Population Estimates, 1980–1990*. Available on-line from www.census.gov/population/www/estimates/nat 80s detail.html, accessed March 20, 2000; U.S. Bureau of the Census. *Projections of the Resident Population by Race, Hispanic Origin, and Nativity: Middle Series, 1999 and 2000 (Table NP-T5-A), 2050–2070 (Table NP-T5-G), and 2075–2100 (Table NP-T5-H)*, Population Division. Available online from www.census.gov/population/projections/nation/summary/, accessed March 19, 2000.

HIGHLIGHTS OF THE TIME LINE

Despite its limitations, the time line reveals a number of significant processes and events in the history of race, class, gender, and sexuality struggles in the United States. Primarily, it shows that the struggles of oppressed groups for full inclusion in a democratic society have been continuous. And often the gains secured by a single group broaden the inclusiveness of the society for everyone. The Civil Rights Acts of 1964, 1965, and 1968, for example, were won primarily through the efforts of African-American citizens to expand representation in government and to secure fair treatment in education, in the workplace, and in housing. When written, the Civil Rights Acts outlawed discrimination on the basis of race (including all racial groups), sex, color, religion, and national origin. The protection against sex discrimination prohibits sexual harassment, and some gay and lesbian students harassed in school have successfully brought suits by charging that their civil rights to equal protection were violated (cf. Lambda Legal Education and Defense Fund 2000).

But even when political rights are secured legally, realizing and maintaining those rights often remain a struggle and are more difficult for oppressed groups because dominant groups use their power to find new ways to oppress. For example, after *Roe v. Wade* in 1972 guaranteed women the right to an abortion, actually securing an abortion has been made more difficult, particularly for poor women, by a series of political actions: the 1977 Hyde amendment that eliminated federal funds for abortions, legislation placing restrictions on abortion such as parental approval and 24-hour waiting periods, and harassment of doctors and clinics that provide abortions (Woliver 1998). Likewise, after the Fourteenth and Nineteenth Amendments to the Constitution extended the right to vote to all citizens, discriminatory practices, such as poll taxes, dual registration, and literacy tests, made it difficult to exercise that right for many years. Significant numbers of women and people of color were not elected to state or federal offices until the very recent past and still constitute only 21 percent of Congress (113 of 539 members) (CIS Congressional Universe 2000).

The same processes of oppression are evident in education. Even after the *Brown v. Board of Education* decision of 1954, ruling that separate but equal educational facilities were unconstitutional, it was not until the pressures of the Civil Rights movement in the 1960s and even into the 1970s that governments began to intervene to eliminate the practice. Today, racially segregated and unequal schooling remains a problem for the poor, people of color, and inner-city and rural residents.

Finally, gays, bisexuals, and lesbians have faced numerous obstacles to obtaining full and equal rights, privileges, and treatment in U.S. society. Although they were never denied some citizenship rights such as the vote, realizing full civil rights has still been extremely difficult because of pervasive hostility, repression, and discrimination.

HISTORICAL TIME LINE OF RACE, CLASS, GENDER, AND SEXUALITY CONTESTS IN THE UNITED STATES

Education

Education is a central site of contests over race, class, gender, and sexuality in the United States both because knowledge is key to resisting oppression and because educational credentials are essential to getting good jobs, salaries, benefits, and better quality of life. The time line suggests several critical trends in education contests.

First, because race, class, and gender segregation in schooling has been a primary mechanism for reinforcing hierarchies, school desegregation has been a key goal among oppressed groups. The time line reveals the intense resistance to school desegregation and how quickly the gains made during desegregation can recede when there is no longer intervention to assure that desegregation continues. Significant changes in the racial order occurred with the passage of the Civil Rights Act of 1964, but more recently poorer school districts—typically those in rural and inner-city areas—have also begun to bring lawsuits to challenge the unequal resources that go to schools when school funding is based on property taxes. In Maine and Vermont, for example, where significantly less is spent on school children in rural districts, charges of educational discrimination have led to legal action (Carrier 1999; Young 1999; Burkett 1998). And in the 1990s women successfully desegregated the remaining male-only bastions, the military academies, by charging that they denied women equal educational opportunity, prohibited under Title IX legislation for schools receiving federal funds.

Second, the time line also highlights the fact that the government can be a site both for protecting privilege and for redistribution of power by steering funds to support education. For example, the 1944 G.I. Bill of Rights supported the education and training of thousands of mostly White working- and middle-class men who fought in World War II, but it now serves a much more diverse military. Likewise, funding for the disabled, for bilingual education, and for poor students helps to empower subordinate groups, although seemingly never to the extent that the balance of power shifts significantly.

Finally, it is difficult to record much of the historical struggles of gays, bisexuals and lesbians in education because many gay and lesbian school teachers still do not publicly identify themselves as homosexual for fear of losing their jobs (Carlson 1997). Fear that homosexuals thrive on molesting and recruiting young children to a gay lifestyle, promoted particularly among conservative Christian groups, has led fundamentalists to oppose antidiscrimination measures that would protect homosexuals in schools and to exclude mention of homosexuals from the curriculum (Button, Rienzo, and Wald 1997).

1896	In *Plessy v. Ferguson,* the Supreme Court endorses the principle of "separate but equal." It upholds the segregation of public facilities but asserts that Whites and Blacks should be accommodated on "separate but equal" terms.
1944	The G.I. Bill of Rights, also known as the Serviceman's Readjustment Act, is passed, creating a massive socioeconomic shift upward for the American working class. The G.I. Bill establishes a system to reintegrate military personnel into the civilian economy and a system to compensate veterans of World War II for their service. The bill provides tuition, fees, books, and a monthly subsistence payment to the veterans while they are in school, as well as providing them the opportunity to set up their own businesses, to buy their own homes, and to receive financial aid.
1948	The Supreme Court rules in *McCollum v. Board of Education* that there may be no religious instruction or activity in public school facilities.
1954	In *Brown v. Board of Education* of Topeka, Kansas, the Supreme Court strikes down the "separate but equal" doctrine of *Plessy* and orders all public schools to be desegregated.
1955	The Supreme Court orders the implementation of *Brown,* stating that all public facilities and accommodations be desegregated "with all deliberate speed."

*See Appendix: Historical Time Line References on pp. 183–89 for a more comprehensive listing.

1964 Despite the Supreme Court's order, desegregation is not widely implemented until the Civil Rights Act of 1964.

1965 Congress passes the Elementary and Secondary Education Act. It is the first law to extend federal funding to elementary and secondary schools. It also provides grants for the purchase of library materials and textbooks.

Congress passes the Higher Education Act, providing federal scholarships and federally guaranteed student loans for poor students. It also provides for funds for college libraries, for graduate fellowships for prospective elementary and secondary school teachers, and for a teacher corps, whose members will augment the faculties of schools in poverty-stricken areas.

1966 Congress passes a bill establishing the program of school breakfasts for poor children, extending the existing school milk and lunch programs.

1968 The Bilingual Education Act, an amendment to the Elementary and Secondary Schools Act, provides assistance to local educational agencies in establishing bilingual educational programs.

1969 The Navajo establish Navajo Community College in Arizona, the first college operated by Native Americans.

1970 College students receive $2 million grants, loans, and interest subsidies for guaranteed loans compared to $247,000 in 1964. The money reaches one in four students.

1971 The Supreme Court rules in *Swann v. Charlotte-Mecklenburg Board of Education* that busing to achieve racial balance is constitutional in cases where segregation has received official sanctions and officials have offered no alternatives.

1972 Congress passes Title IX of the Education Amendments of 1972, prohibiting discrimination on the basis of sex in most federally assisted educational programs and related activities, including sports. Title IX opens the way for increased participation of women and girls in athletic programs and professional schools.

1973 The Vocational Rehabilitation Act mandates that no handicapped individual shall be excluded from any program or activity receiving federal financial assistance.

1975 The Education for All Handicapped Children Act passes, guaranteeing all handicapped students aged 3 to 21 a right to free public education.

1978 For the first time, more women enter college than men.

In *Regents of the University of California v. Bakke,* the Supreme Court upholds the constitutionality of affirmative action, while not affirming racial quotas in admissions processes.

1979 The Supreme Court rules unanimously that federally funded colleges do not have to admit all handicapped applicants or make extensive modifications to accommodate them.

1983 In U.S. colleges and universities, women earn more than one-half of the undergraduate degrees, one-half the master's degrees, and one-third of the PhDs. However, women make up only 27 percent of the full-time faculty and 11 percent of the full-time professors.

1988   In response to the Supreme Court's ruling in *Grove City College v. Bell,* Senate Bill 557 is passed, stating that Title IX of the Civil Rights Act applies to all higher education programs regardless of whether they draw federal funds.

1994   Congress adopts the Gender Equity in Education Act to train teachers, promote mathematics and science learning by girls, counsel pregnant teens, and prevent sexual harassment.

1996   California passes a law banning the use of race and sex in college admissions, contracting, and public employment.

The Supreme Court rules that Virginia Military Institute must admit women to its student body. The Citadel follows suit.

In *Hopwood v. Texas,* a federal court invalidates the program of affirmative action in admissions at the University of Texas Law School.

1997   University of California, Berkeley, reports a 57 percent drop in Black admissions and a 40 percent decline in Latino/a admissions. For the University of California, Los Angeles, the decline is 43 percent for Black students and 33 percent for Latinos/as.

At the University of Texas Law School, five African-American students are offered admission, down from 65 in 1996.

The Supreme Court expands the meaning of Title IX by ruling that to qualify for federal support, college athletic programs must actively involve fairly equal numbers of men and women.

1999   Nancy Mace is the first woman to graduate from the Citadel. In the fall semester, the Citadel enrolls 32 women in an incoming class of 550, bringing total female enrollment to 69 of the 1,771 member corps of cadets.

U.S. District Court Judge Robert Potter rules that Charlotte, North Carolina, educators can no longer use race when deciding where to assign school children. Amid concern that backing away from this policy will only hurt efforts to provide an equal education for all children, educators must find a way to dismantle Charlotte's 30-year-old policy of school integration mandated by *Swann v. Charlotte-Mecklenburg Board of Education.*

In *Weaver v. Nebo School District* (Utah), a federal judge rules that a school district cannot prevent a gay or lesbian teacher from being "out" in his or her life outside the classroom.

Some recent indicators of educational attainment for various groups can perhaps give another perspective on the ways that inequality is played out in the educational arena. Perhaps the single most important credential to qualify for most middle-class, professional, managerial, and administrative jobs is a college degree. Table 2.2a and Table 2.2b display the percentage of men and women in the five major racial designations who are over 25 and who have completed college from 1970 to 1998. The data show several patterns:

- The college-educated population has increased dramatically in the 28-year period, either doubling or tripling for almost every group.

TABLE 2.2a. Percentage of Males 25 Years and Over Who Have Completed College, by Sex and Race, 1970 to 1998

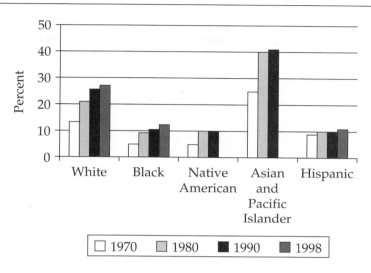

TABLE 2.2b. Percentage of Females 25 Years and Over Who Have Completed College, by Sex and Race, 1970 to 1998

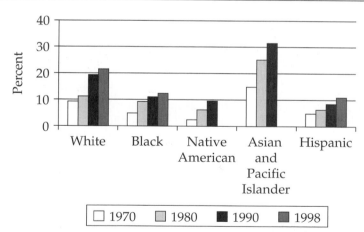

Source: U.S. Bureau of the Census. 1998 Current Population Survey. "Educational Attainment in the United States," March 1998 (Update) pp. 20–513. Table A2.: Percent of People 25 Years Old and Over Who Have Completed High School or College, by Race, Hispanic Origin and Sex: Selected Years 1940 to 1998. Available online: www.census.gov/population/socdemo/education/tablea–02.txt, accessed December 10, 1998.

Note: 1970 data for Asians are based on the 1 in 1000 Public Microdata Samples. 1998 data for Native Americans and Asian, Pacific Islanders are not available.

- Black women are the only group of women whose educational attainment is higher than that of men in their group. In 1998, 15.4 percent of Black women and 13.9 percent of Black men had completed college.
- In 1998, only 68 percent as many Black women and 48 percent as many Hispanic women had attained college degrees as had White women. Only 51 percent as many Black men and 41 percent as many Hispanic men had attained college degrees as had White men.
- In 1990, Asian Americans, although less than 2 percent of the total U.S. population, had the largest college-educated population of all racial groups. They also experienced the greatest percentage point increase in college education from 1970 to 1990 (16.8 percent for men and 17.2 percent for women compared to 11.2 percent and 10.4 percent for White men and women, respectively). This increase is in part the result of the Immigration and Naturalization Act of 1965, which allowed immigration of people who worked in targeted high-technology occupations such as engineer and computer specialist that require a college degree. Immigration produced a 75 percent increase in the Asian or Pacific Islander population between 1960 and 1970, a 127.5 percent increase between 1970 and 1980, and a 107.8 percent increase from 1980 to 1990 (Roberts 1995).

The Hispanic population increased 61 percent between 1970 and 1980 and 53 percent between 1980 and 1990 (Roberts 1995). By 1990, 42 percent of the Hispanic population and 70 percent of the Asian population between the ages of 18 and 24 were born in a foreign country. In contrast, only 2 percent of the White, 4 percent of the Black, and 2 percent of Native American populations 18 to 24 years old were foreign born (Hogan and Lichter 1995). In part because Latin Americans have been recruited to low-wage jobs in the Southwest (e.g., farm labor), the percentage of the Hispanic population that has completed college remains low (10.3 percent for males and 8.3 percent for females in 1996) while the college-educated Asian population, recruited for high-tech and managerial jobs, remains high. This systemic difference is important to remember when Asian educational attainment is held as a standard to compare against other minorities. Many educated Asians were not educated in the United States whereas African Americans, Native Americans, most Hispanics, and native-born Asian Americans attend a race and class-structured school system in the United States.

Polity

Several patterns stand out in the political time line. The pattern of patriarchal privilege that White, property-holding men had known in Europe was written onto the American landscape after the initial struggle for settlement was over. Whites took firm hold of the land and of the rights to make decisions about the lives of its occupants. Citizenship rights, including the right and the ability to vote and hold office, were first extended to property-owning White men and were denied to all women, to Native Americans, to African Americans—slave and free—and to White men who owned no property. These oppressed groups have worked for over

200 years to achieve in law and in practice what property-owning White men claimed at the founding of the nation.

One way to assess changes in the balance of power among groups is to track representation in government offices and in the military. The time line reveals a story of slow progress that nonetheless changes to a "war of position" after World War II when the force of racial and gender liberation movements significantly changed the position of groups.

Gay and lesbian representation has been slower to come. Gays and lesbians have historically been the target of particularly oppressive government actions, such as being excluded from immigrating to the United States after the passage of the McCarran-Walter Act of 1952, identified as traitors during the 1950s, expelled from the military, and harassed by the police (Blasius and Phelan 1997; D'Emilio 1983; Duberman, Vicinus, and Chauncey 1989). Recent research has shown that the United States and its allies continued the imprisonment of homosexuals they found in Nazi concentration camps on the grounds that their incarceration was justifiable (Duberman, Vicinus, and Chauncey 1989).

Cities such as Tampa, Florida, and Boulder, Denver, and Aspen, Colorado, that passed antidiscrimination measures in the early 1990s witnessed extensive political mobilization to reverse the measures, including passing statewide legislation to nullify the antidiscrimination measures. Barney Frank was elected as a gay congressman in 1988, but only after he had been "outed" and had already served his district successfully for seven years. In 1998 Tammy Baldwin of Wisconsin became the first "out" lesbian elected to Congress.

Citizenship

1778   The United States Constitution limits the right to vote to taxpayers or property owners, who make up a large proportion of the White male population. By the time Andrew Jackson is elected president in 1828, the right to vote is extended to include almost all White males.

1790   In a first effort to define American citizenship, Congress passes the Naturalization Law, which states that only free White immigrants are eligible for naturalized citizenship.

1830   The Indian Removal Act mandates the removal of Native Americans (including Seminoles, Choctaws, Creeks, Chickasaws, and Cherokees) from east of the Mississippi River to the newly established Indian Territory in present-day Oklahoma. In 1838 the Cherokee tribe is driven along the "Trail of Tears" after being forcibly removed from its land.

1848   The Treaty of Guadalupe-Hidalgo ends the Mexican War and incorporates half the land area of Mexico (i.e., the states of Texas, New Mexico, Arizona, and California and parts of Nevada, Utah, and Colorado) into the United States. Mexicans remaining in the new territory are granted full citizenship rights. Because language or cultural rights of the new citizens are not protected, over the next 50 years language laws inhibit Mexican American participation in voting, judicial processes, and education.

1857   The Supreme Court rules in *Dred Scott v. John F. A. Sanford* that a slave is not a citizen of the United States and has no right to sue in federal courts.

1866   The Fourteenth Amendment is ratified, guaranteeing newly freed slaves the right to vote, but also limiting the vote to males.

1870   The Fifteenth Amendment is ratified, guaranteeing all citizens the right to vote regardless of race or color. Nevertheless, men of color continue to face obstacles to voting, such as literacy tests, dual registration, and poll taxes.

1875   In *Minor v. Happersett,* the Supreme Court rules that the clause guaranteeing equal protection under the laws of the Fourteenth Amendment does not include women. The Court concludes that although women are citizens, the right to vote is not a privilege of citizenship. Most states continue to disenfranchise women, although some, notably Western, states extend them the franchise.

1882   As a direct result of economic downturn and White workers' competition with Chinese men for jobs in agriculture; railroads; and the shoe, rope, and cigar industries, anti-Asian sentiment flares and leads to the passage of the Chinese Exclusion Act. The first legislation to restrict immigration for any group bans Chinese immigration and denies future citizenship to all Chinese already in the country. It is broadened by 1900 and renewed indefinitely in 1902.

1887   The Dawes Allotment Act grants the president the right to break up reservations and allot land to individual Native Americans. More than 80 million acres of land belonging to Native Americans is opened for settlement. Every Native American receives 160 acres of land and any land left over is sold. The act forces individuals to live on small farms, destroying the communal lifestyle of Native Americans.

1902   The Reclamation Act dispossesses many people of Mexican descent living in the Southwest from their lands.

1920   The Nineteenth Amendment is ratified, giving all citizens regardless of sex the right to vote. But when trying to vote, men and women of color still face property tax requirements, dual registration, literacy tests, and other obstacles.

1924   The National Origins Law, also know as the National Quota System, seeks to maintain Western European ethnic dominance in the United States by imposing limits on the number of immigrants coming into the country. The limits are quite stringent for immigrants from Eastern and Southern Europe, but much broader for Western Europeans. To provide cheap labor in the Southwest, Latin American countries are exempt from this law. Asian immigration is banned.

         Native Americans are granted citizenship in the United States, but some states continue to disenfranchise them.

1926   The American Eugenics Society is founded. American eugenists believe that the wealth and social position of the upper classes is justified by a superior genetic endowment. They support restrictions on immigration from nations they consider inferior such as Italy, Greece, and the countries of Eastern Europe. They argue for the sterilization of insane, retarded, and epileptic citizens in the United States. As a result of their efforts, sterilization laws are passed in 27 states, and isolated instances of involuntary sterilization continue into the 1970s.

1934   Since 1887, 62 percent of the Native American land base has been transferred to Whites.

1942   The War Relocation Authority is established to administer the forced evacuation of all persons of Japanese ancestry living on the U.S. West Coast and their relocation to inland detention centers; over 110,000 persons of Japanese ancestry are placed in 10 war relocation centers, victims of mass hysteria following the Japanese attack on Pearl Harbor in 1941. These war relocation centers, where military police are armed with machine guns, are like concentration camps.

The U.S. Army decides to enlarge Camp Gruber, a military installation with an extensive reservation not far from Muskogee, Oklahoma. To accomplish its plan, the government sees to it that eight tracts of restricted Cherokee property, including the homes of 45 Cherokee families, are condemned. The government forcibly removes the Cherokee from the land and orders that the land be vacated within 45 days.

1945   The War Relocation Centers that housed persons of Japanese ancestry during World War II are closed.

1948   For the first time, Native Americans in Arizona and New Mexico are allowed to vote in state and national elections.

1952   The McCarran-Walter Act allows the naturalization of non-White immigrants. Asian immigration is legalized but kept to low levels. England, Ireland, and Germany represent two-thirds of the quota for the entire world. The Western hemisphere, including Latin America, is exempt from limits except that applicants must clear a list of barriers designed to exclude homosexuals, Communists, and others.

1957   Utah allows Native Americans living on reservations to vote. It is the last state to do so.

1965   The Immigration and Naturalization Act gives all nations equal opportunity to immigrate to the United States. An annual limit of 20,000 immigrants is set for any given country, including countries in Latin America.

The Voting Rights Act becomes law. By suspending racially discriminatory voting practices, this act is chiefly intended to reverse the disenfranchisement of African Americans, but obstacles to voting continue to affect all people of color.

1975   The Voting Rights Act Amendment requires bilingual ballots in certain areas.

1983   United States English is established, an organization seeking to secure the passage of the English Language Amendment that would declare English as the official language in the United States. In 1995 this organization will have 400,000 members and an annual budget of $5 million.

1984   Wilma Mankiller becomes the first woman installed as principal chief of a major Native American tribe, the Cherokee in Oklahoma.

1988   The U.S. government apologizes for the internment of Japanese Americans during World War II and passes legislation providing reparations of $20,000 each to the approximately 60,000 surviving Japanese Americans who had been interned.

1990   The Immigration Act continues to permit immigration of immediate relatives of U.S. citizens but puts a flexible cap of approximately 700,000 for the fiscal years 1992–1994 on all immigrants. A preference system is based on family relationships, employment, and diversity. (See Figure 2.1 for a historical picture of the immigration patterns in the United States.)

1992   Congress passes the Voters Assistance Act, which mandates that bilingual voting information be readily available.

Government Offices

1822   Joseph Marion Hernandez (Whig, Florida) is the first Latino/a elected to Congress.

1870   During Reconstruction, the first African-American men, Hiram R. Revel (Republican, Mississippi) and Joseph Hayne Rainey (Republican, South Carolina) are elected to Congress.

1892   Charles Curtis (Republican, Kansas) is the first Native American to serve as a representative in Congress (1893–1907) and as a Senator (1907–1913). He later served as Vice President during Herbert Hoover's presidency (1929–1933).

1917   Jeanette Rankin (Republican, Montana) is the first woman elected to Congress.

1958   The first Japanese American, Daniel Inouye (Democrat, Hawaii), is elected to Congress.

1969   The first African-American woman, Shirley Chisholm (Democrat, New York), is elected to Congress.

1970   The first Asian-American woman, Patsy Mink (Democrat, Hawaii), is elected to Congress.

1974   The numbers of women in elective office begins to rise. Women hold 8 percent of the seats in state legislatures and 16 (3 percent) of the 535 seats in Congress.

1976   Daniel K. Akaka (Democrat, Hawaii) is the first Chinese American elected to Congress.

1981   The first woman Supreme Court justice, Sandra Day O'Connor, is seated.

1986   Women hold 14.8 percent of the seats in state legislatures and 24 (4.5 percent) of the 535 seats in Congress.

1988   After publicly disclosing his homosexuality in 1987, Barney Frank (Democrat, Massachusetts) becomes the first openly gay person to be elected to Congress. First elected in 1980, he is elected to his tenth term in 1998.

1989   Following the death of Claude Pepper, Ileana Ros-Lehtinen (Republican, Florida) is the first of three Latinas and the first Cuban American to be elected to Congress.

FIGURE 2.1. Immigration Trends by Region and Decade, 1820–1998.

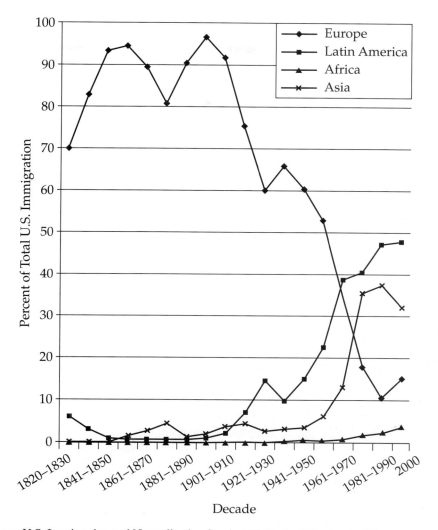

Source: U.S. Immigration and Naturalization Service. "Statistical Yearbook of the Immigration and Naturalization Service, 1998," available from, www.ins.usdoj.gov/graphics/aboutins/statistics/ybpage.htm, accessed March 19, 2000.

1992   The first Korean American, Jay C. Kim (Democrat, California), is elected to Congress.

　　　　　Ben Nighthorse Campbell (Republican, Colorado) becomes the first Native American elected as Senator in more than 60 years.

　　　　　Nydia Velazquez (Democrat, New York) is the first Puerto Rican woman to be elected to Congress. Lucille Roybal-Allard (Democrat, California) becomes the first Mexican-American woman to be elected to

Congress. Carole Moseley Braun (Democrat, Illinois) becomes the first African-American woman to be elected to the Senate.

1997   Madeleine Albright's appointment as the first woman Secretary of State makes her the highest ranking woman in the history of the U.S. government.

1998   Tammy Baldwin of Wisconsin becomes the first "out" lesbian elected to Congress.

1999   Women hold 67 (12.4 percent) of the 539 seats in Congress; 20 (3.7 percent) are held by women of color. Men of color hold 46 (8.5 percent) congressional seats.

2000   1,669 (22.5 percent) of the 7,424 state legislators are women; 251 (3.4 percent) are women of color.

The U.S. Congress is the primary body establishing policy for the nation. Control of this body has a tremendous impact on the health and well-being, rights, and opportunities of all U.S. citizens. Congress has 539 members whose composition in 1999 is displayed in Table 2.3.

While White men constituted only 35 percent of the total U.S. population in 1999, they controlled 77 percent of the seats in the U.S. House of Representatives, more than doubling their power over their actual population representation. In the U.S. Senate, their control is even greater—constituting 88 percent of that body of 100. Only three men of color (one Native American and two Asian Americans) and nine White women were senators in 1999 (CIS Congressional Universe 2000).

Military

1792   Although more than 5,000 African-American men served during the Revolutionary War, the United States requires only that all White males between the ages of 18 and 45 take up arms and report for training. The states that previously admitted free African Americans into their militia interpret the law as a ban and expel them.

1812   Like the militia, the new National Army accepts no African Americans until the War of 1812 compels it to do so.

1917   The Selective Service Act is passed, authorizing conscription for the nation's armed services and requiring all males between the ages of 21 and 30 to register for the draft.

1948   President Truman issues Executive Order 9981, directing the armed forces to provide equal treatment and opportunity regardless of race.

The Women's Armed Forces Integration Act incorporates the women's armed service nursing corps into the regular services, further opening military careers to American women.

1973   "Women-only" branches of the U.S. military are eliminated. But women are still barred from participating in combat.

1976   The first women are admitted to the U.S. military academies.

1980   The first women graduate from the service academies: Coast Guard, 14; U.S. Military Academy, 61; Naval Academy, 55; Air Force Academy, 97.

TABLE 2.3. Race and Gender Composition of the United States Congress and the U.S. Population, 1999

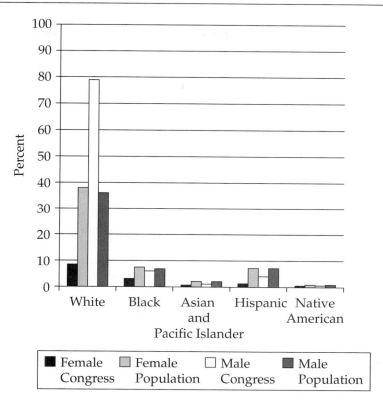

Sources: CIS Congressional Universe. 2000. Text from: Member Profile Reports. Available from: Congressional Universe (On-line Service). Bethesda, MD: Congressional Information Service.
U.S. Bureau of the Census. 1999. Resident Population Estimates of the United States by Sex, Race, and Hispanic Origin: April 1, 1990 to November 1, 1999. Available on-line: www.census.gov/population/estimates/nation/intfile3-1.txt

1991	Over 40,000 women serve in the Persian Gulf War; 7 percent of the active duty troops and 17 percent of the reserve forces and National Guard are women—the largest deployment of women in U.S. history.
1993	100 percent of the positions in the Coast Guard, 99.4 percent in the Air Force, 91.2 percent in the Navy, 67.2 percent in the Army, and 62 percent in the Marine Corps are open to women.
1994	The "Don't ask, don't tell, don't pursue" policy goes into effect, requiring that military personnel may not inquire about a service member's sexual orientation. It also requires that gays and lesbians not identify themselves as homosexual.

1999   Women in the military (including the Coast Guard) number 194,219—
14 percent of the total active force. The Air Force has the highest
percentage of women (18.3 percent) and the Marine Corps the lowest
(5.8 percent). The Army has the highest percentage of African-American
women (43 percent of women); the Marine Corps has the highest
percentage of women of Hispanic origin (13.6 percent of women). The
Navy is the only service with a higher percentage of women serving in
its officer ranks (14.3 percent) than in its enlisted ranks (12.8 percent).

Since the enactment of the "Don't ask, don't tell, don't pursue"
policy, 5,412 service members have been discharged from the military
under this policy, representing a 73 percent increase since the policy
went into effect five years earlier. Of the service members discharged,
31 percent are women.

Work/Economy

This section of the time line emphasizes legal changes that alter the status of various categories of workers. At first, laws and policies tended to focus on making
work policies and practices uniform across the country [e.g., child labor laws, unemployment compensation, Aid to Families with Dependent Children (AFDC)].
Later, the focus shifted to address concerns about inequities in the workplace (e.g.,
hiring practices, pay, and discrimination).

1848   A New York state law, the Married Women's Property Act, grants
married women the right to own property in their own name, to sue and
be sued, to run their own business, to work outside the home and claim
the wages as their own, and to make a will disposing of their own
property as freely as their husbands. This law serves as a model for
subsequent married women's property acts passed across the country
between 1848 and 1895. Before this law, the property of a woman
became her husband's to control upon marriage.

1904   The National Child Labor Committee forms in 25 branches in 22 states,
demanding that child labor be outlawed.

1910   It is estimated that more than two million children are employed in an
industrial setting.

1933   Congress authorizes the Civil Works Administration to give work to the
unemployed.

1935   Known as the cornerstone of the New Deal, the Social Security Act is
passed, providing monthly payments for Americans aged 65 and older.
This act and the others that follow ensure federal responsibility for
public welfare.

Aid to Dependent Children (ADC), initially a minor provision of
the Social Security Act, provides single mothers with a means to subsist.
In the 1960s its name would be changed to AFDC (Aid to Families with
Dependent Children) as part of President Johnson's "Great Society."
AFDC is built on the existing tradition of state pensions for widows
who were mothers of small children.

President Roosevelt establishes the Works Progress Administration (WPA). During its eight-year existence, the WPA put some 8.5 million people to work (more than 11 million were unemployed in 1934) at a cost to the federal government of approximately $11 billion. The agency's construction projects produced more than 650,000 miles of roads, 125,000 public buildings, 75,000 bridges, 8,000 parks, and 800 airports. The Federal Arts Project, Federal Writers' Project, and Federal Theater Project—all under the aegis of the WPA—employed thousands of artists, writers, and actors in such programs as the creation of art work for public buildings, the documentation of local life, and the organization of community theaters.

1938 Congress passes the Fair Labor Standards Act, limiting work to 40 hours a week, after which workers must be paid overtime, and establishing a minimum wage of $0.25 an hour. This law affects 12.5 million workers. The establishment of the minimum wage significantly discourages the employment of minors.

1939 The Department of Agriculture introduces food stamps.

1941 In part as a response to a threatened march on Washington to demand jobs for Blacks, President Roosevelt issues Executive Order 8802, designed to end racial discrimination in government agencies, job training programs, and industries with defense contracts. It also establishes the Committee on Fair Employment Practices.

1947 Congress passes the Taft Hartley Act, written by the National Association of Manufacturers, to cripple unions that had gained strength during the labor shortages of World War II. The act outlaws closed shops (which required all employees in workplaces with unions to be union members), sympathy strikes, and secondary boycotts; requires union representation to be determined by a percentage of the workforce as a whole, not just of those voting; prevents foremen from joining unions; allows strikebreakers to vote in union elections and to vote to decertify a union; allows the President of The United States to halt strikes; makes union leaders subject to arrest for failing to break wildcat strikes; and requires union leaders to sign loyalty oaths stating that they are not Communists.

1962 President Kennedy issues an Executive Order that requires federal employees to be hired and promoted without regard to sex. Before this order, federal managers could restrict consideration to either men or women.

1963 The Equal Pay Equity Act is the first federal law that prohibits sex discrimination and guarantees to men and women the same wages for the same work performed under the same conditions. It does not cover those employed in domestic or agricultural positions, executives, professionals, or administrators.

1964 Congress passes Title VII of the Civil Rights Act, prohibiting discrimination in employment because of sex (but not sexual orientation), race, color, religion, and national origin.

1968   The Fair Housing Act of 1968, also known as Title VIII of the Civil Rights Act, is passed, making it for the first time illegal to advertise any preference, limitation, or discrimination based on race, color, religion, or national origin. It will be amended in 1974 to prohibit sex discrimination in financing, selling, or renting housing or in the provision of brokerage services.

1969   Congress passes the first of three major Tax Reform Acts (others follow in 1976 and 1986) purportedly designed to reduce tax loopholes for the rich. It didn't work. Between 1969 and 1989 the number of persons with incomes over $200,000 who paid no income taxes rose from 155 to 1,081.

1970   Women make up 38 percent of the civilian workforce, rising to 42.5 percent by 1980, 45.2 percent by 1990, and 46.2 percent by 1996.

1972   The Equal Pay Act of 1963 is amended to include executive, professional, and administrative positions.

   East Lansing, Michigan, is the first community to protect its workers from discrimination on the basis of sexual orientation. As of January 2000, however, the state of Michigan still does not protect its workers from this discrimination.

1974   The Equal Credit Opportunity Act is passed, allowing married women for the first time to obtain credit cards in their own name.

1975   For every $1.00 earned by White men, Black men earn $0.74; Hispanic men, $0.72; White women, $0.56; Black women, $0.55; and Hispanic women, $0.49.

1986   The Supreme Court declares sexual harassment to be a form of illegal employment discrimination.

1988   Employment and training, transitional health and day care benefits for persons leaving public assistance, and extension of public assistance to families with both parents present are only a few of the reforms that the Welfare Reform Act enacts. The law also provides for improved enforcement of child support orders.

   The Fair Housing Act of 1968 is amended to prohibit discrimination against the elderly, mentally or physically handicapped, and families with children.

1994   One person in every two-parent family who receives payments under AFDC must participate in job searches.

1995   For every $1.00 earned by full-time, year-round employed White men, Black men earn $0.76; Hispanic men, $0.63; White women, $0.71; Black women, $0.64; and Hispanic women, $0.53.

1996   The Personal Responsibility and Work Opportunity Reconciliation Act replaces the previous welfare system with block grants to states through the Temporary Assistance to Needy Families (TANF) program. There is a lifetime limit of five years on receiving benefits. Welfare recipients are required to work after 24 months of benefits, or they become ineligible for further assistance.

Indicators of Economic Inequality

To highlight current levels of economic inequality, a set of indicators follows.

National Income Inequality. Key to the well-being of groups is control over material resources, particularly income and wealth, and freedom from poverty. A major distinguishing characteristic of the U.S. economy is the vast gap between the material resources of the rich and the poor. Andrew Hacker (1997:54) reports that of the 14 industrial nations he studied, the United States has by far the highest level of income inequality—with the top 10 percent of income-earning households receiving almost six times the earnings of households in the bottom 10 percent of the income distribution (see Table 2.4).

The United States has the greatest income disparity, in part because the rich receive more here than elsewhere but mostly because the poor receive so much less. In the United States, the poor earn 35 percent of the U.S. median income—three-fourths of what the poor receive in Canada (the next lowest country), two-thirds of what they receive in England, and slightly over one-half of what they receive in the Netherlands.

Who Controls Material Resources? Race, class, gender, and sexuality hierarchies are maintained in part because dominant groups have greater control over the material resources of society. Therefore, women, people of color, and working-class people have higher poverty rates, lower incomes, less wealth, fewer prestigious occupations, and pay a greater portion of their earnings in taxes (Barlett and Steele

TABLE 2.4. Share of National Income: Ratio of Rich to Poor*

Best-Off Tenth (%)	Poorest Tenth (%)	Country	Inequality Index
153	59	Finland	2.6
152	56	Sweden	2.7
163	59	Belgium	2.8
175	62	Netherlands	2.9
162	55	Norway	2.9
185	54	Switzerland	3.4
187	54	New Zealand	3.5
193	55	France	3.5
194	51	United Kingdom	3.8
187	47	Australia	4.0
184	46	Canada	4.0
198	49	Italy	4.1
209	50	Ireland	4.2
206	35	United States	5.9

*Percentages show the proportion of each nation's median income received by the midpoint household within its poorest 10% and also for its best-off 10%. The index of inequality is the ratio of the two percentages for each country.
Source: Andrew Hacker, *Money: Who Has How Much and Why* (New York: Scribner's, 1997), p. 54.

1994; Hacker 1997; Harrison and Bennett 1995; Oliver and Shapiro 1995). Although the economic status of gays, bisexuals, and lesbians as a group is not reported in government documents, some clear material advantages are denied to homosexuals, among them the special economic privileges that accrue to married couples: spousal benefits on the job, survivor benefits in Social Security, and tax advantages. Furthermore, promotions and other forms of advancement in many work settings are still difficult to obtain for gay men and lesbians (Badgett 1995).

Who Are the Poor? Since 80 percent of the U.S. population in 1990 was White, there are of course more poor Whites than any other group. However, families of color and especially women of color who are single parents and their children bear a much greater portion of the poverty burden than their share in the population would indicate. As Table 2.5 reveals, families of color have higher poverty rates than the White family rate of 8.0 percent in 1998: Asians, 11.0 percent; Hispanics, 22.7 percent; and Blacks, 23.4 percent.

Single-parent mothers and their children have the highest poverty rates of any family group, but single-parent women of color and their children are most likely to be poor. Poverty rates for families headed by single mothers are Whites, 24.9 percent; Blacks, 40.8 percent; and Hispanics, 43.7 percent (data for Asian, Pacific Islanders, and Native Americans are not available).

TABLE 2.5. Poverty Rates by Race, 1998.

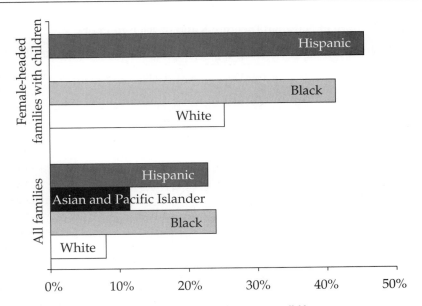

Note: Data for Asian and Pacific Islander female-headed families are not available.
Source: U.S. Bureau of the Census, *Statistical Abstract of the United States* (Washington, DC: U.S. Government Printing Office, 1999), Poverty 1998: Poverty by Selected Characteristics. Available on-line: www.census.gov/hhes/poverty98/pv98est1.html

Who Has the Wealth? As of 1996 only two White women were chief executive officers (CEOs) on *Fortune* magazine's list of the top 1,000 corporations in the United States—Jill Barad, the CEO of Mattel, the toymaker, and Linda Wachner, head of Warnaco, a women's apparel company (Hacker 1997). In 1999 *Forbes* magazine reported the top 200 billionaires in the world: 48 were from the United States and all but two were white men. The list included such familiar names as Bill Gates, Sam Walton's family, Warren Buffett, Ted Turner, Ross Perot, David Rockefeller, and Ralph Lauren (Dolan 1999).

Who Gets the Income? Most of the population, however, makes a living not through corporate ownership but through the wages earned from working for an employer. The income distribution of the United States also reveals the effects of race, class, and gender inequality. One major economic disadvantage to people of color and working-class people is that they have higher rates of unemployment, part-time work, and seasonal work. White women, while they do not have higher unemployment rates, are more likely to work part-time and seasonally than White men. However, even comparing only people working full time and year-round, White men continue to earn significantly more than White women or people of color.

Men earn significantly more than women in every racial group. Asian men are the only group that approximates White men, earning $0.96 for every $1.00 earned by White men. Every other group earns at least 25 percent less than White men, and Hispanic and Native American women earn only about one-half the earnings of White men. Table 2.6 presents median income data in 1998 for all race and gender groups.

Marriage/Reproduction

Controlling marriage and reproduction and its attendant privileges has been a primary mechanism of race, class, gender, and sexuality oppression throughout the history of this country. The data in this section implicitly show the story of attempts to control women and some of the ways that those controls vary by race, class, and sexual orientation. For example, after *Roe v. Wade* legalized abortion, the Hyde Amendment effectively took away that right for many poor women, in practice more frequently for women of color, by eliminating federal funding for abortions. The contests over sexuality have also been fought largely in this arena. For example, gays and lesbians still have not realized the legal right to marry and obtain related rights, including spousal health benefits, joint tax filing, and, in almost all states, adoption. And many lives were lost because the government was slow to respond to HIV/AIDS, which was initially believed to be a disease affecting only homosexual men.

1873   Congress passes the Comstock Law, defining contraceptive information as "obscene material" and making it a crime to import or distribute any device, medicine, or information designed to prevent conception or induce abortion and even to mention in print the names of sexually transmitted diseases. Connecticut makes use of contraceptives illegal; 24 states

TABLE 2.6. Median Income for Full-Time Year-Round Workers by Race and Gender, 1998.

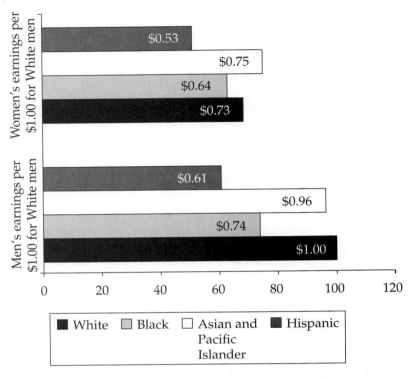

Source: U.S. Bureau of the Census, 1999. Income 1998: Historical Income Tables—People (Tables P = 36B, P = 36C, P = 36D, P = 36E). Available on-line: www.census.gov/hhes/income/histinc/incperdet.html.

prohibit publication or advertising of abortion or birth control information; and 14 other states also prohibit speech about birth control and abortion.

1921   Margaret Sanger organizes the American Birth Control League, which later becomes the Planned Parenthood Federation of America. She does this to assist the poor because birth control is primarily available to the wealthy. Sanger arranges to get doctors for the poor and to educate them about birth control.

1922   The Cable Act passes, discouraging Chinese Americans from marrying immigrants who could gain exemption from naturalization laws and laws preventing them from owning land by marrying citizens. This act intimidates Chinese Americans and severely restricts their ability to establish families in the United States.

1931   The Cable Act of 1922 is amended to allow American-born Asian women to regain their American citizenship upon termination of their marriage to a noncitizen.

1936   The Cable Act is repealed.

1965   In *Griswold v. Connecticut,* the Supreme Court upholds the right of married couples to use contraceptives.

1966   Seventeen states have laws against interracial marriage. All 50 states regulate marriage between Whites and other races.

1967   In *Loving v. Virginia,* the Supreme Court overturns all antimiscegenation laws (against marriage between different races), deeming them a violation of the Equal Protection Clause of the Fourteenth Amendment.

1972   In *Eisenstadt v. Baird,* the Supreme Court invalidates state laws restricting the access of single persons to contraceptives.

1973   The Supreme Court decides in *Roe v. Wade* that the decision to have an abortion must be left solely to a woman and her physician.

1977   The Hyde Amendment is passed, cutting off federally funded abortions for low-income women.

1978   The Pregnancy Discrimination Act of 1978 is passed as an amendment to Title VII of the Civil Rights Act, requiring all firms of 15 or more employees to treat pregnancy the same as any other medical disability. As a result, discrimination against women because of pregnancy, childbirth, or related conditions is prohibited.

1981   The first cases (422 in the U.S.) of AIDS (acquired immunodeficiency syndrome) are identified in Los Angeles, California. Initially, most cases of AIDS in the United States were diagnosed in gay men and intravenous drug users.

1987   After a six-year silence, President Ronald Reagan uses the word "AIDS" in public for the first time. Of the 71,176 AIDS cases diagnosed in the country, 41,027 people have died.

1988   The Reagan administration sends an eight-page booklet, "Understanding AIDS," to every household in America. According to the Centers for Disease Control (CDC), the epidemic will not spread widely in the heterosexual population.

1990   The 1990 Census shows that about 1.1 million interracial couples live in the United States, constituting approximately 2 percent of married couples.

In *Ohio v. Akron Center for Reproductive Health,* the Supreme Court upholds a state law requiring teenagers who seek abortions to notify one parent before doing so.

1992   The Supreme Court affirms in *Planned Parenthood v. Casey* that it is the right of states to restrict abortions, if the restrictions do not pose an "undue burden." Specifically, the Court upholds 24-hour waiting periods and mandatory antiabortion counseling for women seeking abortions.

1993   The Pregnancy Discrimination Act is superseded by the Family and Medical Leave Act, requiring employers with 50 or more employees to allow time off for pregnancy, a medical condition, or care of a sick family member.

All 50 states have revised their laws so that men can be prosecuted for sexually assaulting their wives, cohabitants, or dates.

1994   The Freedom of Access to Clinic Entrances Act, the first abortion rights legislation, imposes severe fines and jail sentences and makes it a potential felony to block access to clinic entrances and to intimidate or harass clinic workers.

1996   Hawaii becomes the first state to recognize that gay and lesbian couples are entitled to the same privileges as heterosexual married couples.

        The Defense of Marriage Act is passed, acknowledging that states will not be obligated to recognize gay and lesbian marriages performed in another state.

1998   Hawaii voters approve a constitutional amendment that expands the power of state lawmakers to restrict marriages to opposite-sex couples, thereby invalidating the 1996 Hawaiian court ruling.

1999   Since 1995, 29 states have enacted antimarriage laws targeting gay couples.

        The Vermont Supreme Court grants gay and lesbian couples the right to enter into legal contracts that confer the same rights and protections as state-sanctioned marriage.

        Thirty-four states enact 70 antichoice measures (e.g., waiting periods, conscience clauses, counseling bans, insurance prohibitions), up 300 percent since 1994 when 13 states enacted 18 antichoice measures.

        Deaths worldwide from AIDS total 16.3 million. An estimated 33.6 million people worldwide are living with HIV/AIDS. The major mode of HIV transmission is heterosexual intercourse, which accounts for 70 percent of all HIV infections. The overwhelming majority of people (95 percent of the world total) with HIV live in developing countries.

2000   The Vermont House of Representatives passes a bill to create "civil unions," giving gay and lesbian couples virtually all the benefits of marriage.

        Fifteen states continue to provide public funding for abortion in all or most circumstances; 29 states provide public funding for abortion only in cases of rape, incest, or life endangerment.

SUMMARY

The historical record of oppressed groups in U.S. society reminds us that this nation was built by first extracting the land from Native Indians, by building the agricultural base through the forced labor of African slaves and the cheap labor of Mexican migrants, by expanding the land base through the conquest of Mexico and building the railroads with the cheap labor of Chinese workers, and by the factory, farm, and service work of the White working class. Women of each of these groups worked in these arenas while they cared for families and raised their children to participate in the society, without themselves being fully accepted as equal participants. The historical time line gives us a sense of the persistence of both oppression and of the struggles of oppressed groups for full access to the rights, privileges, and opportunities of U.S. society.

Current social and economic indicators such as poverty, income, wealth, education, and congressional representation confirm that race, class, gender, and sexuality systems of oppression are persistent, pervasive, and severe. They persist through time, pervade every institution in society, and have severe consequences for oppressed groups. These historical markers and statistical indicators alert us that race, class, gender, and sexuality oppression exists. How these systems are created, maintained, challenged, and transformed is not apparent in these indicators. The remainder of this book seeks to describe how these systems operate in the United States today.

A Conceptual Framework: Five Themes

This section presents a conceptual framework for understanding race, class, gender, and sexuality as interrelated systems of oppression by identifying five major themes in the growing scholarship focusing on the interplay of these systems. The themes serve as guides for conducting analyses of race, class, gender, and sexuality dynamics. The section begins in Chapter 3 with the case of Margaret Welch, whose life illustrates both overtly and subtly the dynamic relationships of race, class, gender, and sexuality. Welch's case is also used to illustrate the different kinds of questions asked when only a single instead of multiple dimensions of inequality are considered in an analysis. Chapters 4 and 5 introduce the themes of the framework in detail. To facilitate future analyses of the interrelated systems of race, class, gender, and sexuality, the section concludes with a set of questions derived from the conceptual framework.

CHAPTER 3

The Story of Margaret Welch: A Case Study

Everyone thinks that if you try hard enough, you can make it in America. I thought so too, but when I found myself a widow at age thirty-three, with two children to support, and forced to go on public aid, I discovered how the welfare system works.

I have tried hard to make a better life for myself and my girls. I have studied hard to get an A average after being out of school for sixteen years, and it hurts to have to give up my dream, but the system won't let me out of the "welfare class." There are a great many of us who want out of the welfare class, but the system won't let us out.

—MARGARET WELCH
Chicago Tribune, Letters to the Editor, March 26, 1987

Margaret Welch is a White woman who moved to Chicago from Tennessee in 1982 after the death of her first husband. When her second husband "walked out" five years later leaving her with two girls, ages nine and five, she was forced to go on public aid. What follows is an excerpt from an interview conducted with Margaret Welch by Studs Terkel, a Chicago writer.

An Interview by Studs Terkel

The image people have of public aid is black women with a lot of kids. Before I went on public aid, I had that impression: the more babies you have, the more money you get. I realized that you get three dollars a day if you have another baby. That's not going to raise a kid. I thought they were freeloaders, who like to live off other people. But when I was forced on public aid, my opinion changed. I was on an even keel with them. We all sat there in the office and waited five or six hours at a time. They weren't getting special treatment. They were having hard times, too.

What gets me is this: I'm on public aid. I'm trying to stay in school and

---

61

(continued)

apply for all these scholarships. Blacks and Hispanics have hollered so much, they've got these scholarships. Even single white men can get scholarships if they have kids. But it's hard for a single white woman to get a scholarship, because you're not a minority.

If you're a woman, you're supposed to take care of your kids if you're left alone with them. If men are left with kids, it's "Oh, that poor guy.". . .

I've just registered for my last year in nursing school. I won't be able to go back because the scholarship I got last year was just denied me. They said it was a Hispanic scholarship, and enough Hispanics applied, so I lost out. . . . I can't afford the tuition, so I don't know if I'm ever going back. . . .

I went on public aid when my job at the hot-dog stand ended and my house burned down. I lost everything. On public aid, they gave me $711. That was supposed to get me an apartment, replace all my furniture and all the kids' clothes. The cheapest apartment called for a $600 deposit. It doesn't leave anything.

I noticed a poster on the wall: public aid helps returning to school. I had a GED. I took the test and placed into the highest class. They were telling me about the scholarships and said I was a cinch. I got one last year and carried straight A's. But I found out last week I'm not a minority and out.

There goes . . . my dream of becoming a registered nurse. . . . I got so close. "I'm sorry, but this time we have enough Hispanics."

This is the first time in my life I'm really mad this way. . . .My boyfriend is Mexican and my best girlfriend is Puerto Rican and very black. I've never been prejudiced, but why the hell are you doing this to me? I've been through enough. I was widowed at seventeen and married again and my husband took off, leaving me with two kids. Just because I'm white, I don't get something? . . .

I feel like I've been robbed of a chance to finish school. . . . I already had a job promised me in a hospital. I would be making $15 an hour for the first time in my life. I could feed my kids without begging, borrowing, or stealing. Selling food stamps is considered stealing. I get $308 a month to live on. My rent's $250. So that leaves me $58. You can't pay lights and gas and everything else. So you end up selling a few food stamps to buy laundry detergent.

For food, you buy a lot of rice and flour, make tortillas. That's all your kids have. They're the ones who are punished, whether you're white, black, or anything else. I was so sure that in a year, I'd have a job where I could feed my kids without feeling the way I do. I wouldn't have them laughed at in school because they get free meals. They wouldn't have to suffer that any more. Now . . .

My Puerto Rican black friend and I always applied for the same scholarships. We were always among the top in grades. . . . We were promised jobs at the same hospital. We were in school together since the first day. This year, she got the scholarship, I didn't. She came to the house and said, "Don't be mad at me." I'm not. She's still my best friend. It's just—*why?*

(continued)

We were sitting in my truck. I told her I got my letter. She ran out, checked her mail, and she's gotten hers. We didn't open them until we were together. She could tell by the look on my face. "What's the matter?" "I didn't get it. Did you?" She mumbled, "Yeah," and wouldn't let me see her letter. For a minute I was so mad at her. "I just want to kill you." [*Laughs*] We're still great friends. I'm glad she's making it, she deserves it.

I think blacks are going ahead. They speak out, they fight for their rights, and they're getting them. We're almost afraid of them and let them push us back.

If you see one black guy walking by, it's okay. But if you see three or four standing on a corner, you cross to the other side of the street. I was mugged about two years ago by a couple of Hispanic guys. Now if I see several Hispanics standing together, I cross the street.

TERKEL: *Suppose there were three or four tough-looking white guys?*

I'd just walk through them. . . . I've never been scared of a fight. I'm a big woman. I can handle myself.

Not far from my house is a motorcycle gang, Hell's Henchmen. . . . When I was tending bar, I'd walk past them at two, three in the morning by myself and not think anything of it. But there's no way I'd walk by a black club.

I myself really don't feel hostility, but I feel that a lot of whites are becoming more and more afraid of blacks. . . .

Somehow, people have to talk about this. You shouldn't feel "I'm too dumb to get up and say something"; talk in your words, say whatever. If enough people talk, good ideas may come out of it. Nobody wants to give up whatever power they got. To me, that's the whole thing, power. . . .

You see the old slave-day movies. They were scared of their masters, their owners. They did what they were told. It seems like they've almost turned the tables. It's like we're scared to stand up against them. . . .

TERKEL: *Would you prefer it the old way?*

No-o-o-o! When I went to City-Wide College, my supervisor was a black lady. She just knew when there was something wrong. I'd sit at my desk half-crying. I'd gotten my second five-day notice that month to move out of my apartment. One of my classmates told her. When I came back from my break, there was a check on my desk to cover my rent. I tried to pay her back, but she said, "No, that's my gift to you." I would never have dreamed there was a black person like that when I was in Tennessee [*where she grew up*].

I don't believe black people should be pushed back. But I don't feel because I'm white, I should be either. It goes both ways. I don't think the gap is that big on a street level, not in my neighborhood. But when you get into the bureaucracy, business, and school, it's those big people making the noise. . . . (Terkel 1992:69–73).

INTERPRETING MARGARET'S STORY

Margaret Welch is angry. She is also hurt, discouraged, resentful, envious, confused, empathetic, proud, and self-confident. In short, she is a complex person trying to comprehend her life circumstances in light of the race, class, gender, and sexuality hierarchies in society, in the welfare system, in her college, in her neighborhood, and in her most intimate relationships with her boyfriend and her best girlfriend. She vents her anger at a social system that leaves her without the resources to finish her education and get off welfare. More intensely, she vents her anger at people of color, who have secured scholarship programs to which she is told she cannot apply, even as she struggles to control and understand that anger. In the same breath she says that she wants "to kill" her Puerto Rican best friend, that she is glad for her, and that she deserves the scholarship.

- Is Margaret racist?
- Is her lack of effort or talent the reason she is on welfare?
- Will cutting back her welfare payments or requiring that she work or go to school solve Margaret's dilemma and get her off welfare?
- If she were Black or Puerto Rican and had been turned down for a scholarship, where would she place her anger?
- Why did someone attribute the denial of Margaret's request for a scholarship to Latino/a students' funding?
- Is Margaret a criminal for selling food stamps?
- If Margaret were living in the 1950s or 1960s, how would her situation have been different?
- Why is she afraid of anonymous Black men on the street, but not of White Hell's Henchmen?
- If Margaret were lesbian, would her children be taken from her?
- What does it mean to be a White, heterosexual mother on welfare today?

These are but a few of the many questions raised by Margaret's life that are centered in race, class, gender, and sexuality hierarchies. These questions have no simple answers. I raise them, in part, to illustrate the complexity of race, class, gender, and sexuality in our everyday lives and to provide you with an avenue to explore the many ways that social location in these hierarchies shapes how we experience the world and how we view the experiences of others.

Race, class, gender, and sexuality are fundamental features of social organization and personal identity. They are deeply embedded in society's basic political, economic, and ideological institutions: the state, the economy, the family, and the educational and religious systems. They are also fundamental elements of personal identity, how we define who we are. Yet every day, the meanings of these hierarchies are negotiated and renegotiated as individuals like Margaret encounter institutions such as the college or the welfare office and attempt to understand, conform to, and challenge the patterns of behavior and beliefs that are associated with race, class, gender, and sexuality.

As Margaret begins to react to her scholarship denial, she believes she is a victim of discrimination because she is a White woman. Yet, as the data in Chapter 2 show, the major institutions of society are primarily structured to support the advancement of White people, not people of color. White women are 1.6 times as likely to graduate from college as Black women and 2.8 times as likely as Puerto Rican women (Ortiz 1994). Living in poverty are 40.8 percent of Black female heads of families with children, 43.7 percent of Hispanic female heads of families with children, and 24.9 percent of White female heads of families with children, such as Margaret (See Table 2.5). But because of scholarships targeted to increase enrollments of these groups, Margaret still feels discriminated against as a White woman.

Interestingly, Margaret doesn't overtly consider the role of class in shaping her situation. Instead, class appears more in the background of her life. She doesn't question the fact that higher education isn't free and open to all, as elementary and secondary schools are. Like most Americans, she takes that for granted. Instead, she needs financial aid because college costs money and she is poor. Yet she seems to feel "put down" and blocked not as much by these class realities as by Blacks and Latinos/as—other oppressed groups—who collectively and successfully have pushed for rights in the political arena and have won key struggles, including those for college financial aid.

Because Margaret was told that her scholarship was for Latinos/as, it is not surprising that Margaret would blame Black and Latino/a progress for her own ill fortune. But one of the things that an analysis of race, class, gender, and sexuality reveals is that in any social situation the way we define the situation, what we take to be real, is shaped by our social location. Thus, any particular situation can be described as having multiple "truths"—realities, understandings—representing the interpretations that different actors make based on the earlier experiences and perspectives they bring to the encounter.

Consider for a moment Margaret's interpretation, her "truth." Margaret said she was told that

- the scholarship she had received in the past was in fact a Latino/a scholarship
- "enough" Latinos/as had applied this semester
- because she was White and not Latina she could not have a scholarship.

A Mexican or Puerto Rican student, upon hearing of Margaret's plight, might see the situation from a different perspective, have a different "truth," and wonder

- if the money was reserved for Latinos/as, why was Margaret given a Latino/a scholarship in the first place?
- if the money could have been held until enough eligible Latinos/as applied.
- why were there not enough applicants?
- if Latinas on welfare knew the money was available.
- what the welfare office was doing to encourage Latinos/as to attend college.

A financial aid officer might wonder

- why would funds earmarked for Hispanic students be given to a White student?
- if restricted funds are being commingled (a violation of proper procedure and law in many cases).

- if Margaret has been told of the scholarship money that was available and open to *anyone* based on need or merit.
- why Margaret was told that a scholarship was denied her because Hispanics applied when she was never really eligible for that form of aid in the first place.

Based on the message she was given, we have seen the way Margaret feels: "All of a sudden, they're [the minorities] giving me the short end," and the questions she asks:

- Just because their skin's darker than mine, why should they get it and I don't?
- I've never been prejudiced, but why the hell are you doing this to me?
- Just because I'm White, I don't get something?

What are the "truths"—the understandings, the interpretations—that each of these actors takes from this situation? Margaret believes that White women don't have a chance. Even though her best girlfriend and her boyfriend are Latina and Latino, her neighborhood is racially mixed, and she has had many positive experiences across racial lines, Margaret appears to see her disadvantage as directly connected to a presumed advantage of people of color—and she is angry. Interracial hostility, even though it is very uncomfortable for her, is an understandable, if not desirable, outcome. Margaret also raises the issue of the welfare system's not wanting people to get off welfare. Here she implies, but does not directly state, that if welfare is designed to help people become self-sufficient, she, as a poor person, should be able to get the financial aid she needs to finish her education and to get a job as a nurse. Race is not her focus. Poverty and the class structure of the educational system are. And this "truth," while part of Margaret's world view, is not the one that is reinforced in the way that her denial was explained to her. This truth lacks the power, therefore, of the racial advantage "truth" and appears to recede in Margaret's understanding of the situation.

How people interpret their "truths"—their lives, the meanings they take from their experiences—is also revealed as much in their silences and the things they take for granted as in their spoken words. Those silences are most likely to occur in areas where we experience privilege. So one of the issues that Margaret doesn't consider is her heterosexuality—because it poses no special problem for her here. Because she is heterosexual and White, Margaret is presumed (by the welfare office and larger society) to have the capacity to be a good mother if she could change her class position by getting a degree and a good job and providing for her children (cf. McIntosh 1998). If Margaret were lesbian, however, she would face the prospect of having her children taken away from her by child protective services as many lesbian mothers do (Benkov 1994). If she were lesbian, she might be less likely to even go to the welfare office to seek aid, and she and her children would suffer even worse economic hardship as a result. But these problems don't emerge in Margaret's life. She takes for granted that her sexual orientation had nothing to do with the scholarship denial, that her children won't be taken away or harassed in school because of her sexual orientation. It's simply not an "issue" for her. It is a silence in her story, but it is a powerful "truth" in her life.

And what of Margaret's best girlfriend? What truths might she take from this situation? First, she obviously feared that her friendship would be damaged by the attribution of Hispanic responsibility for Margaret's being denied the scholarship. She implored, "Please don't be mad at me." When she reflects on the situation, she might also feel justifiably angry that Hispanics are blamed for the ineptitude and/or policies at the scholarship office. She might also feel angry that the limited funds earmarked for Hispanic students were used to support a White student.

- Facing Margaret's racial anger, will she become hurt and angry herself and begin to think of Margaret as racist, as the enemy?
- Will she blame the welfare office for its racially divisive practice or blame herself for taking a scholarship that Margaret might have deserved?

PARTIAL TRUTHS: RACE, CLASS, GENDER, AND SEXUALITY AS SEPARATE SYSTEMS

Clearly, there are many ways of understanding Margaret Welch's dilemma, many truths in her life. Dominant perspectives in modern social science as well as in the media tend to interpret complex lives in very isolated and limited ways by attending to only a single dimension. To illustrate the important—but partial—insights that might be gained by such perspectives, the following are examples of issues that might be raised, questions that might be asked, and truths that might be unearthed when Margaret's complex life is examined through the lens of only a single dimension of oppression.

Race

Race scholars would emphasize the ways that ideas about and structures of race influence Margaret's life. Her story, in fact, was originally printed in *Race: How Blacks and Whites Think and Feel About the American Obsession*, a book of interviews conducted by Studs Terkel (1992). By focusing on the racial dimension alone, we might explore

- the racial animus expressed by a White toward Blacks and Latinos/as. The power of racial "otherness" or racial stereotypes was clearly illustrated in Margaret's generalization of her denial of a scholarship intended for Latino/a students to hostility toward and fear of both Blacks and Latinos/as inside the academic setting, on the street in her neighborhood, and in the public political arena.
- the institutional practice that promotes racial animosity between Whites and other racial groups by pitting them against one another for scarce resources such as scholarships.
- the ramifications of the fact that Whites make up the majority of welfare recipients—despite the stereotypical association between welfare and people of color—even though Blacks and Latinos/as are much more likely to be poor, reflecting their racial disadvantage in the economy.

- whether it is appropriate to label Margaret as racist. What is a racist? Can a person *be* racist? Do people incorporate racial beliefs into their personalities as permanent and unchangeable character traits? Or are configurations of racial beliefs, attitudes, and behaviors more malleable—subject to change in different situations, at different times?
- the seeming irony that a racially privileged group member would perceive herself as the victim of racial discrimination. How might that happen? What are the implications for how Whites come to see their race? How do their views of themselves affect their views of people of color? And how do the views and resistance of people of color shape how White people view their Whiteness?
- the significance of nursing as a predominantly White profession, with 88 percent of registered nurses being White (U.S. Statistical Abstract 1999: table 645). When Margaret finally does receive her nursing degree, she is unlikely to face *racial* discrimination in the job market while her Puerto Rican friend is much more likely to face it. Yet if Margaret has difficulty finding a job, how will she understand it? Whom will she blame? What will she do about it?
- how White people maintain their position of power in the racial hierarchy by structurally excluding people of color from political and economic advancement and by promoting and maintaining stereotypes of racial ethnic peoples, including notions that they are inferior, less deserving, and to be feared.

Class

Class scholars would emphasize the way that ideas about and structures of economic class influence Margaret's life. What questions might be raised and class truths extracted from Margaret's story?

- How are Margaret's difficulties in meeting the basic survival needs for her family a product of her class position and her poverty? Because she worked at a hot dog stand and then lost her job, she was forced onto public aid to survive. Can Margaret and others like her find a way out of poverty in the current economy where the increase in job opportunities is largely for part-time work and even full-time workers in minimum wage jobs receive wages that are lower than the poverty level (Freeman 1994; Mishel and Bernstein 1994)?
- If education and training are to be seen as an answer to Margaret's and other workers' low wages, what social forces are inclined to further this cause when much of the economy is dependent on low-wage work?
- The American labor movement is at a historically weak point (e.g., union membership is at an all-time low), in part because of the global portability of large-scale capital and the immobility of labor here and across the globe. What is the relationship between the plight of American workers, like Margaret, and the weak position of labor today? What avenues do workers have for improving their collective position in the economy?
- What are the processes through which our class system is reproduced and challenged? How do the privileged classes, the middle and upper classes, re-

strict access to higher education, particular positions in the labor market, or inherited wealth? How are controlling images (stereotypes) of the poor and working classes—as exerting less effort and being less talented and less deserving than those in the privileged classes—maintained? How do the poor and working classes resist those images?

Gender

Gender scholars would emphasize the ways that ideas about and structures of gender influence Margaret's life. If we were to focus solely on gender, what are some of the questions we might ask and the truths we might reveal?

- Women earn 76.3 percent of male wages in the labor market (U.S. Bureau of Labor Statistics 1999). Margaret feels responsible and the state (the whole political and governmental domain) sees her as responsible for child–rearing, but she is not provided with the financial wherewithal either from the state or in the job market to support her family. What does Margaret's poverty have to do with her being both widowed and divorced and a single mother?
- Margaret plans to enter nursing, a female-dominated profession, that pays much lower wages and takes fewer years of schooling than male-dominated health professions, such as medical doctor. Why? What are the social and psychological processes that produce sex-segregated labor markets?
- She fears for her personal safety in the streets of her neighborhood. What is the connection between violence against women and patriarchy, the system of male dominance?
- If Margaret and her friend were Mike and Juan and if Mike were denied a scholarship to engineering school while his Puerto Rican friend Juan got one, would they have reacted as the women did? How might their reactions have been different?
- What are the processes through which men maintain their position of power in the gender hierarchy? How do men and gender systems structurally restrict women's advancement in the economy, threaten women with violence, and promote stereotypes of women as weak, as more suited to home and family than to market work, and as less competent than men?

Sexuality

In addition to race, class, and gender, ideas about and structures of sexuality also shape Margaret's life. In the hierarchy of sexuality—the system of heterosexual privilege—cross-sex relationships are defined as the norm, and same-sex relationships are defined as abnormal or deviant and are rigidly restricted. Strong sanctions against homosexuality, in fact, help to maintain rigid and extremely different versions of what is "masculine" and what is "feminine." People conform to rigid sex roles—expectations for acceptable behavior for women and men—in part out of homophobia, the fear that they will be associated with gays or lesbians and will be mistreated as a consequence. What questions can be raised and truths revealed about Margaret's life arising from her position in the sexual hierarchy as a heterosexual woman?

- How would her story be different if Margaret decided to live with another woman to make ends meet? Would she be suspected of being lesbian and be treated differently by her friends, the school, the welfare office, her children? What would happen if she were lesbian or bisexual?
- What are the processes through which heterosexuality is socially constructed and legally enforced as a prerequisite for being seen as a "good mother"? What are the implications of being a heterosexual, bisexual, or lesbian mother for such issues as child custody, welfare benefits, and employment?
- To what extent is Margaret's reproductive life controlled by the low benefits afforded her for each child under AFDC/welfare? How are social policies constructed to control the sexual behaviors of poor women?
- To what extent is the hyperaggressive behavior of Hell's Henchmen based on the need to claim masculine power by asserting forcefully that they are not "feminine," not gay?

These are only a few of the questions raised and insights or "truths" that can be gleaned from Margaret's life. Each of these questions may reveal a significant aspect of Margaret's life, but when juxtaposed with the total complexities of Margaret's life and with each other, they seem at best to be very partial truths—for each ignores the other. And Margaret's own attempt to make sense of her situation reveals clearly that when she thinks of her situation, she does not—and cannot—separate her race from her class from her gender from her sexuality.

Margaret is like each of us in that her race, class, gender, and sexuality are all fundamental sources of her identity. Margaret is a woman. She is also White, poor, and heterosexual. All of these factors shape how she views herself and her situation, how others view her, and how the policies and practices of social institutions affect her. We can ignore some aspects of our social location at any time, but because they are fundamental elements of society's organization, we cannot render them inactive or unimportant.

FIVE THEMES: AN OVERVIEW
OF THE CONCEPTUAL FRAMEWORK

Rather than analyze Margaret's or any other life or group experience through a single lens alone, a much richer analysis is achieved through the analysis of race, class, gender, and sexuality as interrelated systems of oppression. Five common themes characterize these interrelated systems and can be used as a framework for analysis. The systems are (1) historically and geographically/globally contextual, (2) socially constructed (3) power relationships that operate at (4) macro social structural and micro social psychological levels and are (5) simultaneously expressed. They are described in detail in the chapters that follow, but are briefly summarized here.

1. *Historically and Geographically/Globally Contextual.* Race, class, gender, and sexuality can be understood only in their *historical and geographic contexts.* So analyses focus on specific times and places and avoid the search for common meanings of race, class, gender, and sexuality that would apply in all times and places.

   Remember Margaret's life. Her dilemmas would have been very different in the 1950s when the welfare system was almost solely serving White women. She would not have been told that she lost a scholarship to a Hispanic woman, but would the education scholarships have been available for women at all?

2. *Socially Constructed.* Race, class, gender, and sexuality are *social constructs* whose meaning develops out of group struggles over socially valued resources. While they may have biological or material referents, race, class, gender, and sexuality are not fixed properties of individuals nor of materially defined groups. Their meaning can and does change over time and in different social contexts.

   Think again of Margaret. Part of her lament is that it no longer *means* the same thing to be White as it once did, and this raises key questions for her. She asks: "I don't get something because I'm White?" One could almost finish her thought, "Then what does it mean to be White anymore?"

3. *Power Relationships.* Race, class, gender, and sexuality are *power relationships* of dominance and subordination, not merely gradations along a scale of resources—who has more than whom—or differences in cultural preferences or gender roles. They are based in relationships of exploitation of subordinate groups by dominant groups for a greater share of society's valued resources. They change because oppressed groups struggle to gain rights, opportunities, and resources—to gain greater control over their lives—against dominant groups who seek to maintain their position of control over the political, ideological, and economic social domains—over their own lives as well as over others' lives.

   Margaret Welch's story is certainly a story of power relationships—structural, external powers that shape her life because of her gender, sexuality, race, and class: the power she had to provide for her children while married, the power she lacked to do the same when widowed and divorced, the power she lacked to command a decent wage in the economy, and the power she had to keep her children while on public aid, when women of color and lesbian mothers might lose theirs. And there are her internal, psychological senses of power—her sense of powerlessness to overcome the obstacles to completing her degree, her fear of and sense of powerlessness relative to Black men and Latinos, and yet the power she feels to walk without fear through a group of Hell's Henchmen.

4. *Macro Social Structural and Micro Social Psychological Levels.* These power relationships between dominant and subordinate groups are embedded in society's *macro* social institutions and in the *micro* face-to-face interactions that constitute the everyday lives of individuals. Specifying the linkages between these two levels is a key component of a race, class, gender, and sexuality analysis.

Margaret's plight can be understood by looking at the opportunities and restrictions, the options and limits that social systems of race, class, gender, and sexuality place on her—from occupational restrictions, to low wages, to legal and social expectations for poor White heterosexual mothers. And these macro systemic patterns are played out in her everyday interactions with her boyfriend, her best girlfriend, her children, the school, and the welfare office.

5. *Simultaneously Expressed.* Race, class, gender, and sexuality *operate simultaneously* in every social situation. At the societal level, these systems of social hierarchies are connected to each other and are embedded in all social institutions. At the individual level, we each experience our lives based on our location along *all* dimensions, and so we may occupy positions of dominance and subordination at the same time.

For example, many of the ways that macro systems of class and gender shape Margaret's life are relatively apparent. But race and sexuality systems—systems in which she occupies a *privileged location*—also shape her life in critical ways, even though they are somewhat more obscured. Her racial privilege is masked by a dominant ideology that blames racially oppressed groups for White's class disadvantages. So Margaret is told—and she accepts—that her inability to pay for college is because scholarships are available for racially oppressed groups. Further, because Margaret is heterosexual and has not violated sexual norms, the system of heterosexual privilege is somewhat hidden in her story, but it nonetheless supports her in a way that she doesn't see, as is typically the case with privilege.

SUMMARY

Margaret Welch's story illustrates the importance of social location in shaping what we come to see as real, in shaping our understandings of the world. And since our social location represents our position in all the social hierarchies—including race, class, gender, and sexuality—within which we live our lives, analyses that focus on only a single dimension, while useful for some purposes, are ultimately partial. To develop understandings that are more useful in the pursuit of social justice, we need complex analyses that attend to the multiple social hierarchies as they intersect with one another both in individual lives like that of Margaret and in the society as a whole.

To analyze race, class, gender and sexuality as intersecting systems of oppression, this text puts forth a conceptual framework. The framework represents these systems as socially constructed, historically and geographically specific power relations that simultaneously operate at the macro social structural and micro social psychological levels.

Themes: Historically and Geographically/Globally Contextual, Socially Constructed Power Relations

In this chapter I examine the first three themes in the analysis of race, class, gender, and sexuality: They are (1) historically and geographically/globally contextual, (2) socially constructed (3) power relations. I begin by reviewing some of the historically and geographically varying meanings of each of these systems. That the meanings of these constructs vary over time and place implies that they are socially constructed. Next, I explore in more detail what is meant by social construction. Finally, I highlight how conceiving of these dimensions as power relations pushes us to see them as relational and thus to examine both privilege and oppression.

Race, class, gender, and sexuality are interdependent, socially constructed power relations. Their meaning develops and changes in group struggles that are firmly rooted in particular geographic locales and in particular historical time periods. From these group contests, new racial groups, new social classes, new gender constructions, and new sexual communities arise, transform, and dissolve. Through similar processes of biologizing, dichotomizing, and ranking, race, gender, and sexuality systems of power and privilege are created and challenged. The social class system produces a similar dynamic of oppression through a slightly different process of construction: not biological determinism but an extreme notion of individual determinism where notions of ability and effort are used to justify dominant groups' position of power.

HISTORICALLY AND GEOGRAPHICALLY/GLOBALLY CONTEXTUAL

Although they persist throughout history, race, class, gender, and sexuality hierarchies are never static and fixed but are constantly changing as a part of new economic, political, and ideological processes, trends, and events. Their meaning varies not only across historical time periods but also across nations and regions during the same period. Because these systems must always be understood within a specific historical and geographic context, race, class, gender, and sexuality analyses tend to avoid the search for common meanings of the systems that would apply in all times and places.

Race

Consider for a moment the major shifts in the dominant conception of race that have taken place in the United States over the last century. The concept of race—the grouping of people with certain ancestry and biological traits into categories for differential treatment—emerged initially in the United States as a justification of slavery (Fields 1990; Omi and Winant 1994). People of many different African tribes were defined as belonging to one group, and that group was associated with evil, sin, laziness, bestiality, sexuality, and irresponsibility. This new racial conception of Africans rationalized the exploitation of their labor in slavery and justified holding humans in bondage, whipping them, selling them, separating them from their families, and working them to death. In "The Illogic of American Racial Categories," Paul Spickard (1992:18–19) illustrated the historical and geographic way that races are defined and redefined by the state from 1870 through 1980. The U.S. Bureau of the Census used the following racial classifications:

1870	White, Colored (Blacks), Colored (Mulattoes), Chinese, and Indian.
1950	White, Black, and other.
1980	White, Black, Hispanic, Japanese, Chinese, Filipino, Korean, Vietnamese, American Indian, Asian Indian, Hawaiian, Guamanian, Samoan, Eskimo, Aleut, and other.

More recent shifts include:

1990	*Five races:* White, Black (or African American), Asian or Pacific Islander, American Indian, Eskimo, Aleut.
	Two ethnicities: Hispanic, non-Hispanic (O'Hare 1992).
2000	*15 races:* White; Black, African American or Negro; American Indian or Alaska Native; Asian Indian; Japanese; Native Hawaiian; Chinese; Korean; Guamanian or Chamorro; Filipino; Vietnamese; Samoan; other Asian; other Pacific Islander; some other race.
	5 ethnicities: Mexican, Mexican American, Chicano; Puerto Rican; Cuban; other Spanish/Hispanic/Latino; not Spanish/Hispanic/Latino (U.S. Bureau of the Census 1998b).

As late as the 1980s, racial groups were differently defined in different countries:

England	White, West Indian, African, Arab, Turkish, Chinese, Indian, Pakistani, Bangladeshi, Sri Lankan, and other.
South Africa	White, African, Coloured, and Asian.
Brazil	The many gradations of *white* and *black* were: *preto* (black), *cabra* (slightly less black), *escuro* (dark, lighter than preto), *mulato escuro* (dark mulato), *mulato claro* (light mulato), *pardo* (light mulato), *sarara* (light skin, kinky hair), *moreno* (light skin, straight hair), and *branco de terra* (some Black heritage, seen as White) (Degler 1971).

While some of these U.S. and British categories are also nationality labels, many people in the United States and Great Britain treat them as domestic racial units (Spickard 1992). And census classifications directly affect access to housing and employment, social program design, the organization of elections, and the disbursement of local, state, and federal funds (Omi and Winant 1994). Each of these national systems of racial classification, in fact, reflects a different social, economic, and political reality. When these social conditions change, so do racial categories. For example, Brazil has a history of extensive miscegenation and for years was touted as a "racial democracy," free of the racism so extensive and intense in the United States (Degler 1971; Skidmore 1993b). However, scholars have recently begun to change their view of Brazil as less racist because, despite structural changes in the economy, peoples of African descent in Brazil remain on the bottom of the economic hierarchy (Skidmore 1993a). Analyses of the everyday lives of Afro-Brazilians also reveal the discrimination and subtle forms of racism they confront everyday (Twine 1998).

In the post–civil rights era in the United States, the racial signifiers "Latino/a," "Asian American," "People of Color," and "Native American" developed when people from different cultures, tribes, and national origins were treated as a single racial group by a dominant culture that failed to recognize differences among "racial" ethnic groups (Omi and Winant 1994). Many members of these groups subsequently organized politically to resist their joint oppressions, and out of those political movements new racial identities were forged. These labels did not exist before the 1960s, and even today some people identify with them and others do not, signifying the fluid, political, historically specific, and social meaning of race.

Also, following the 1967 repeal of the last laws against miscegenation (race mixing), a "biracial baby boom" began to be recorded in U.S. census data (Root 1992). Even though interracial and intergroup marriages constituted only 4 percent of the total in 1990, the 1990 census reported about 1.1 million interracial couples, up slightly from 1.0 million in 1980 and more than triple the 321,000 in 1970 (Harrison and Bennett 1995). The growth of this racially mixed population is literally transforming the face of the United States and is directly challenging the foundation of a social order predicated upon the notion of biologically distinct and fixed races:

> The increasing presence of multiracial people necessitates that we as a nation ask ourselves questions about our identity: Who are we? How do we see ourselves? Who are we in relation to one another? . . . such questions of race and identity can only precipitate a full-scale "identity crisis" that this country is ill equipped to resolve. Resolving the identity crisis may force us to reexamine our construction of race and the hierarchical social order it supports (Root 1992:3).

The beginnings of this identity crisis can be seen in the refusal of many mixed race people to identify themselves on such things as job applications and school records as Black, White, Hispanic, Native American, or Asian. Many multiracial people argue that because they are more than any one of these, having to choose one of these designations negates their identity—and they are insisting on a new designation: mixed race or multiracial. Their impact is being felt: The 2000 census allows citizens to check off as many racial designations as they desire (U.S. Bureau of the Census 1998b).

Class

The social class system is also historically specific. Today, for example, most scholars—even those studying class from a Marxist perspective—no longer contend, as Marx originally did, that the proletariat (workers) and the bourgeoisie (capitalists/owners) are the only two major classes in modern capitalist societies. And although they disagree about the exact composition of the new class, almost all modern class theorists agree that today's capitalist class system contains a third major actor, the "new middle class" that exists between labor (workers) and capital (owners) (cf., Vanneman and Weber Cannon 1987; Van den Berg 1993; Wright 1997).

The middle class controls workers both directly and indirectly. Managers and supervisors exert direct control; mental workers (e.g., lawyers, teachers, social workers) exert indirect control. The middle class sells its labor to the capitalist/owning class (sometimes defined as the upper class) and exerts control over the workers below them. For controlling workers, for increasing production and profits, and for promoting the ideas that justify the current class system, the middle class is rewarded with higher wages, job security and benefits, prestige, and respect.

As evidence of their location as a class "in the middle" and not as the most powerful economic class, the middle class since the 1970s has been challenged and transformed by changes in the economy that have shifted greater power and resources to the owning/upper class:

- Increasing technological control (and a decreasing need for supervisory control) over the workforce.
- Corporate downsizing.
- Shifting of the tax burden away from corporations and the wealthy to individuals in the middle, working, and lower classes.
- Stagnating or declining wages.
- Internationalization of markets and the workforce.
- Increasing costs of housing, health care, and higher education.

The negative economic effects of these shifts have been mitigated somewhat in two-parent, heterosexual, middle-class families by the increased participation of women in the workforce and by the declining number of children in families. But the standard of living among single mothers and among the poor—particularly among people of color—and their children declined significantly during the period (Barlett and Steele 1994; Farley 1996).

Just as the power of the middle class relative to the owning or upper class has declined in recent history, so too has the power and standard of living for the working class and the lower class or poor. In addition to being affected by many of the same processes as the middle class, working class and poor people were affected by the increase in part-time employment; the loss of high-paying, blue-collar jobs; the decline of unions; and reductions in government programs such as welfare benefits and college grants and scholarships. As a result of these changes and as more resources are concentrated at the top of the class system, each of these classes has become less able to resist further changes that benefit the wealthy. Thus, for example, the ability of workers to demand and obtain higher wages, better working conditions, and better benefits is in most industries less than it was 30 years ago (cf. Farley 1996; Freeman 1994).

In short, the social class structure changes over time as new classes are created and existing classes gain or lose power in their struggles with other classes for resources. Further, the class system is structured by race, gender, and sexuality as women and men, people of color and Whites, heterosexuals, and gays, bisexuals, and lesbians have different opportunities to attain higher class positions, to reap the full benefits of those positions, to stay in those positions, and to pass those advantages on to their children (cf. Badgett 1995; Higginbotham and Weber 1992; Oliver and Shapiro 1995; Wright 1997).

Gender

Although gender—the socially structured relationships between women and men—is constructed, like race, with reference to biological categories (male and female), its meaning too has drastically changed throughout different historical eras. Not until the Industrial Revolution of the 19th century did the workplace become increasingly separated from the home and today's dominant conceptions of masculinity and femininity begin to take shape. During this time, dominant culture (White, heterosexual, middle and upper class) conceptions of femininity became associated with the warm, personal, "private" sphere of home while masculinity became associated with the cold, "public" sphere of the labor market. The daily lives of women and men began to diverge as dominant-culture men were increasingly pulled away from the home to work in factories and were extended the "family wage," a wage large enough to support their entire families. Dominant-culture women were expected to remain out of the paid labor force and to tend to the home (Coontz 1992).

Carol Tavris describes these newly emerging heterosexual conceptions of masculine and feminine:

> People began to attribute to inherent male and female characteristics what were actually requirements of their increasingly separate domains. Thus, women were expected to provide warmth, nurturance, and care, and forgo achievement; men were expected to provide money and success, and forgo close attachments. The masculine ideal, tailored to fit the emerging economy, was to be an independent, self-made, financially successful man. Masculinity now required self-control: no gaudy displays of emotion; no weakness; no excessive self-indulgence in feelings. Femininity required, and soon came to embody, the opposite (Tavris 1992:265).

Despite the pervasiveness of the images, numerous race, class, gender, and sexuality scholars have noted that not *all* women and men were included in these ideals of masculinity and femininity. Men of color were not extended a family wage, and women of color were already in the paid labor market, doing domestic work, other low-wage service work, or agricultural work (Amott and Matthaei 1996). The ideal traits held up for men and women of color contrasted sharply with those for White women and men. After Reconstruction (ca. 1865–1877), for example, the ideal dominant culture image of the "good" African-American man was the Sambo stereotype: a happy-go-lucky, silly, stupid darky who was often afraid of the dark (Goings 1994). The image provided a justification for slavery and at the same time reduced the perceived physical and sexual threat posed by real African-American men. The Mammy image was the female parallel to Sambo: a happy asexual servant who so loved the master's family—and servitude itself—that she would willingly give over her life to the care and nurturance of White families (Collins 1991a; Goings 1994). Just as the ideal White man was strong, independent, and emotionless, Sambo—like White women—was weak, dependent, and full of emotion. White women were to nurture their families, whereas emotionally strong Mammies could have no families of their own, just as they could have no sexuality.

In sum, gendered social relationships between women and men are constructed differently throughout history, among different social groups, and in different locations through social processes that consistently produce and maintain a patriarchy—a system of male dominance—that is racialized, class-bound, and heterosexist.

Sexuality

For as long as recorded history, we know that people have engaged in heterosexual and homosexual sexual relations. Only recently, however, has sexuality come to be constructed as a fundamental element of social structure, as a source of community, and a source of personal identity. Just as late-19th-century shifts in the economy brought changes in gender meanings, they also brought about the conditions that made possible for the first time the development of a homosexual community and identity. John D'Emilio (1993) argues that as wage labor spread, work became dissociated from family and the household. And families and heterosexual expression came to be a means of establishing intimacy, promoting happiness, and experiencing pleasure—not a means of surviving. The free labor system thus released sexuality from the "imperative" to procreate (to produce more workers for the family) and made it possible for men and women to survive outside the household economy. These changes in heterosexual relations made possible the appearance of a collective gay life:

> By the end of the [nineteenth] century, a class of men and women existed who recognized their erotic interest in their own sex, saw it as a trait that set them apart from the majority, and sought others like themselves. . . . In this period, gay men and lesbians began to invent ways of meeting each other and sustaining a group life. Already, in the early twentieth century, large cities contained male homosexual bars. . . . In St. Louis and the nation's capital, annual drag balls brought together large numbers of Black gay men. Public bathhouses and

YMCAs became gathering spots for male homosexuals. Lesbians formed literary societies and private social clubs. Some working-class women "passed" as men to obtain better paying jobs and lived with other women—lesbian couples who appeared to the world as husband and wife (D'Emilio 1993:470).

Yet the communities that developed in the early 20th century remained rudimentary and difficult to find until World War II severely disrupted traditional patterns of gender relations and sexuality and temporarily created new situations conducive to homosexual expression—in sex-segregated settings as GIs or as WACs (Women's Army Corps) and WAVEs (Women Accepted for Volunteer Emergency Service) and in same-sex rooming houses for relocated workers. Through the 1950s and 1960s, the communities grew particularly in urban subcultures and became easier to find as newspapers, magazines, and novels published stories about gay life and as bars and other gathering sites increased.

The modern gay rights movement was ignited by the Stonewall Riot in New York City in 1969 when a group of gay men in the Stonewall Inn fought back when police raided the bar to harass and arrest them. The movement was generated in part because a gay community already existed and as a response to the severe oppression and scapegoating of gays during the Cold War era of the 1950s and 1960s:

- President Eisenhower imposed a total ban on employment of gay men and lesbians by the federal government.
- The FBI instituted widespread surveillance of gay organizations.
- Purges of gays from the military had risen sharply (D'Emilio 1993).

In sum, the nature of the system of heterosexual privilege and the experience of homosexuality has varied extensively from its early expressions in the 19th century to the much more open and stable communities of the post–Stonewall era. Race, class, and gender as well as geographic location (especially rural-urban and coastal-interior differences) also critically shaped the nature of communities and the life experiences of gay people. For example, one gay man, Mama Rene, arrested at Stonewall was a Filipino who was interviewed 25 years later along with other Filipino gay men for a study by Martin Manalansan IV of gay transnational politics. When asked how he felt about that historic event, Mama Rene said:

> They say it was a historic event. I just thought it was funny. Do I feel like I made history? People always ask me that. I say no. I am a quiet man, just like how my mom raised me in the Philippines. With dignity (Manalansan 1995:433).

Manalansan found that Mama Rene's belief that "coming out," or the public avowal of identity, is not necessary for self-fashioning was common among Filipino gay men:

> They see "coming out" as the primary preoccupation of gay men from other ethnic and racial groups. In fact, visibility can be dangerous for gay Filipinos. Until the late 1980s, U.S. immigration laws both criminalized homosexuality and categorized it with Communist Party membership. And not all gay venues are open to these immigrants . . . . Some tell of being "hounded" out of predominantly white or black gay bars (Manalansan 1995:434).

More important, Manalansan argues, the closet and the coming-out process are not culturally constituted in the same way:

> Filipino gay men argue that identities are not just proclaimed verbally, but are "felt" (*pakiramdaman*) or intuited as well. The swardspeak expression *ladlad ng kapa*, which literally means unfurling the cape and has been translated as "coming out" reveals gay identity to be something "worn" and not necessarily "declared." And it is this act of "wearing" identity that makes other public modes of gay identity articulation superfluous for many of my informants (Manalansan 1995:434).

Thus, even the political and personal nature of "coming out," which has been a cornerstone of the political and personal liberation strategies of U.S. White gays and lesbians, has very different, and even contradictory, implications for Filipino gay men and other men of color (cf. Almaguer 1993). What liberates Whites might be viewed as repression by people of color. Neither strategy for fighting oppression is "right"; no single strategy alone can work. Likewise, since lesbians also face gender oppression, their experience of sexual oppression is different in many ways. For example, since women face discrimination in the labor market—earning less, having fewer options for high wage employment, and higher poverty rates—the loss of a job due to sexual discrimination can have a potentially greater impact on lesbians than on gay men, making them more likely to face poverty as a result. The lesson to be heard is that race, class, gender, and sexuality as intersecting systems of oppression are created and maintained in specific historical and geographic contexts and within specific groups. They cannot be fully understood or applied as abstract constructs independent of specific times and places.

SOCIALLY CONSTRUCTED

These brief examples of the historical and geographic specificity of race, class, gender, and sexuality systems of oppression foreshadow the second major theme in the scholarship on these dimensions: that they are *socially constructed*. Race, class, gender, and sexuality are historically and geographically specific because they are social constructs whose meaning develops out of group struggles over socially valued resources. These struggles vary over time and in different places as the abilities of dominant groups to maintain their position change as a result of numerous forces, most notably the effectiveness and strength of subordinate groups' resistance to oppression but also because their own strength at any given time is affected by factors such as global competition and internal group cohesiveness.

I discuss race, gender, and sexuality first because there are some shared elements—biological determinism and dichotomizing—in the ways that race, gender, and sexuality systems are socially constructed. Social class is socially constructed on slightly different building blocks—a ladder, not dichotomous categories, and individual choice, not biological determinism—and yet the result is a similar system of oppression. The case of social class makes it clear that systems of oppression can be constructed on somewhat different grounds and still achieve similar ends.

The dominant culture defines the categories within race, gender, and sexuality as polar opposites—White and Black (or non-White), men and women, heterosexual and homosexual—to create social rankings: good and bad, worthy and unworthy, right and wrong (Lorber 1994). It also links these concepts to biology (most clearly with race and gender, less consistently with sexuality) to imply that the rankings are fixed, permanent, and embedded in nature. That is, dominant groups define race, gender, and sexuality as ranked dichotomies where Whites, men, and heterosexuals are deemed superior. Dominant groups typically justify these hierarchies by claiming that the rankings are a part of the design of nature, not the design of those in power. Subordinate groups often resist the binary categories, the rankings associated with them, and the biological rationales used to justify them. Critical examination of either process—polarizing or biologizing—reveals that race, gender, and sexuality systems are based neither in polar opposites nor in biology but are social constructs (Frankenberg 1993; Garnets and Kimmel 1991; King 1981; Lorber 1994; Omi and Winant 1994).

When we say that the meanings of race, gender, and sexuality are not fixed biological traits, we also mean that we cannot *fully* capture their meaning in everyday life in the way that social scientists often attempt to do by employing them as variables in traditional quantitative research. When race, gender, and sexuality are treated as discrete variables, individuals are typically assigned a single location along each dimension, which is defined by a set of presumably mutually exclusive and exhaustive categories. This practice reinforces the view of race, gender, and sexuality as permanent characteristics of individuals, as unchangeable, and as polarities; that is, people can belong to one and only one category. So race, gender, and sexuality are not treated as social constructions whose existence and meaning depend on social relations among groups opposing one another for societal resources but rather as fixed and permanent characteristics of individuals—more like eye color than group membership.

This practice also fails to grasp the historical specificity and the conflicting meanings of race, class, gender, and sexuality that arise in everyday life (Omi and Winant 1994). "Mixed race" people, for example, often have no place in the schema provided. And what of the people who are bisexual or heterosexual at one time of life and gay or lesbian at another? Neither do people who identify themselves as transgender—living part or all of their lives in a gender expression different from their sex (Feinberg 1996)—have a place in these schemas.

Race

Biologists and physical anthropologists recognize that all humans have an essential commonality, that there have never been any pure races. What we call races are geographic and biologically diverging populations that in particular locales are distinguished by statistically significant frequencies of various genetic or physical types—from blood types to sickle-cell anemia. Yet the variations within these divergent populations are greater by far than the variations among them. As geneticist James King states:

Whether two individuals regard themselves as of the same or of different races depends not on the degree of similarity of their genetic material but on whether history, tradition, and personal training and experiences have brought them to regard themselves as belonging to the same group or to different groups . . . there are no objective boundaries to set off one subspecies from another (cited in Spickard 1992:16).

More importantly, the presence of similarities or differences in physical makeup is significant only when social meaning becomes attached to those differences and society's valued resources are allocated on the basis of them (Spickard 1992:15).

As Michael Omi and Howard Winant (1994:96) suggest, race is a social phenomenon that "suffuses each individual identity, each family and community, yet also suffuses state institutions and market relations." Struggles over the meaning of race are fought in the political, economic, and ideological arenas as subordinate racial groups press for full incorporation in all aspects of society. In the modern era, the 1960s witnessed the success of social movements that were racially based and inspired and that transformed the meaning of race. Racial equality had to be acknowledged as a desirable goal, but its meaning and the proper means to achieve that equality were open for debate.

In the economically troubled period since the 1960s, the dominant culture has reacted to the gains of the 1960s by claiming to favor equality and a "color-blind society." But many of the rights won in the 1960s have been opposed at the level of implementation, just as affirmative action has come under vehement attack. Today, the rise in Native American, Asian-American, and Latino/a populations is again changing the nature and meaning of race, as these groups become large enough to press demands and as Whites seek to maintain control by implementing repressive policies aimed at limiting their power.

Gender

Even though gender is socially defined by referring to biological differences related to reproduction, the physical similarities between women and men far outweigh the differences. Gender too is socially constructed in the struggles between groups over society's scarce resources.

Even in the area of reproduction and mothering, the biological relationships of women to children are socially constructed and given meaning in race, class, gender, and sexuality hierarchies. For over a century, social expectations of women's work and family roles, for example, have been rationalized by the biological fact that women can bear children. Middle-class mothers who stay at home to care for their children are often viewed by the dominant culture as "good mothers," yet poor women who do the same are viewed as lazy or "welfare queens." How can women's biological reproductive capacities prescribe their roles as mothers when we have different expectations for mothers of different classes, races, and sexual orientations?

Furthermore, the biological connection of women to their children is far more complex than ever before and is now being challenged—particularly by White, middle-class, heterosexual women and some lesbians and gay men who seek to adopt children—as a basis for legal rights to motherhood (Solinger 1998). Today, when women and men have so many different biological and social relationships to their children, the courts are increasingly asked to mediate questions of who should rear children—of who can *be* mothers. Consider the following "mothers:"

- *Traditional mothers,* who have a genetic, gestational, and legally sanctioned social relationship to the child.
- *Lesbian mothers,* whose biological relationship may or may not be the same as that of traditional mothers and yet whose legal status as mothers is often challenged and denied because of their sexual orientation.
- *Surrogate mothers: genetic and gestational mothers,* who provide an egg and bear the child but do not raise the child, and *gestational mothers,* who have no genetic relationship to it but bear the child for another couple.
- *Social mothers: foster mothers,* whom the state assigns as temporary mothers but who have no genetic or gestational relationship to the child; *adoptive mothers,* who are legally recognized mothers but who have no genetic or gestational relationship to the child; *"other" mothers,* who have no legal, genetic, or gestational relationship to the child but who play a significant role in raising the child (cf. Collins 1991a).

Each of these ways of mothering is constructed in race, class, gender, and sexuality hierarchies that shape the meanings attached to them and the legally prescribed rights of these mothers to rear children. The rights of some women to be mothers depends, in fact, on the lack of rights among other women to retain their status as mothers. In the era of "choice" following the *Roe v. Wade* Supreme Court decision in 1971, for example, large numbers of White, unmarried girls in the United States began to choose abortion or to keep their babies. These choices reduced the pool of adoptable White babies, producing both an increase in the market value of available White babies (and increased "trading" in the underground sale of those babies) and a boom in foreign adoptions. As Rickie Solinger states:

> Probably most Americans did not realize how profoundly the motherhood "choices" of (White) middle-class women—to get abortions, or to become single mothers (both of which choices diminished the pool of babies who might have been available to others), or to become adoptive mothers—indirectly created or directly depended on the definition of other women as having weak, or coercively transferable, motherhood rights. Nor was it always clear how much motherhood "choices" had to do with money, for both the women who had it and the women who did not (1998:390–91).

Annette Appell's (1998) research focuses on one of those groups with weak and transferable motherhood rights: the mothers of the roughly half-million children in foster care in the United States—mothers whose children were removed because the mothers failed to meet a government agency's standard of proper mothering. They are disproportionately poor and women of color. Appell notes that only a small minority of these women have physically harmed or abandoned their children. The rest lose their children because they use illegal drugs, consume too much alcohol, are abused by husbands or boyfriends, or leave their children with family or friends without making a "proper" care plan. Yet these women have their children taken away in part because their poverty means that their lives intersect with official entities and bureaucracies on a number of levels: The government pays their medical bills; public hospitals, clinics, and emergency rooms provide their health care; public building inspectors and police enter their homes. Middle-class mothers have private health care, privacy in their homes, and are more likely to use alcohol and prescribed antidepressants than crack cocaine. Poor mothers with problems come into contact with the legal system and face losing their children; middle-class mothers seldom do.

In discussing why we have the phenomenon of surrogate mothers, Phyllis Chesler also highlights the impact of race, class, gender, and sexuality on motherhood:

> Racism is the issue, and why thousands of babies are "unsuitable" [for adoption]. Ownership is the issue, and the conceit of patriarchal genetics. "Barren women" are the issue, and why some women must come to feel an excruciating sense of failure because they cannot bear a child. . . . And guilt and money, and how women can earn both, are the issues that need honest attention (1986:280).

In sum, while our biological relationship to children can be determined fairly easily (even in cases where one party denies the connection) with DNA testing, it tells us very little about the way that relationship shapes our lives. The meaning of our biological relationship to children is socially constructed in race, class, gender, and sexuality hierarchies and cannot be understood independent of these systems.

Sexuality

Despite evidence to the contrary, dominant culture perspectives on race and gender contend that they are biologically distinct categories and that their biological base does—and should—affect the social position of people in different race and gender groups. Dominant group perspectives on sexuality, however, are currently undergoing debate in the political and ideological arenas. Some contend that sexual orientation—heterosexual, gay, lesbian, bisexual—is genetically determined. Others view sexual orientation as a personal lifestyle choice. Much like the issue of choice in the decisions of pregnant women to abort or to bear a child, the notion of choice in the debate in the United States is typically viewed as a free choice that individuals make. This notion pays scant attention to the social structural constraints—powerfully shaped by race, class, gender, and sexuality systems of oppression—within which these choices are made (Solinger 1998). "Choice" in the dominant culture context implies individual responsibility. If the choices individuals make are not the choices that dominant groups prefer to see made, then individual responsibility implies blame, and blame sets the stage for unequal treatment.

Thus, whether homosexuality and, of course, heterosexuality are viewed as genetically determined or as lifestyle choices to a large extent shapes how homosexuals and heterosexuals will be treated in the social order. Despite extensive biological and genetic research, there is, in fact, no strong evidence that gay, lesbian, bisexual, transgender, or heterosexual orientations are genetically determined. In no way could the people who identify themselves and are seen by others as gay, bisexual, lesbian, or transgender be classified on the basis of physical traits, just as heterosexuals cannot be so identified. Yet many groups (some religious groups, for example, who view homosexuality as morally wrong) have based policies of tolerance for gays and lesbians on the belief that sexual orientation is genetically determined and is not a matter of choice and thus responsibility. In September 1997, for example, the National Conference of Catholic Bishops made clear they believe homosexual sex is wrong yet urged parents of gay children to demonstrate love for their sons and daughters and to recognize that "generally, homosexual orientation is experienced as a given, not as something freely chosen" (Cloud 1997). Many gays and lesbians have also promoted this idea in the hopes of finding greater acceptance in society at large.

Yet, as John D'Emilio (1993) points out, this strategy is ultimately self-defeating because it doesn't attack the underlying belief that homosexual relations are bad, a poor second choice. The gay, lesbian, transgender, and bisexual political movements of recent times have in fact made it easier for people to make the choice. As a consequence, there are more self-identified homosexual people and better developed and more visible communities now than ever in history.

Out of the struggle to define sexuality, the images, rights, and treatment of gays, lesbians, and bisexuals emerge. And race, class, and gender significantly shape the experiences and perspectives that homosexual groups bring to the conflict (Anzaldua 1987a, 1987b; Duberman, Vicinus, and Chauncey 1989; Sears 1989; Smith 1993; Williams 1997). The largest and politically most visible group, for example, is White, middle-class, gay men. They have the economic self-sufficiency to survive outside of heterosexual marriage, and they have the gender and racial advantages that enable them to combat and overcome many of the restrictions imposed on their lives by homophobic social policies and practices (D'Emilio 1993).

Other groups, such as lesbians of color, may have less institutionally supported economic or political power—for example, to press for biological or choice ideologies of sexuality, but since their status as women of color makes clear that biologically based ideologies can be equally constraining, they may also be less likely to exert their political energies to push for a genetic explanation as a way to greater social acceptance of homosexuality.

Social Class

Social class provides an instructive contrast to race, gender, and sexuality ideologies. The dominant ideology of social class is that it is not binary, polarized, or biological. Instead, the United States is represented as having an open economic system where talent and hard work—not inherited physical traits—are the primary determinants of one's economic location (Hochschild 1995). Our system is not depicted as polarized between rich and poor, capitalists and workers, or middle and working classes. Rather it is portrayed as a continuous ladder of income and resources, where people can slide up and down based on their own efforts and abilities, not on their biology (Vanneman and Weber Cannon 1987). Because anyone is presumed to be potentially able to "make it," people can be held personally responsible for where they land in the class system. This ideology is labeled the *American Dream* to contrast with the economic ideologies in other industrial nations, particularly in European nations, where the aristocracy and the presumably more rigid class systems are deemed to be more closely tied to biology and inheritance.

The belief that biology and inheritance do not and should not determine class is deeply ingrained in American dominant culture ideology. While this belief in the American Dream was far more prevalent when the economy was expanding during the 1950s and 1960s, some social scientists even today assert that the American economic system is so open that classes do not exist (Clark and Lipset 1991). Research on the relative ease with which individuals can move up the class hierarchy suggests, however, that the American class system is not uniquely open (Kerckhoff 1995). Comparing the United States with Canada, a capitalist economy, and with Sweden and Norway, more social democratic and less purely capitalist economies, Mark Western and Erik Olin Wright (1994) found that the United States exhibits similar patterns of openness to class mobility. They also found that in the United States and Canada, friendships and intermarriage across class lines are no more prevalent than in Sweden and Norway. In short, class transmission has as much to do with inheritance in the supposedly more open United States system as it does elsewhere.

If class location is largely inherited, is class biological? A long-standing tradition in the United States does link poverty to genetically inherited traits, beginning with the Social Darwinism of the late 19th and early 20th centuries and continuing to the present in works such as Richard Hernstein and Charles Murray's *The Bell Curve* (1994). In that widely read book, the authors argue that genetic differences explain the fact that poor people have consistently low IQ scores, that IQ measures intelligence, and that low IQ explains the poor's lack of achievement and poverty. However, Hernstein and Murray, as well as others who have made similar claims, provide no direct evidence of the connection between genetics and IQ because they do not study genetics at all and ignore evidence of cultural, class, race, and gender bias in the IQ test. But even this biological class argument runs counter to the dominant ideology of class as substantially an "earned or achieved," not biologically determined, position. The upper classes presumably "earn" their position because of their superior traits (values, intelligence, skills, effort), and the lower classes "earn" their inferior location.

Neither of these two extreme positions—that class is either genetically determined or purely a function of individual talent and effort—captures the more complex reality of social class. Like race, gender, and sexuality, social class is a pattern of hierarchical social relationships that is deeply ingrained in the social order and that shapes the lives, options, and opportunities of individuals from birth. It is also deeply intertwined with other dimensions of inequality.

Consider, for example, the ways in which social class influences and is maintained in college and law school admissions along with gender and race. As Susan Sturm and Lani Guinier (1996) conclude about affirmative action in college and law school admissions, procedures that are not targeted to Whites, men, and the affluent and admit people of color and women but that have more universally applicable standards (such as admitting any applicants who finished in the top 10 percent of their class regardless of the school they attend) will increase the racial and gender diversity in admissions more than most affirmative action policies employed to date. Standard admissions procedures that are based in large part on cultural knowledge (estimated through tests with known race, class, and gender biases), on attendance at elite private schools, and on social connections (e.g., special consideration given to the children of law school graduates) are strongly biased in favor of White men from affluent backgrounds.

If we actually changed the standards to base them more on experience (e.g., grades) and not on prediction through tests, people from less culturally and socio-economically advantaged backgrounds would be admitted in much greater numbers than any affirmative action adjustments could achieve. Evidence from schools such as City College in New York that have had open admissions programs suggests that these students will succeed at similar if not higher rates than other students admitted in traditional ways (Sturm and Guinier 1996). This is not to say that progress toward greater inclusion for oppressed groups lies in the elimination of affirmative action, but rather that it lies in social change of a more fundamental sort—addressing the interactions of these dimensions—change that may also be more powerfully resisted.

Although American social class ideology disavows biology and categorical binaries, it justifies hierarchy and dominance nonetheless. The case of social class makes very clear that ideologies are created to justify hierarchies and need not be constructed as binaries or biological, nor need they be internally consistent or logical. To justify the power and control of the dominant group, ideologies of dominance develop in different ways over time and in different social contexts and can rest on fundamentally very different, even seemingly contradictory, beliefs.

In sum, race, class, gender, and sexuality are social constructions that are constantly undergoing change at both the level of social institutions and at the level of personal identity. They are not fixed, static traits of individuals as is implied when they are treated both as biological facts and as categorically fixed variables in a research model. They are, however, deeply embedded in the practices and beliefs that make up our major social institutions. The permanence and pervasiveness they exhibit illustrate their significance as major organizing principles of society and of personal identity.

POWER RELATIONSHIPS

Race, class, gender, and sexuality are historically and geographically specific, socially constructed *systems of oppression*—they are *power relationships*. Race, class, gender, and sexuality do not merely represent different lifestyle preferences or cultural beliefs, values, or practices. They are power hierarchies where one group exerts control over another, securing its position of dominance in the system, and where substantial material resources (e.g., wealth, income, or access to health care and education) are at stake (Baca Zinn and Dill 1996; Connell 1987, 1995; Glenn 1992; Vanneman and Weber Cannon 1987; Weber 1995; Weber,

Hancock, and Higginbotham 1997; Wyche and Graves 1992). Race, class, gender, and sexuality are thus fundamental sources of social conflict between groups.

The centerpiece of these systems is the exploitation of one group by another for a greater share of society's valued resources. That they are based in *social relationships between dominant and subordinate groups* is key to understanding these systems. There can be no controlling men without women whose options are restricted, there can be no valued race without races that are defined as "other," there can be no owners or managers without workers who produce and deliver the goods and services that the owners own and the managers control, and there can be no heterosexual privilege without gays and lesbians identified as "abnormal," as "other."

Race, class, gender, and sexuality are not just rankings of socially valued resources—who has *more* income or prestige. They are power relationships—who exerts power and control over whom—how the privilege of some results from the exploitation of others (Baca Zinn and Dill 1996; Connell 1987, 1995; Glenn 1992; Griscom 1992; Vanneman and Weber Cannon 1987; Weber 1995; Weber, Hancock, and Higginbotham 1997; Yoder and Kahn 1992). The groups that have power in a social system influence the allocation of many types of resources. In one sense, then, the procurement of socially valued resources can be seen as the end product—the spoils to the victors—of struggles for power. To maintain and extend their power and control in society, dominant groups can and do use the resources that they command. So socially valued resources such as money and prestige both accrue to those in power and, once procured, serve as tools for maintaining and extending that power into future social relations.

Heterosexism like racism, classism, and sexism is, for example, a system of power relations where to justify the privileges of heterosexuality, heterosexuals gain and maintain control over gays, lesbians, and bisexuals by defining them as "other," as less than fully human, as "deviant." Heterosexual marriage is established as the standard against which all other ways of conducting adult intimate life are measured (Scanzoni et al. 1989). People who depart from this script are commonly seen as deviant and (except in rare cases) are denied the legal privileges afforded heterosexuals, including the right to marry, to adopt children, to receive survivor benefits from social security, to file taxes as married, to receive health insurance from a spouse's employer, to inherit from one's partner, to claim a legal family connection in medical emergencies (Harvard Law Review 1990).

Scholars studying race, class, gender, and sexuality tend to see these systems as power relations, but this perspective is not universally accepted. The ethnicity approaches to race (reviewed in Omi and Winant 1994), gradational perspectives on class (reviewed in Vanneman and Weber Cannon 1987), sex differences and sex roles approaches (reviewed in West and Fenstermaker 1995), and moral or biological perspectives on sexuality (reviewed in D'Emilio and Freedman 1988) conceive of these dimensions as differences that are not ultimately power based. In these alternative approaches, differences between women and men, gays and straights, and among racial and ethnic groups are taken as primarily centered in women's and men's social roles and in cultural variations in traditions such as food, clothing, rituals, speech patterns, leisure activities, child-rearing practices, and sexual practices.

These perspectives, however, often downplay or ignore the very real struggles over scarce resources that accompany location in these different groups and systems of oppression. The "gradational" approach, for example, sees class inequality as represented by relative rankings along a scale of prestige or income (a ladder image), not by the struggle between opposing groups for scarce resources (for reviews see Lucal 1994; Vanneman and Weber Cannon 1987). No oppositional relationships exist between positions on a scale—some people simply have more than others. And these approaches see race as a group of ethnicities, different cultural practices and preferences that have roughly equal value. White is treated more as an absence of color—race is a term used to refer to people of color—a process that hides the privileged status of Whites and their relationship of dominance with other races (Lucal 1996). In a similar process, heterosexuality is also viewed as an absence while gays, lesbians, and bisexuals represent the "presence" of sexuality (Herek 1987; Lucal 1996).

Perhaps because race, class, gender, and sexuality studies emerged primarily from the experiences and analyses of groups who face multiple dimensions of oppression and perhaps because power relationships are simply much more apparent when more than one dimension of inequality is addressed, the "cultural difference," "gradational," or "ranking" perspective is almost nonexistent in race, class, gender, and sexuality studies. The view that power relations are central is almost universal.

Looking at the *relational* nature of these systems of inequality—not simply at the differences in rankings of resources that accompany these systems—forces us to focus on *privilege* as well as on oppression. Because the one cannot exist without the other, any analysis of race, class, gender, and sexuality must incorporate an understanding of the ways that the privilege of dominant groups is tied to the oppression of subordinate groups. The scholarship in this field has, therefore, begun to explore the social construction of Whiteness (cf. Frankenberg 1993; McIntosh 1998; Roediger 1991), of masculinity (cf. Brod and Kaufman 1994; Connell 1995; Messner 1992), and of heterosexual privilege (Giuffre and Williams 1994; Rich 1993). One common theme is that the experience of privilege is associated with a failure to understand the connection between privilege and oppression but that the experience of exploitation gives a unique angle of vision on the nature of oppression (Collins 1991a). As Albert Hourani, an Arab philosopher, described it:

> To be in someone else's power . . . induces doubts about the ordering of the universe, while those who have power can assume it is part of the natural order of things and invent or adopt ideas which justify their possession of it (quoted in Terkel 1992).

To understand these relationships of privilege and oppression, we must ask who gains and who pays in the events and processes we observe. How are the economic, political, and ideological resources and control of privileged groups produced by the low wages, labor, political disenfranchisement, and controlling images and devaluation of others? By focusing on power relations among groups, we move away from dominant culture conceptions of race as only about people of color, gender as about women, class as about the working classes and the poor, and sexuality as about gays and lesbians. Instead, we make visible the invisible norms, the dominant groups, the standards against which others are judged to be inferior: Whites, middle and upper classes, men, heterosexuals.

To understand power dynamics, it is revealing to look closely at social critiques and social policies that fail to take these power relationships into account. For example, many political analysts consider the most significant legacy of many politicians of the 1990s—from President Clinton to Mayor Rudolph Giuliani of New York—to have been the spearheading of welfare reform and removing as many as one million welfare recipients from government support during the decade—400,000 in New York alone (DeParle 1998). And these politicians consider welfare reform an unprecedented success. As Giuliani stated, "This is by far the best thing we're doing for the city. It is much more significant than the reduction in crime" (DeParle 1998:53).

But if we look beyond the declarations of the politicians who embrace the policies to look through the lens of race, class, gender, and sexuality, we consider power relationships and we ask, "Success for whom?" Is the policy a success for the (mostly) women whose lives have been changed by it? Have they benefited? Most are working minimum wage for many of the service industries that exploded in the 1980s and 1990s and rely on a cheap and unskilled labor force: fast-food restaurants, retail sales, domestic work. A growing number of reports contend that women receiving welfare much prefer to work, yet they cannot live independently on the wages they make in minimum wage jobs (Edin and Lein 1997).

Barbara Ehrenreich, a journalist, lived and worked in Florida for a month to find out if it is "really possible to make a living on the kinds of jobs currently available to unskilled people." She found out—it isn't. She began by cleaning hotel rooms, and before the month was up, she had taken a second job. Essentially she was working all of her waking hours and could not afford to get sick. She had become so tired and run down that she finally "broke" and simply walked out on her restaurant job when, after a particularly grueling day, a customer entered the kitchen to complain about the slow service. She left feeling a failure and concluded:

> How former welfare recipients and single mothers will (and do) survive in the low-wage workforce, I cannot imagine. Maybe they will figure out how to condense their lives—including child-raising, laundry, romance, and meals—into the couple of hours between full-time jobs. Maybe they will take up residence in their vehicles, if they have one. All I know is that I couldn't hold two jobs and I couldn't make enough money to live on with one. And I had advantages unthinkable to many of the long-term poor—health, stamina, a working car, and no children to care for and support (Ehrenreich 1999: 50).

Economists and sociologists at the Center for Research on Women in Memphis, Tennessee, studied what it takes to earn a "living wage" in Memphis in 1999 (Ciscel 1999). They defined a living wage as the level of income it takes for women to live independently of government subsidies, private charity, and other assistance. Even assuming a bare-bones budget—one that allowed for no extras such as eating out in a restaurant, going on a vacation, buying a new car, or saving for children's college—a single parent with one child working full-time would need to earn

$22,306 a year or $11.15 an hour—more than double the minimum wage. In fact, the living wage was about double the official federal poverty thresholds for 1999, meaning that the government does not even define a family as in poverty, and therefore eligible for assistance, unless it makes less than one-half the living wage.

When we think about the race, class, gender, and sexuality power dynamics at work in this story, it is difficult to see the welfare recipients—mostly White women but disproportionately women of color—as benefiting from the "success" of welfare reform. When the policies were instituted, few welfare recipients were consulted. They lacked power, a voice. Barbara Ehrenreich's attempt to live on the minimum wage and the Memphis research team's study of the living wage lead us to question the benefits for the women themselves. Furthermore, in their study of the impact of welfare reform on single mothers, Kathryn Edin and Laura Lein (1997) report that for a variety of reasons women on welfare faced less hardship than women who left welfare rolls for low-wage work, particularly because work brought new expenses that their low wages could not offset, such as child care and transportation. They also lost income and incurred higher expenses because other government supports were reduced when their incomes increased when they took jobs—Medicaid, housing subsidies, and food stamps.

If the poor women did not benefit, who did?

- The owners of businesses who employ workers at low wages.
- The politicians who claimed credit for a "social engineering" victory.
- The groups whose taxes will be cut as a result of revenue surpluses in government.
- The agencies and programs that receive funding that might otherwise have gone to welfare benefits: hospitals, schools, highways, businesses.

Yet how is this process debated and discussed in the public arena? Women who receive welfare are racialized—pictured as women of color (even though the majority are White women, as Margaret Welch came to understand)—and dehumanized, for we are asked to believe that their poverty is centered in their lack of skills, motivations, and values, not in the choices that the powerful make. Consequently, the policy of requiring women to work seems to be a viable solution to rid the country of not just welfare recipients but poverty itself. It denies, however, the real work, energy, and creativity that it takes to survive in poverty, whether on welfare or in low-wage employment as well as the benefits that accrue to the powerful when a large sector of the nation is either unemployed or employed in low-wage work.

A race, class, gender, and sexuality analysis pushes us to confront the power relationships at the core of these systems of inequality. These systems are sometimes described as interlocking dimensions in a matrix of domination where race, class, gender, and sexuality represent axes. Individuals and groups can be identified by their location in a position of dominance (power) or subordination (lacking power) along each dimension (cf. Collins 1991a; Baca Zinn and Dill 1994). However pictured, thinking of these systems as relational encourages us to consider the nature of their relation to each other. They are not completely independent but rather are interdependent, mutually reinforcing systems. One of the ways that sexuality, gender, and race privilege and power is maintained by White male heterosexuals, for example, is by maintaining power in the social class system and by restricting access to valued economic resources (e.g., wealth, jobs) by other sexuality, gender, and racial groups as the case of women and welfare so aptly suggests.[1]

SUMMARY

Race, class, gender, and sexuality are historically and geographically/globally specific, socially constructed power relations of dominance and subordination among social groups competing for society's scarce valued resources in the economic, ideological, and political domains. The structures of oppression and groups' differences within systems vary over time and in different social locations. Because race, class, gender, and sexuality are social constructions, their nature and meaning is generated in significant patterns of human social interactions, not predetermined by biology, not fixed at birth, but still persistent and pervasive. Race, class, gender, and sexuality are also significant because they represent power relations of dominance and subordination, not simply cultural preferences, gradations on a scale of prestige or money, gender role expectations, or moral or biological sexual differences. Dominant groups have access to greater economic, political, and ideological resources and employ these resources to control subordinate groups and to maintain their power. At the same time, subordinate groups resist economic, political, and ideological oppression. It is in this struggle between dominant and subordinate groups that the meaning of race, class, gender, and sexuality is transformed in different places and at different times.

[1]For descriptions of this process in graduate and professional schools, see Guinier, Fine, and Balin 1997; Granfield and Koenig 1992, for law; Margolis and Romero 1998, for sociology.

CHAPTER 5

Themes: Macro Social Structural and Micro Social Psychological Levels, Simultaneously Expressed

In this chapter I discuss the final two themes of the framework: that race, class, gender, and sexuality systems operate at both the macro social structural (institutional) and micro social psychological (individual) levels and that they are simultaneously expressed, intersecting systems. These themes remind us that these dimensions are embedded simultaneously in both societal structures and our personal identities. Analyses should look for the connections and intersections of macro and micro levels as well as of the dimensions of inequality.

Race, class, gender, and sexuality relations are simultaneously embedded and have meaning in the macro level of community and social institutions as well as in the micro level of people's everyday lives. As Table 1.1 in Chapter 1 summarized, we can think of society as organized into three major domains, each supported by major social institutions:

- *Ideological*   Education, media, religion
- *Political*   The state, law
- *Economic*   Industry, work.

Institutions represent the social arrangements and practices in a domain that are relatively stable and pervasive and that persist over time. The primary ways in which education, government, and work are conducted in U.S. society are relatively stable. For example:

- Education is required in most states through age 16.
- College is not required.
- The main model for teaching is a teacher with a class (ideal size 15 to 20).
- Common tests are used to measure performance.

Embedded in the arrangement and practices of each institution, race, class, gender, and sexuality systems are created, maintained, and transformed as dominant and subordinate groups struggle for self-definition, self-valuation, empowerment, full participation in political processes and outcomes, and a fair share of society's valued

93

economic resources. The practices and arrangements exist at both the macro social structural level of institutions—broad societal and community-level patterns—and also at the micro social psychological levels of families and individuals—small groups and personal identity. A key aspect of a race, class, gender, and sexuality analysis involves explicating the linkages between broad societal level structures, trends, and events and the ways in which people in different social locations experience and interpret the structures and make meaning of their lives.

Macro social structural trends often are represented analytically as a set of lifeless statistics about different populations. For example, when we look at statistics summarizing national trends in economic or political indicators, such as those presented in Tables 2.3–2.6, it is difficult to know exactly what they mean about how people actually live their lives—their micro reality. This understanding is especially difficult when the people whose lives we study occupy different social locations than our own in the race, class, gender, and sexuality systems. On the other hand, when we closely follow the micro trends in everyday life for a group of people, we may see how they live with financial constraints: how they feed their families, how they deal with life's stresses, how they manage work and family life, how they stay healthy.

But when we focus in detail on the lives of a small group of people, we have difficulty knowing how representative or pervasive the patterns that we observe may be. Thus, to understand race, class, gender, and sexuality, we must examine both macro societal processes and the everyday lives of people in different social locations in race, class, gender, and sexuality systems. And we must explore connections between both levels—how people's everyday lives reinforce and/or challenge the macro systems and how the macro systems influence people's individual lives.

We can pursue this understanding by

- identifying trends in the major social institutions and the race, class, gender, and sexuality relations in them
- looking for patterns and themes in the ways that individuals and groups in similar and different social locations confront the options, opportunities, and strictures posed by their location in these race, class, gender, and sexuality systems within major institutions
- recognizing that individuals may respond differently to similar circumstances—even individuals in the same locations in race, class, gender, and sexuality systems
- sharing in an ongoing dialogue the patterns and themes that we observe with the individuals and groups whose lives we seek to understand. This dialogue enables us to evaluate the validity of our understandings and to support the self-definition, self-actualization, and empowerment of the people we study as well as ourselves
- reflecting on the macro social structural and micro social psychological influences in our own lives.

MACRO-MICRO PROCESSES IN THE IDEOLOGICAL DOMAIN

Macro Processes

Ideologies represent sets of beliefs that help us to make sense of the contradictions in our social world. Leith Mullings describes ideologies:

> How ideologies—used here in the sense of production of meanings—are generated, maintained and deployed is intimately related to the distribution of power. Dominant ideologies often justify, support and rationalize the interests of those in power: they tell a story about why things are the way they are, setting out a framework by which hierarchy is explained and mediating contradictions among classes, between beliefs and experiences (1994:266).

If few people believe them, ideologies serve no purpose and cannot exist. Social systems built on inequality thus rely heavily on ideologies disseminated in institutions such as education and the media to provide the explanation for inequality that will justify the status quo and discourage people from challenging it. The American Dream is one such ideology—it explains all forms of inequality by suggesting that the privileged are more talented and work harder and, by implication, that those who are in subordinate positions work less hard, have less talent, and deserve less.

Dominant ideologies (also referred to as hegemonic ideologies) are pervasive societal beliefs that reflect the dominant culture's vision about what is right and proper. *Controlling images* (stereotypes) are dominant culture ideologies about subordinate groups that serve to restrict their options, to constrain them. Although society has many conceptions of working women, for example, only one is dominant, hegemonic, taking precedence over other conceptions and serving as the standard against which the value or worth of "other" conceptions of working women is measured.

When you hear the phrase "today's working woman" mentioned in the media or in a popular magazine, what kind of woman comes to mind? In all likelihood, no matter what your race, class, gender, or sexual orientation, you thought of a White, heterosexual, professional woman working hard in a position of some power in the labor force. She is most likely married, but if she is single, she is certainly young. This image of today's working woman is not only atypical, it is antithetical to the reality of work for most women today. Only 28.7 percent of working women are in professional, managerial, or administrative positions, and many of those hold little real power in the workplace. Furthermore, 9.8 percent of those women are not White (U.S. Bureau of Labor Statistics 1995), some are over 50 years old, and many (although we cannot know exactly how many) are lesbian or bisexual.

Why would such an atypical image come to mind? Because this image is the dominant, hegemonic, conception of working women. It represents the image of the most powerful race, class, and sexual orientation group of women. It is grossly overrepresented in the media, because it is set up as the model, the ideal against which other working women are to be judged. By its repeated presentation in the media (e.g., *Ally McBeal, Murphy Brown, Judging Amy*) the image distorts the public perception, leaving the impression that the attainment of positions of power among women is far more possible than is actually the case. By masking the true nature of race, class, gender, and sexuality oppression, the image helps to preserve the status quo.

Ideologies such as this that pervade the macro structures of society affect how people come to view themselves and others: the micro level. This hegemonic controlling image of working women further sets up a standard for judgment that most women cannot possibly attain. So the experience of most women does not match the prevailing ideas about who working women are. Ideologies, then, are meant to explain the contradictions—talent and hard work place some women above the rest. If most women come to believe their failure to measure up is a product of their personal limitations—lack of talent, desire, effort—they internalize the oppression. They may experience a loss of self-esteem and a lower sense of self-worth, and because they feel less worthy, they may accept the obstacles they face in trying to improve their position in the labor market.

Because of the distorted images of subordinate groups that pervade education and the media, members of these groups are often viewed as weak human beings who passively accept—and even deserve—less of society's socially valued resources. To comprehend the human agency, resilience, creativity, and strength of oppressed group members, however, one must view their actions and motivations through their own lenses, not through the lenses of dominant culture controlling images. When we do so, it is clear that oppressed groups actively resist oppression and devaluation in numerous ways every day. Not all women, for example, come to view themselves as less worthy as workers if they do not attain the hegemonic ideal.

Daily acts of resistance range from an individual's rejecting negative images and replacing them with positive ones (e.g., a domestic worker's taking great pride in her work) to mass social protests. Acts of resistance also range from passive forms such as work slowdowns or excessive and carefully planned use of sick leave (to ensure maximum disruption of the workplace) to active measures such as public protests, marches on Washington, strikes, or violence (Bookman and Morgen 1988).

Recognition of the history of oppressed group resistance helps to counter myths and beliefs in the dominant culture that oppression is a "natural" aspect of social life. Through public protest and the persistent demand for civil rights laws that made racial discrimination in education, housing, and employment illegal, for example, African Americans were able to shift greater educational and economic opportunity and earning power in their direction and in the direction of other oppressed groups (e.g., other people of color, White women, religious groups). Social movements such as the civil rights movement; racial and ethnic pride; gay, bisexual, and lesbian pride; the labor movement; and women's movements are collective manifestations of resistance to negative and controlling images of and structures constricting oppressed groups. It is in part through these movements that individuals become aware of the ideological nature and the structural barriers to attaining the "ideal." They resist internalizing the oppression and have the potential for self-definition and self-valuation, a process critical to the survival of oppressed groups.

Micro Processes

Identity

At the individual level, race, class, gender, and sexuality are fundamental sources of identity formation for all of us: how we see ourselves and who we think we are. They are so fundamental that to be without them would be like being without an identity at all.

Racial group membership, for example, not only shapes how we see ourselves but how others view us. People of color are often viewed in limiting ways based on controlling images—stereotypes of who they are and how they ought to act. When White people say to a Native American, "You don't seem Indian to me," or "I don't think of you as Indian," they are acknowledging that the Native American is acting out of sync with the stereotypic images of Native Americans. Statements such as these also imply that although contradictory evidence may make Whites willing to change their views of a single person (you're not like them), it does not challenge their stereotypes and indeed reinforces the power of these controlling images (they can't possibly be like you).

Members of oppressed racial groups may also seek to control the behavior of group members by holding them accountable to *oppositional* expectations for group loyalty and resistance to oppression—that they *not* act like the dominant White group. Most racial groups, for example, have developed derogatory terms to refer to members of their own group who may deny or devalue their racial identity. *Oreo, coconut, apple,* and *banana* are terms for African Americans, Latinos/as, Native Americans, and Asian Americans, respectively, who "act White"—appear to devalue their heritage by denying or ignoring it. In short, both dominant and subordinate groups hold expectations for the way racial group members should be. And even though these expectations often differ across class, gender, and sexuality systems, they are powerful structures in our lives.

Psychosocial Resources

While the barriers of oppression are both material and ideological, the resources associated with one's social location in the matrix of dominance and subordination are both material and psychological (Collins 1991a, 1998; Weber, Hancock, and Higginbotham 1997). Nonmaterial psychosocial resources have important consequences for social and psychological well-being that in turn affect one's ability to secure material resources. Psychosocial resources associated with one's social location include positive feelings of well-being and self-respect that result from a strong connection to and identity with a group of people who share a common history and life experiences (Comas-Dias and Greene 1994).

Developing positive identity and feelings of self-respect is made easier for dominant groups whose own experiences serve as the public model for how *all* people should live their lives. Because social institutions such as schools are structured to support the White middle class, for example, White, middle-class children are usually raised with successful role models and in families with greater access to the resources that will help the children succeed in school. They enter school with greater expectations for success; teachers expect their success and give them more attention. Teachers' positive orientations enhance the children's sense of self-worth, thus improving their performance and their chances for school success (Oakes 1985; Ornstein and Levine 1989; Polakow 1993).

Occupying a subordinate location in the race, class, gender, and sexuality systems does not, however, necessarily equate with a lack of psychosocial resources (Comas-Dias and Greene 1994). Research has consistently demonstrated that African-American adolescent girls, for example, have higher self-esteem and a stronger sense of self than White adolescent girls (American Association of University Women 1991, 1994). Working-class, Latino/a children growing up in the barrio may develop a strong sense of self-worth if they are surrounded by loving family members and neighbors who convey a sense of each child's special worth as an individual and as a Latino/a. And this psychosocial resource can serve as the foundation for a healthy defense against negative or rejecting messages from the dominant society. Resistance to pressures of structured inequality within subordinate group communities can, in fact, be a psychosocial resource that can be used in a collective struggle against oppression and in a personal journey toward self-appreciation and good mental health.

MACRO-MICRO PROCESSES IN THE POLITICAL DOMAIN

Macro Processes

As the historical time line in Chapter 2 suggests, the struggle for full citizenship rights, for inclusion in the political process, and thus for an equal voice in public policies—from defining racial groups to taxation to family, welfare, immigration, school, and international policies—has been long and difficult. Participation in the political institutions of society defines groups' relationships to the policy enforcement institutions: law, criminal justice, the police, and the military. Control over the political domain also increases control in the ideological and economic domains by increasing power over the production of controlling ideologies about subordinate groups and by increasing access to greater economic resources. The prevalence of upper-class, White, heterosexual men in the U.S. Congress, for example, enables them to pass tax laws, business legislation, and other policies that support the continued dominance of this group in the economy.

But macro political processes also affect other domains that seem less obvious, such as a group's physical health. Thomas LaVeist (1992) demonstrates that the political empowerment of communities of color is an important determinant of their health. In communities with more people of color on the city council, health indicators (e.g., life expectancy, disease rates) for communities of color were better than for communities with few people of color on the councils. When people of color are elected to city councils, their presence affects the community's health in at least two ways:

- Council members can direct resources that improve health to communities of color (e.g., health clinics).
- Council members can divert projects that might threaten community health (e.g., toxic waste dumps).

Subordinate group resistance through political action can and has affected the well-being of oppressed communities. But for these macro community level changes to take place, individuals must also feel empowered and involved enough to participate in the process: running for office, lobbying, protesting, voting, working for candidates, talking to others in the community about the issues and candidates, writing letters.

Micro Processes

When people in oppressed groups internalize the negative views and limits on their lives in the political realm, they may feel unable to effect change in their environments and be unlikely to act in ways that would change their own or the group's status. They lack a sense of control over their environment and a sense of efficacy—the belief that what you do can make a difference. So they are unlikely, for example, to participate in the political process. When large numbers of people in a community don't participate in the political process, political change that favors their community is unlikely to take place. During the last 36 years, for example, the voting participation in federal elections has declined precipitously:

- *For President*—from 62.8 percent of the voting age population in 1960 to 49 percent in 1996.
- *For Congress*—from 58.5 percent of the voting age population in 1960 to 32.9 percent in 1998 (U.S. Bureau of the Census 1999: Table 489).

This decline in popular voting coincides with the period of a great shift of wealth and power away from segments of the middle class, working class, and poor populations. Still, White, middle-class, educated, middle-aged voters remain the most likely to turn out, in part because dominant group status provides people with access to resources and options that enable them to influence the political process and thus increases their sense of personal control and efficacy. To achieve the same end—a sense of personal control, efficacy, empowerment—members of oppressed groups must reject negative images, self-blame, and limitations.

Patricia Hill Collins discusses the ways in which Black women's empowerment involves rejecting the dominant view of reality, including the pervasive cultural stereotypes of Black women as subjugated and devalued people in American society. Collins describes the creation of a separate reality for Black women as

they confront and dismantle controlling negative images of themselves as matri-
archs, mammies, welfare mothers, physically unattractive women:

> When Black women define themselves, we clearly reject the assumptions that
> those in positions granting them the authority to interpret our reality are entitled
> to do so. Regardless of the actual content of Black women's self-definitions, the
> act of insisting on Black females' self-definition validates Black women's power
> as human subjects (Collins 1991a:106–7).

When Black women and other oppressed groups feel validated as human beings,
they will be empowered to act in many ways to further their own lives as well as
those of others.

MACRO-MICRO PROCESSES IN THE ECONOMIC DOMAIN

Control over economic resources (e.g., wealth, income) enables dominant groups
to control other critical social resources: housing, education, transportation, health
care, and jobs—the primary means by which most adults obtain their financial resources and by which many define their sense of self-worth. So a critical race,
class, gender, and sexuality analysis must examine economic resources (wealth
and income) and jobs, both how they are distributed across different groups and
how the distributions have changed in the recent past. Recent changes indicate a
shifting balance of power across different race, class, gender, and sexuality groups
and thus foretell different everyday struggles for people in different locations in
these systems.

Macro Processes

Since the 1970s, economists, sociologists, and even politicians agree that changes
in the U.S. economy have seriously reduced the standard of living for most Americans (Hacker 1997; Mishel and Bernstein 1994). Doug Timmer, Stanley Eitzen,
and Kathryn Talley (1994:85–89) summarize those changes:

- The decline of manufacturing and the increase in the service sector (from
  50 percent to 78 percent of the economy between 1947 and the 1990s) that
  brought permanent layoffs, the loss of higher-paid, blue-collar jobs, and the
  creation of lower-wage, white-collar jobs.
- The rapid technological advances, especially the applications of the computer
  chip, that have led the push to a service economy and have cost many jobs in
  other sectors of the economy.
- The increased global competition from foreign companies that have cheaper
  labor costs.
- The loss of union strength; private-sector unionization dropped from 40 percent of the labor force in the 1950s to 11 percent in the 1990s (see also Freeman 1994:16).

- The job cutbacks in the defense industry to reduce the huge national debt produced largely by lavish military spending in the 1980s.
- The increased corporate debt whose interest payments have greatly reduced the amount of money businesses have for new investment in plants and equipment.
- The numerous takeovers, mergers, and leveraged buyouts of competitors or businesses in unrelated industries that were conducted in the 1980s—deals that typically involved enormous interest payments. Companies often went bankrupt or sold off assets to pay interest on loans, and many workers lost their jobs.
- The flight of businesses to locations abroad to seek cheap labor and to reduce their U.S. taxes (see also Barlett and Steele 1994:51).
- The shift in the tax burden from corporations to individuals and from the wealthy to the middle class, working class, and poor (see also Barlett and Steele 1994).

Income and Jobs

The power structures of race, class, gender, and sexuality put groups in different positions both to shape these processes and to structure their relationship to them, producing advantages for some and disadvantages for others. During the 1980s and into the 1990s, both wealth and income inequality increased and the middle class declined for the first time since the 1920s and the Great Depression of the 1930s:

- The very rich got richer.
- Middle-income groups lost numbers, wealth, and income.
- The ranks of the poor grew, and the people in them got poorer (Barlett and Steele 1994; Hacker 1997; Mishel and Bernstein 1994; Timmer, Eitzen, and Talley 1994).
- The only major wage gap to *decline* during the 1980s and early 1990s was the gender gap in wages. Between 1979 and 1989 the gap declined by 10.6 percentage points from 62.8 percent to 73.4 percent; 75 percent of this shift was the result of a decline in men's wages, not of an increase in women's wages (Mishel and Bernstein 1994:124).

These shifts in the class structure were also differentially distributed across race, class, gender, and sexuality: The ranks of the poor were increasingly comprised of women (particularly women of color) and children. Growing poverty and a shrinking middle class were produced primarily by job loss, by lower wages in the new jobs created in the 1980s (more women's than men's jobs), and by reduced wages in the remaining jobs. In the 1990s, the fastest-growing jobs were retail salespeople, janitors, maids, waiters, receptionists, hospital orderlies, and clerks (Timmer, Eitzen, and Talley 1994).

Since the 1980s U.S. workers have seen long-term deterioration in job quality:

- Part-time and temporary employment increased, constituting 20 percent of all private-sector jobs created. In 1997 *Fortune* magazine reported that the largest private employer in the United States is MANPOWER, Inc., a temporary worker service.

- Low-paying self-employment increased.
- Multiple job holding increased, primarily because workers earned insufficient wages in their primary jobs.
- A larger proportion of the workforce is either underemployed, overemployed, low paid, or trapped in unfavorable job situations (Mishel and Bernstein 1994:203).

The economic downturn that created these unfavorable job conditions uniquely affected the white-collar workforce, many of whom are middle class. During previous recessions, the blue-collar workforce bore the brunt of job layoffs and wage cuts. But in the 1980s the rise in unemployment was greater among white-collar than among blue-collar workers. For the first time, the growth in unemployment in services was nearly as high as in manufacturing, signaling the end of the service-sector boom. Between 1987 and 1991, 12.3 million workers lost jobs as a result of a facility's closing, job elimination, or slack work—5.7 million were white-collar (Mishel and Bernstein 1994:209).

During the late 1990s incomes increased slightly among middle-income groups and even among the poor, fueled by technology, stock market, and consumer-driven expansions at the end of the decade. The long-range implications for inequality are, however, still unclear because some of the gains were the result of increased stock owning and a significant increase in debt—with the median amount owed jumping more than 42 percent and the median mortgage debt growing strongly (Kennickell, Starr-McCluer, and Surette 2000).

Women and Work. Women's labor force participation rates have dramatically increased since the 1970s. In 1998, 45 percent of the workforce was female, and 59.8 percent of all women in the United States were employed outside the home (U.S. Bureau of the Census 1999: Table 651). Historically, the number of Black women employed outside the home has been high because they had to work to offset their husbands' low pay, which resulted from discrimination in hiring and in wage structures (Ortiz 1994). The number of White women employed outside the home, however, has increased until their rates (59.4 percent) almost equal those of Black women (62.8 percent) (U.S. Bureau of the Census 1999: Table 650). This increase has been especially dramatic among women with children. Only 27.6 percent of married women with children were employed in 1960 but 70.6 percent were employed by 1998. Only 56 percent of divorced, separated, and widowed women with children were employed in 1960, but 79.7 percent were employed by 1998 (U.S. Bureau of the Census 1999: Table 659). Employment rates among Mexican-American, Cuban-American, and Asian-American women have also increased since the 1960s (Weiss 1991). As these figures show, most families are now composed of two wage earners.

Wealth

Wealth is in many ways a better indictor of economic well-being than income because it is the total, at a given moment, of a person's accumulated assets (e.g., ownership of stocks, money in the bank, real estate, business ownership) less the debt held at one time. Income is less inclusive and refers only to the flow of dollars (salaries, wages, and payments from an occupation, investment, government transfer) over a set period, typically a year (Oliver and Shapiro 1995). The richest people earn very little of their wealth through wages. Wealth is thus a good indicator of the relative economic power of race, class, gender, and sexual groups:

- The inequality of wealth (representing total financial assets) between White people and people of color—the racial wealth gap—has remained very high in the 1980s and 1990s. By 1989 the median wealth for families of color was only 5 percent that of the median wealth of White families, and the average wealth among families of color was only 29 percent that of White families (Mishel and Bernstein 1994:250–52).
- Wealth inequality grew more among people of color than among Whites. The economic divide between rich and poor people of color grew more than the wealth or income divide between rich and poor Whites, signaling the increasing importance of class in communities of color.

The racial wealth gap also varies according to gender and family status. In 1989 the average wealth among people of color who were

- married was 35 percent that of Whites who were married
- single, male heads of household was 62 percent that of White single, male heads of households
- single, female heads of household was 20 percent that of White single, female heads of households.

These gaps are different from income differences between the races, but they present a more accurate picture of the total financial resources available to families. In this picture, single women of color who are heads of households are by far the most disadvantaged group financially—relative to White women and men, to men of color, and to women of color who are married (Mishel and Bernstein 1994:252).

Micro Processes

These changes in the macro structure of the economy have clearly affected everyday life in the United States for everyone. Occupying a privileged location in the economic class system facilitates one's life in many ways. As a consequence of the macro economic shifts in the last 30 years, for example, many poor and working-class people have lost their jobs, work multiple part-time jobs, can no longer afford higher education, have transportation problems getting to work, cannot afford quality child care, may lack or have minimal health care coverage, cannot afford to own their own home, and need multiple incomes in a family to meet basic needs.

For many middle-class and upper-class people, likely none of these needs is likely to be a cause for concern—their economic resources either render them nonexistent (difficulty getting to work) or easily remedied (finding child care or paying for college). Consequently, dominant group people often fail to grasp the realities of life for those living on the economic margins. They also can feel validated by a dominant system that in many ways equates money with success and success with worth. In contrast, people in subordinate groups must, as Patricia Hill Collins

(1998) points out, resist the negative association in our society between lack of material/economic resources and lack of worth as human beings.

Communities often resist this dominant culture association between wealth and worth by putting forth alternative systems of valuation such as valuing loyalty, honesty, hard work, respect for elders, and nurturing others. People who show these valued traits can receive community validation and develop a positive sense of self-worth, even in the face of a dominant society that actively devalues them.

SIMULTANEOUSLY EXPRESSED

Race, class, gender, and sexuality are interrelated systems at the macro institutional level—they are created, maintained, and transformed simultaneously and in relationship to one another. Therefore, they cannot be understood independently of one another. At the micro level of the individual, these systems are experienced in our lives simultaneously. Each contributes to our identities, our views of the world. In a very real sense they cannot be separated. This feature has been highlighted by women of color involved in feminist movements who are often asked to place their gender before their race in deciding where they will work for social justice and the kinds of positions they should take on social issues. In a similar vein, the Black Power movement of the 1960s was undermined and lost women's participation in part because of its patriarchal demands that racism, not sexism, was the primary oppressor and that Black women should play traditional women's roles in the organization. As former Black Panther Elaine Brown said, the party was "a very misogynistic organization" (Jackson 1998:45). The pressure to separate one's self into different (and competing) parts was eloquently resisted in the often-quoted title of one of the first anthologies about Black women's studies: *All the Women Were White, All the Blacks Were Men, but Some of Us Are Brave: Black Women's Studies* (Hull, Scott, and Smith 1982).

Although one system may appear prominent in a particular historical moment or social situation or in an individual's identity, close examination will always reveal the relevance of the other dimensions. While race, class, gender, and sexuality systems of oppression often reinforce one another, they are also unique systems of dominance with unique histories and current manifestations. What is unique about a race, class, gender, and sexuality *analysis* and what differentiates it from analyses of a single dimension of inequality is that it

- simultaneously examines all four dimensions and may also incorporate other related dimensions such as ethnicity, nation, disability, or age. In this way the analysis is much more complex than one that isolates a single dimension for examination.
- focuses attention on the unique expressions of social reality that exist at the points of connection—the intersections of the four dimensions. Thus, the lives of groups such as women of color are not excluded from but become the central focus of much research.

One's social location in the intersecting systems of race, class, gender, and sexuality produces varying social experiences:

- One can be privileged in all social systems—White, heterosexual, middle-class, professional males.
- One can be privileged in some social systems yet disadvantaged in others—middle-class people with a subordinate racial ethnic position, working-class men, and middle-class White women. Gay, middle-class, White men, for example, have the advantage of race, class, and gender privilege, yet this advantage cannot protect them from negative social sanctions aimed at controlling their sexual expressions.
- One can be disadvantaged in all the social systems—lesbian women of color who have few job skills and little formal education.

That we almost all occupy both dominant and subordinate positions and experience advantage and disadvantage in the race, class, gender, and sexuality systems means that there are few pure oppressors or oppressed in our society. Race, class, gender, and sexuality are not reducible to immutable personality traits or seemingly permanent characteristics. They are social constructions that give us power and options in some arenas while restricting our power and options in others.

We cannot argue from this principle, however, that "we are all oppressed" so that our oppressions can simply be added up and ranked to identify the most oppressed group or the most victimized. Nor can we say that disadvantage on any two dimensions is the same as on any other two. No simple mathematical relationship can capture the complexity of the interrelationships of these systems. Yet recognizing that we each simultaneously experience all of these dimensions can help us to see the often obscured ways in which we benefit from and are disadvantaged in existing race, class, gender, and sexuality social arrangements. Such an awareness can be key in working together across different groups to achieve a more equitable distribution of society's valued resources.

SUMMARY

Race, class, gender, and sexuality systems of oppression are generated, extended, and challenged in the ideological, political, and economic societal domains. At the micro level, the everyday actions of individuals as they live their lives in unequal social relations both generate those systems and challenge them. The macro structures of oppression provide a powerful framework—a hierarchy that persists through time and across places and that has serious consequences for social life. Understanding the ways that our individual lives are shaped by larger social forces is a key process in coming to understand race, class, gender, and sexuality as systems of oppression that shape all of our lives, all of the time. Further, these systems are interrelated and so are our identities and places within them. Because we simultaneously experience our location along all dimensions, they must all be taken into account in every analysis of social life.

Questions to Ask When Analyzing Race, Class, Gender, and Sexuality

As you read the rest of the book, I hope that you develop and strengthen your ability to analyze the interconnected systems of race, class, gender, and sexuality and see how to use your analyses to further your personal development and for social betterment. When you analyze situations and events, remember that the tools that you bring to the analysis are the questions you ask and the knowledge you have of the dynamic character of race, class, gender, and sexuality oppression: that these systems are historically and geographically/globally contextual, socially constructed power relations that are simultaneously expressed at both the macro level of social institutions and the micro level of individual life and personal identity. When we think of race, class, gender, and sexuality systems of oppression in this way, a more complete and more complex understanding of social life provides us with a firmer foundation on which to develop effective strategies for promoting social equity and a more humane social order.

When you conduct your analyses, recall the five basic themes in a race, class, gender, and sexuality analysis. Each theme can be associated with some general questions you might want to consider. The questions posed here are not meant to be comprehensive but to be general guides, a starting place. We will also revisit the case of Margaret Welch by raising a few questions that highlight the simultaneous and interrelated dynamics of race, class, gender, and sexuality in her life.

HISTORICALLY AND GEOGRAPHICALLY/ GLOBALLY CONTEXTUAL

First, race, class, gender, and sexuality are *contextually rooted in history and geography.* When we examine situations, it is important to know the histories and global contexts of particular groups so that we can come to understand their current situations and their interpretations of events. Taking a broad historical and global view also enables us to see the tremendous changes that have taken place in each of these systems over time and the diversity across social geography and to recognize the potential for change in situations we face every day. Ask yourself:

- How have the relevant ideologies controlling images developed over time? In this location?
- What political processes have shaped these relationships over time? In this location?
- What historical economic conditions have affected these relationships? Regional economic conditions?
- How would these relationships be understood at a different historical time? In different regional and geographic locations?

About Margaret Welch, we might ask:

- How have controlling images of poor women and welfare recipients developed over time in the United States? How do they differ for White women and women of color and for heterosexuals, bisexuals, and lesbians? How have the political forces that shape today's wel-

(continued)

fare policies (e.g., prescribed schooling and work for benefits) developed over time? Margaret lives in Chicago—do rural poor women face different obstacles? How have the economic shifts of the last 30 years in the United States affected the lives of poor women? If Margaret were lesbian, would she have better protection against discrimination in New York or San Francisco than in Chicago, Des Moines, or the rural South?

SOCIALLY CONSTRUCTED

Second, race, class, gender, and sexuality are *socially constructed,* not biologically determined. Their meaning develops out of group struggles over socially valued resources. Ask yourself:

- Are race, class, gender, and sexuality taken to determine how people should be out of some notion of biological imperative or of inherent inferiority?
- Are race, class, gender, and sexuality seen as immutable "facts" of people's lives or of social situations?
- Are people's economic resources, power, prestige, education, health— their total status—seen as something they earned through individual effort?
- How might you view the situation if people of different race, class, gender, and sexuality locations were in it?

In Margaret's life, we might ask: Does the welfare system operate under the assumption that women like Margaret can actually improve their life condition? Does Margaret blame herself for her current plight? Are there any

forces apparent in Margaret's life that believe in her ability to escape permanently from poverty? Suppose instead that Margaret was Chinese American and gay. How would her story change?

POWER RELATIONSHIPS

Third, race, class, gender, and sexuality are *power relationships* of dominance and subordination in which dominant groups exploit the labor and lives of oppressed groups for a greater share of society's valued resources. Try not to confuse personal power with social power. Individuals can be powerful by virtue of their insight, knowledge, personalities, and other traits. They can persuade others to act in ways they want. But this personal power can be achieved in spite of a lack of socially institutionalized power. It is the power that accrues from occupying a position of dominance in the race, class, gender, and sexuality systems that we seek to understand here. Ask yourself:

- What are the institutional arrangements that benefit the powerful and cost others in this situation?
- Which group(s) gains and which group(s) loses in the institutional arrangements we observe?
- Have the participants come to believe (internalized) that they lack power or have power in the situation? How have their beliefs affected their actions?

In Margaret's case, we might ask: What groups gain because Margaret— and others like her (White, heterosexual, women)—are poor? Who benefits from poverty? Does Margaret internalize her lack of power? If so, how does this internalization affect

(continued)

her actions? If Margaret became involved in the Welfare Rights Movement (cf. Abramovitz 1996), would her view of herself and of the causes of her poverty change? How?

MACRO AND MICRO LEVELS

Fourth, race, class, gender, and sexuality systems operate at both the *macro level of social institutions* and the *micro level of individual life.* When you analyze a particular social event, seeing the interpersonal and psychological manifestations of oppression is often easy. The broad macro level forces that shape events are more remote and abstract and are, therefore, more difficult to see.

Which group(s) gains and which group(s) loses in the institutional arrangements we observe? When many people of color and White women look at the White male backlash against affirmative action, for example, they can easily see angry White men trying to push back gains made by people of color and women and to maintain their position of power and control. They can dismiss White men as "oppressors" or bad people. But when we ask about the broader race, class, gender, and sexuality forces that shape this relationship, we also see that the shifts in our economy have rendered many White men vulnerable to loss of jobs, income, and health. White men's anger derives in part from their different expectations—out of their sense of privilege (cf. Newman 1988, 1993).

If we are to collaborate to achieve economic change that benefits most people, we must recognize the real ways in which many White men, along with many other people, are vulnerable in the present economy. Ask yourself:

- What are the ideological, political, and economic institutional arrangements and practices that are shaping each actor's actions and views in the situation?
- Imagine changes in key macro institutional conditions, such as the onset of an economic recession. How would this change alter the situation?
- How does each actor view the situation? Is that view different for people in different race, class, gender and sexuality locations?
- Are oppressed group members aware of the race, class, gender, and sexuality power structures in the situation? Is there evidence that they resist controlling images in their views and their actions? Is there evidence that they have accepted the controlling images—the limits on their lives? Why?
- Are dominant group members aware of their privilege in the situation? What does it mean to them? What views do they hold of oppressed groups? If dominant group members do not refer to oppressed groups, why not?

And thinking of Margaret, we might ask: What are the macro economic conditions that render Margaret poor? The political conditions? The ideological, controlling images? How is Margaret's view of the institutions (e.g., welfare, education) she faces limited by her social location? How would a wealthy White woman view Margaret's situation? Has Margaret inter-

(continued)

nalized the social limits on her life, resisted them, or both?

SIMULTANEOUSLY EXPRESSED

Fifth, these systems are *simultaneously expressed.* All operate to shape everyone's lives at all times. Ask yourself about all of the systems in every situation you examine. Although one system may appear to be in the foreground, go behind the obvious and ask about the less visible dimensions. Ask yourself:

- If we take account of only a single dimension of oppression (e.g., gender) and ignore the others, how might we interpret the situation differently?
- What are the dimensions that are foregrounded (i.e., fairly obvious) in this situation?
- What dimensions are not so apparent? Why?
- How does the power of the individuals involved shape our perspective on what dimensions are important?

And for Margaret, we might ask: Even though race, class, and gender are in the forefront of her story, how does sexuality also shape her life? If Margaret were lesbian, how might her story be different? If Margaret were not White, how might her story be different? If we looked only at her gender, how might we miss key elements in understanding her situation?

IMPLICATIONS FOR SOCIAL ACTION AND SOCIAL JUSTICE

Finally, when you conduct analyses, make the connection between *activism for social justice* and the analyses you conduct. Ask yourself about the implications for social justice of the perspective you have, the questions you ask, and the answers you obtain.

- Do your analyses provide insights that in the current political context would serve to reinforce existing power relations?
- Do your analyses illuminate processes of resistance or avenues for self-definition or self-valuation that could transform the race, class, gender, and sexuality hierarchies?
- How might people in different social locations react to and employ your analyses? To what ends?

When you take race, class, gender, and sexuality into account in every situation, you arrive at a richer, more complete, more complex, and more useful understanding of society.

A Race, Class, Gender, and Sexuality Analysis of Education

When exploring how the intersecting systems of race, class, gender and sexuality are generated, maintained, challenged, and transformed, I seek an analysis that is complex, doesn't rank oppressions, addresses their intersecting nature, and moves us toward social justice. The conceptual framework presented here suggests that the analysis should be historically grounded and address the simultaneous expressions of socially constructed power relationships at both the individual (micro) and societal (macro) levels. In this section I attempt to further explicate the framework by applying it to a specific case, the U.S. system of education. Rather than analyze a particular group's experience in the educational system at a specific historical moment, I seek to illustrate the framework and to guide future work by raising questions and identifying some of the kinds of issues and social relationships that must be addressed in a comprehensive analysis of the reproduction of race, class, gender, and sexuality systems in education in the United States at the beginning of the millenium.

To do this I have structured my discussion as follows. First, in Chapter 6, the discussion opens with two brief educational biographies. Theo Wilson is a teenage, African-American male whom I met and observed in 1996 when he was participating in an after-school program run by faculty from an urban branch campus of a state university in a Northeastern city. Lynn Johnson is an African-American baby boomer who was interviewed nine years earlier for a research project on Black and White professional-managerial women, which I conducted in Memphis, Tennessee. In this segment of her interview, Lynn reflects on her educational experiences in the 1960s and 1970s. Taken together, these two cases reveal many of the complexities of race, class, gender, and sexuality as they are played out between women and men of the same racial group in different places and times.

Second, education is an institution whose primary identity is in the domain of ideology—focused on the production and transmission of ideas that prepare people to work in and to contribute to the smooth functioning of society. Consequently, any discussion of the social processes endemic in the institution of education must first address the cornerstone ideology on which it rests: the American Dream ideology. Chapter 7 presents and critiques the basic premises and paradoxes of the American Dream, particularly as they lay a foundation for the race, class, gender, and sexuality conflicts in and about the U.S. system of education.

Third, in Chapters 8 and 9, I explore the production of race, class, gender, and sexuality in education within the rubric of each of the themes in the framework. I chose not to limit my analysis to a single group, such as Chinese-American women, or to a single social process, such as the resegregation of public schools—a focus that would enable more depth of analysis but would limit the opportunity to raise a variety of issues and questions for further consideration, a purpose of this text. Nor is there space to provide a comprehensive race, class, gender, and sexuality analysis of the U.S. education system. Instead,

these chapters will illustrate the framework by highlighting some of the ways that addressing these themes complicates, illuminates, and renders our race, class, gender, and sexuality analyses more useful in the pursuit of social justice. Hoping to suggest avenues to pursue in more comprehensive analyses, I chose breadth over depth to point to a variety of group experiences.

One of the fundamental social processes through which race, class, gender, and sexuality hierarchies are produced and sustained, particularly in education, is segregating and isolating groups for differential treatment. Understanding segregation processes in education—into different schools, different tracks in schools, different areas of study, different curricula—is key to unraveling the dynamics of race, class, gender, and sexuality. I examine segregation processes in the historical roots of the modern school system as well as in current macro and micro processes. Macro institutional power relations in the economic, political, and ideological domains are illustrated as they play out in education (e.g., in politicization of educational issues, in the curriculum, in labor market outcomes). Micro power relations are examined in classroom dynamics of race, class, gender, and sexuality in kindergarten through grade 12, and the simultaneity of race, class, gender, and sexuality systems is examined through a review of the cases presented in this section.

CHAPTER 6

Theo Wilson and Lynn Johnson: Case Studies

Dream Variations
      Langston Hughes

To fling my arms wide
In some place of the sun,
To whirl and to dance
Till the white day is done.
Then rest at cool evening
Beneath a tall tree
While night comes on gently,
         Dark like me—
That is my dream!

To fling my arms wide
In the face of the sun,
Dance! Whirl! Whirl!
Till the quick day is done.
Rest at pale evening . . .
A tall, slim tree . . .
Night coming tenderly
         Black like me.

THE CASE OF THEO WILSON[1]

I observed the following exchange between Theo Wilson and Marie Carucci during a writing tutoring session in an after-school program in 1996.

> "Write a poem about a dream you have," Marie Carucci said to Theo Wilson, after they read and talked about "Dream Variations."
>
> Puzzled, Theo asked, "What do you mean? Do you mean the things that happen when you're asleep?"
>
> Marie replied, "Well, yes, dreams do happen when you're asleep, but I mean the kind you have when you're awake—perhaps something you might like to do, if you could do anything you wanted."

[1]Theo Wilson is a pseudonym as are all other names in the story. These names and some details of the story have been changed to protect the identities of those involved.

"I don't know," said Theo and his leg began to jitter.

"Just something you really want to do, anything—dance in the sun like Hughes, something serious, something silly." And they talked some more about Hughes' poem.

Finally, Theo said, "Well, I can't do anything I want. Everything takes good math skills, and I'm not good at math."

"Well, just pretend you can."

DREAMS
   Theo Wilson

I would like to be a Secret Service agent,
   Protecting important people,
   Saving lives,
And getting no acknowledgment—
Just knowing that my job and
people
Depend on me.

When Theo got to this point, he quit and shoved the paper at Marie, his leg jittering furiously. Marie asked him why he dreamed this, and he continued:

Why?
To slow down crime or
Make criminals fear me.
To hear thanks or
A smile.

I would love to do this.
But I doubt it would happen.
Bad luck seems to
Follow me.
Whenever I get good at something,
Something or someone messes it up.

Theo stopped, shaking his head and muttering that he just didn't know why "this stuff" happened to him all the time. Marie probed, "What stuff? Give an example."

Take last year in October—
I had the best week of practice all year.
Even the Varsity guys were noticing me.
Coaches tried me out for new things in practice.
But in the JV game versus [Our Town],
I dropped a touchdown pass—
In the end zone.

Theo quit again, hanging his head and trying to laugh off his remembered humiliation. They talked for a while about bad luck and good luck and choices, and Marie said, "How could you change things?"

How could I change things?
Have a magical surgery
To take my hands off me and
Put Jerry Rice's hands on me.

Theo Wilson and Marie Carucci met when she and another faculty member, Bill Nichols, from an urban university campus began to tutor youth in writing and math after school at the community center a few blocks from the campus. They are working against the limits of race, class, gender, and sexuality hierarchies to envision and facilitate a future for Theo that is not a dead end—one that allows dreams.

Theo Wilson is a 15-year-old African-American male who lives in the urban Northeast. Like many young teens, he is of average height, lanky, and a bit awkward and shy. His major interest is sports, especially football. He lifts weights fanatically, hoping someday to make the varsity team. And now he has decided to play lacrosse. Although he was completing his freshman year, his academic performance in high school was already very poor, especially in math. And he was in a technical English class rather than in a college prep one, even a "slow" section.

Like many poor, urban youth, Theo "stays" in a variety of places—sometimes with his father (before he died), sometimes with his paternal grandparents, but mostly with his maternal grandmother. His mother, a drug addict who is in and out of rehab, appears sporadically in his life. Taking advantage of the GI Bill, his father went to college and for a time held a low-wage administrative job. But when Theo was about 10 years old, his father was diagnosed with a rare degenerative disease and spent much of his energy fighting to stay alive. He died less than six months after Theo wrote "Dreams." Before he died, however, Theo's father tried to stay involved in Theo's education. In the spring of 1996, when he learned of the free tutoring sessions, he enrolled Theo.

After his father died, Theo was left even more adrift and turned increasingly to Marie and Bill for parenting and nurturing. Only a few months after his father died, Theo called Marie late one Sunday evening, telling her he had to talk to her "right away." After much stumbling and embarrassed laughing, he blurted out that while everyone was out of the house, he liked to dress up in "different kinds of clothes. Know what I mean?" So in addition to grappling with everything else, Theo—the football player, weight lifter, and lacrosse player—was struggling with this "inappropriate" gender expression and what, if anything, it might mean for his sexual identity. When Marie asked Theo whether his teachers had ever discussed cross-dressing, transgender issues, or homosexuality in class, he burst out laughing, "They couldn't talk about *that* stuff!"

Marie began helping Theo identify sources of information and support. They found a number of sources that offered support for gay, lesbian, and bisexual youth but none for young cross-dressers. For a while, Theo spent much of his free time searching for answers, primarily on the Web but also by calling support and hotline numbers. His search for answers ended, at least for a while, when he called a number he found in his high school newspaper. It promised help for young people with problems. When Theo explained his "problem," the voice at the other end of the phone first denounced him as a sinner and then began reading Bible verses to him. Theo hung up and turned his attention toward girls and having a girlfriend, even to finding a date for the prom. But his "thing," as he calls it, continues to cause him pain and anxiety.

As part of teaching writing to Theo, Marie talked to him about Standard English. When Marie teaches Standard English to poor and working-class students—to anyone other than middle- and upper-class students—she teaches it as a second language. Working with Theo on a grammar assignment—identifying transitive and intransitive verbs, Marie asked an increasingly distracted and frustrated Theo why he thought he had to do this work. She also talked to him about levels of language, about how arbitrary the "rules" are, and about why even though you may say, "I ain't got no money," it's a good idea to know the standard way of saying the same thing. During the conversation, Theo talked a great deal about how useless and how boring this stuff is and how teachers make you do the same stuff year after year.

MARIE: "But why do they make you do it? Why do I think you should know
    Standard English?"
THEO: "I don't know. 'Cause you're a English teacher, too?"
    They both laughed.
MARIE: "Well, here's one good reason why: Unless you're going to be a rock star
    or a professional athlete or a famous artist—if you're going to be a regular
    person who goes to work every day—you make more money if you can speak
    and write Standard English. And if we just work at all of this and you learn it
    this year, you won't have to bother learning it over and over again—just get it
    over with."
THEO: "Why ain't nobody ever told me that before?"

And he set to work with a little more focus and determination.

Unlike the other youth in the program, Theo launched himself into the work from the beginning, never missing a single session and often coming to Bill's office for extra math sessions. And although Marie and Bill gave their work and home phone numbers to all the youth, Theo was the only one to use them, to go after help actively. He even came to math tutoring sessions during the summer.

After a semester of active tutoring and mentoring by Marie and Bill, Theo began to think differently about his options and future prospects—he began to dream. Theo Wilson began to think about college. One thing he learned was that his technical English and basic math courses were not college preparatory classes. In these classes, he wouldn't learn what he needed to know to score well on the SATs or ACTs or to keep up in college. So in his sophomore year in high school, Theo enrolled in college prep courses, continuing to work with Marie and Bill. Bill even began mentoring Theo through the SATs. When he graduated from high school, Theo entered a local community college. But he still faces tremendous obstacles to completing higher education.

THE CASE OF LYNN JOHNSON[2]

Lynn Johnson is a successful 45-year-old, African-American hospital administrator who attended elementary and high school in the 1950s and 1960s in Memphis, Tennessee. She grew up living in public housing projects with her mother, who was on welfare (AFDC), and her six siblings. When she was 16, Lynn had a baby but continued school and graduated with her class from her inner-city, all-Black

---

[2]Lynn Johnson is a pseudonym. Her name and some other details in the story have been changed to protect her identity.

high school. Lynn was among the first African-American students to attend a local, private liberal arts college in Memphis. When she was interviewed in 1987 for a research project I conducted with Elizabeth Higginbotham, she was asked the following questions:

INTERVIEWER: Is there anything about your early childhood and schooling which you think has influenced your career plans?

LYNN: Yeah, the teachers. Elementary school was one of the most outstanding experiences for me. Being a poor kid and going into that environment, you think that the rich people—or the great people of the world—are teachers. They're the ones with the pretty clothes and the big cars and the big money and all that kind of thing. I had in my environment some teachers who really knew you. Who knew about you, took time to find out about you, cared about you, pushed you, who beat your tail if you didn't do it the way that you were supposed to be doing it, who told you what you could do in life. And they always told you that you could do EVERYTHING. Who didn't put limitations on you and who made you excel. I think if a kid does not have that, especially when they grow up in the kind of environment I grew up in, if they don't have that, they'll lose their motivation real quick. The teachers wouldn't allow me to lose it.

INTERVIEWER: Is there anything particular in your high school experience which stands out as important to you?

LYNN: The support that system gave me. I got pregnant when I was 16 years old, and I was supposed to have been kicked out of school.

When I found out I was pregnant, I said, "Oh, my God!" You know, just the embarrassment of it all. And so I was going to stay at home.

My principal came to my house and he said, "What are you doing here? You've been out of school a week. What are you doing at home?"

And I said, "Mr. Springer,"—first I tried to be on my high horse— "I'm not [says her maiden name]."

He said, "Yeah, I heard you got married."

And I said, "Yeah, I did."

And he said, "But I also hear that you're pregnant."

And I said, "Yeah, I am."

And he said, "Well what are you doing here?"

And I said, "I can't come back to school."

He said, "Who said so?"

I said, "Well that's the rule, and I know it's the rule, and I wasn't going to come in there for you to put me out."

He said, " I wasn't planning on putting you out. Get your butt back over here."

I talk about it like it was my experience—but it happened to a lot of girls—I mean, those who weren't going to go anywhere. Teachers in that day and time defined what they had—what kind of young people they were working with. Those that they knew didn't care one way or another, they said, "Get out of here, you done had the baby, you're on your way to having two babies, get out of here." Those who had the potential, who could go somewhere, who made an error or whatever, they worked with them. They worked with them. They said, "All right, you did your dirt. Let us dust you off and you come on back in here and let us see if we can't move you forward." And they did.

. . . Oh, honey, from the 10th grade on you had to take the ACT. They would write the checks themselves cause they'd know we didn't have the money. They had the best people caring about those kids. Not anymore . . .

Lynn is now very active both individually and in programs at work and through her church to provide working-class African-American youth with options, skills, and the motivation to succeed. Lynn mentors Black workers at the hospital, sharing knowledge and information and advising them, in hopes of facilitating their mobility in the workplace. She feels a strong commitment to give back to her community. She was taught that her achievement was not accomplished alone and that it carries with it a responsibility to the community that helped her.

PARTIAL TRUTHS: RACE, CLASS, GENDER, AND SEXUALITY AS SEPARATE SYSTEMS

The stories of Theo Wilson and Lynn Johnson each reveal some of the ways that the social relations of race, class, gender, and sexuality are produced, challenged, and transformed every day in the context of education. They simultaneously highlight both the powerful social forces that guide, steer, and push individuals into particular life paths based on their social location in race, class, gender, and sexuality hierarchies and the powerful personal and group forces that resist, reject, redefine, and overcome structural and psychological limits. We cannot fully understand these forces by isolating them one from another or by treating only one as primary.

Race

Even though Theo and Lynn are of the same race, they have very different senses of themselves. Lynn is optimistic, working to give back to her community and believing that what she does can make a difference. Thirty years later in the Northeast, Theo believed—at least at first—that no matter what he did he could not even dream about a better life, much less envision attaining one. The irony of the racially segregated schools of the South that Lynn attended is that they were grossly underfunded and deemed inferior in many ways. But because they were controlled by local African-American communities, they served as sites of resistance and training grounds for future leaders of that community (cf., Gilkes 1994). In Lynn's story there is a clear sense of community commitment to her success, a commitment missing in the story of Theo and frequently missing in the stories of White working-class women (Weber and Higginbotham 1992).

Class

Even though Theo and Lynn come from working-class families, they appear to be headed for different class outcomes. Lynn, bright and talented, was selected by school officials and tracked for college. She ultimately had relatively easy access to college admission, despite getting pregnant at age 16. But as a working-class African American, Lynn Johnson was not as likely as White, working-class women to marry into the middle class as a way of becoming mobile. Instead she had to rely on her own academic and professional success (Weber and Higginbotham 1992).

Theo made it to college, but the obstacles he faces to completing a degree, especially the weakness of his educational preparation and the high cost of education, are enormous. Making it into the middle class without a college degree is difficult.

Gender

Although Theo is male, male privilege is revealed to have a very class- and race-specific meaning in these stories. It was Lynn, not Theo, who was encouraged in academics and selected by teachers, family, and community for mobility. Despite his lanky build, Theo, like many young African-American boys, was encouraged in sports but tracked for a vocational education in preparation for minimum-wage work (Messner 1992; Oakes 1985).

Lynn's story also reveals the constraints imposed by gender. In Lynn's generation, it was common for teenage girls who became pregnant to be required or pressured to drop out of school and often to give up their babies for adoption (Solinger 1992). Lynn benefited, however, from her African-American community's greater tolerance of pregnant girls, particularly those perceived as having the potential for mobility.

Sexuality

Although Lynn is heterosexual and Theo is still forming his own sexual identity, they both developed their sexual identities in raced, classed, and gendered ways. Lynn's young marriage ended in divorce, and she is now a single, professional, African-American mother. She has a particular orientation toward men, marriage, and motherhood that is shaped by all of these and that differs from that of many upwardly mobile, White professional women (Weber and Higginbotham 1992).

If he chooses to continue to cross-dress and/or to identify as gay, Theo may have an even more difficult time finding positive role models, accurate information, and validation for his sexual practices and identity than if he were White and middle or upper class (D'Emilio 1993; Sears 1992). And to claim masculine privilege, Theo may be even more inclined to pursue contact sports such as football, despite his lanky build, because they represent accepted arenas for achieving masculinity among Black working-class men (Messner 1992).

RACE, CLASS, GENDER, AND SEXUALITY
AS INTERRELATED SYSTEMS: QUESTIONS TO ASK

As these examinations reveal, attempting to look at these two lives solely from the perspective of a single dimension obscures the complex intersections of race, class, gender, and sexuality. To capture the richness and intricacy of Lynn's and Theo's lives, we need to look at them from multiple dimensions and consider the meanings of those dimensions. If we look at their lives from the perspective of the themes of a race, class, gender, and sexuality framework, we might ask the following questions:

Historically and Geographically/Globally Contextual. If Theo, like Lynn, had been growing up in the 1950s or 1960s, how might his situation have been different? Would he have the community support that Lynn got to overcome obstacles to his mobility? How might his sexuality issues have been received? Would he have even spoken of his cross-dressing at all?

If Lynn were growing up now, how might her story be different? What was/is the cost of a college education? What forms of aid were/are available? How have changes in the Black community changed the influences on young people (e.g., Lynn is now middle class but doesn't live near poor African Americans)?

In the 1950s and 1960s, how did southern segregated urban communities differ from northern ones? How do they differ today?

Socially Constructed. What are the social forces at work in the lives of Theo and Lynn that operate to support their personal development? Their social mobility?

How did the schools operate to restrict or support their sexual development? Class mobility? Gender identities?

How might the school and the community respond if Theo were Asian American? If Lynn were?

Power Relations. How is vocational tracking for Theo and other working-class, African-American males related to the success of dominant culture White, middle-class, heterosexual men?

In what ways does Lynn's success challenge a power structure of race, class, gender, and sexuality? Does it also reinforce dominant power relations? How?

How do Lynn's teen pregnancy and Theo's developing gender and sexual identity put them at risk in a heterosexual society?

Macro Social Structural. In what ways did the schools help to create different futures for Theo and Lynn? How did the practice of school tracking—sorting students into different classes (e.g., college prep, basic, technical) in preparation for different futures—affect each of them?

Think of the prevailing stereotypes of young, poor, urban African-American males. How do they restrict options for young men like Theo?

At the hospital, Lynn now has few women and people of color in the ranks above her. How might controlling images of Black, middle-class women affect her chances for further mobility?

Micro Social Psychological. In what ways does Theo resist oppression? What are the implications for Theo of his methods of resistance? In what ways did Lynn resist oppression? What individuals and groups in their environments supported resistance? What are the broader social ramifications of each of their methods of resistance?

What is the evidence that Theo internalized race, class, gender, and sexuality oppression? Is there any evidence that Lynn has? What are possible personal ramifications of accepting restrictive views of their potential? What are the ramifications for society's race, class, gender, and sexuality hierarchies when individuals come to accept society's negative views of their group?

What people and processes support the development of Theo's sexual identity?

Simultaneously Expressed. Where do dreams come from? Why does Theo Wilson have so much trouble understanding the concept of a dream? How is the dream Theo describes a reflection of his social location as a poor African-American male who as a teenager is coming to terms with his sexuality? What is lost when we ignore any aspect of his reality?

How are dreams reflected in the story of Lynn Johnson? In what ways are they consistent with what you might expect, based on her social location? In what ways do they challenge your expectations?

Implications for Social Activism and Social Change. How have social movements (e.g., civil rights, gay, lesbian, bisexual, women's, labor) shaped Lynn's and Theo's experiences of race, class, gender, and sexuality? Lynn Johnson was active in civil rights activities while she was in college. Thus far, Theo shows little interest in political activities. How might their different relationships to social movements affect their life chances and world views?

SUMMARY

The stories of Lynn Johnson and Theo Wilson—and the questions raised by them—highlight a variety of ways that race, class, gender, and sexuality shape and are shaped by people's educational experiences—from school tracking and college attendance to segregated housing and community support for mobility, from the condition of the economy and the cost of higher education to the availability of financial aid and scholarships, from teen pregnancy to sexual identity. Race, class, gender, and sexuality systems are produced and reinforced every day in the domain of education.

CHAPTER 7

Education and the American Dream

The institution of education supports both the political and economic structures of society, but at its core it is an ideological institution—intended to create and transmit the ideas on which the society is organized and which will support its continuation. The American Dream ideology—that those who are talented and work hard can get ahead—depends on a system of education to provide opportunities and to explain its failures. In this way the American Dream ideology, a fundamental belief system rationalizing the current social hierarchies, is intricately intertwined with education. This chapter examines the American Dream ideology and its connection with the system of education to lay the ideological foundation for using the themes of the conceptual framework to explore the ways that race, class, gender, and sexuality hierarchies are produced and challenged in education.

DREAMS AND OPPRESSION

What's in a dream? What do dreams have to do with oppression? A great deal. Dreams contain what we know, what we want, what we think we can and cannot have, what we can imagine is possible. They tell us a great deal about people's lives. They tell us when people are free in their minds—as Lynn Johnson was when she thought she could be anything she wanted to be. They also tell us when people are controlled, contained, or trapped in their minds—as Theo Wilson was when he could not dream because "Everything takes good math skills, and I'm not good at math," and

> *Bad luck seems to*
> *Follow me.*
> *Whenever I get good at something*
> *Something or someone messes it up.*

Writers attempting to convey a central truth about oppression have often relied on dream metaphors. Lillian Smith, a White Southern woman who fought for civil rights, titled her biography *Killers of the Dream* (1949). Langston Hughes, a gay African-American poet, ponders what happens when dreams are shattered by racism:

Harlem (A Dream Deferred)
　　　LANGSTON HUGHES

What happens to a dream deferred?

Does it dry up
like a raisin in the sun?
Or fester like a sore—
And then run?
Does it stink like rotten meat?
Or crust and sugar over—
like a syrupy sweet?

Maybe it just sags
like a heavy load.

Or does it explode?

The connection of dreams and oppression is especially relevant in the American context. The American Dream is a uniquely American ideology—the basic belief that hard work and ability will pay off with personal success. President Bill Clinton described it in a speech to the Democratic Leadership Council in 1993:

> The American dream that we were all raised on is a simple but powerful one—if you work hard and play by the rules you should be given a chance to go as far as your God-given ability will take you (quoted in Hochschild 1995:18).

And the educational system, more than any other social institution, is supposed to be the place of opportunity for all: the institution that makes the American Dream possible.

PREMISES OF THE AMERICAN DREAM

The American Dream ideology gives citizens a basis for continuing to believe that U.S. society provides equality and the promise of financial success to all its citizens, even when people's experiences in no way reflect that belief—most people are not financially successful, and only a few people accumulate enormous wealth. As Jennifer Hochschild (1995) notes, this ideology has four components:

1. *Equality of Opportunity.* The concept of equality means equality of opportunity— our society purports to provide equal opportunity for everyone to pursue money, property, and other desirable social resources. As Bill Clinton suggested, you should be given a *chance* to *pursue* success.
2. *Reasonable Anticipation of Success.* Because, according to the Dream, all Americans have equal opportunity to pursue success, they may reasonably anticipate success—however they define it. As long as resources and opportunities seem to be available to all, people may continue to believe that success is possible for them in the future, even though they may not feel successful now.
3. *Individual Responsibility for Success.* Because, according to the Dream, all Americans have equal opportunity, people who succeed are seen as responsible for their success, and those who fail are held to blame for their failure.

This belief—that because everyone has an equal opportunity to succeed, failures are the fault of the people who fail—is compelling because all people want to believe that they can succeed.

4. *Success as Virtue, Failure as Sin.* Because people who succeed are seen as solely responsible for their success, success implies virtue and, by extension, failure implies sin. The spouse abuse and murder cases of O.J. Simpson graphically illustrate this belief. Because his public success as a football player—and hence his economic success—implied virtue in his private life, many Americans could not believe that Simpson was a murderer. In contrast, many Americans find welfare reform legislation acceptable, even desirable, although it primarily punishes poor women by eliminating their financial assistance, because their poverty is presumed to be a result of their own failure, their sinfulness, their laziness. Punishment thus becomes a way of properly addressing the problem.

David Boaz, executive vice president of the Cato Institute, a libertarian organization, recommended reducing the welfare rolls by increasing the punishment—lowering benefits and increasing the stigma already associated with women welfare recipients by calling their children "bastards":

> We've made it possible for a teenage girl to survive with no husband and no job. That used to be very difficult. If we had more stigma and lower benefits, might we end up with 100,000 bastards every year rather than a million children born to alternative families? (cited in Sidel 1996:6)

PARADOXES OF THE AMERICAN DREAM

Democratic capitalism—the belief in political democracy but not in economic democracy—is based on a paradox:

- Democracy is a political system in which supreme power is vested in the citizens—government *by* the people, justified by the principle of social *equality.*
- Capitalism is an economic system based on the pursuit of profit and private ownership, resulting in pervasive economic *inequality.* Capitalism is organized on social class relations of dominance and subordination—with the upper and middle classes reaping greater economic rewards because they own the workplace and design, supervise, and control the labor of the working and lower classes.

Resolving this basic paradox of democratic capitalism—the belief in social and political *equality* amidst severe economic *inequality*—necessitates reconceptualizing the notion of equality to mean equality of opportunity, not of outcome. The idea of equality of opportunity lends itself to a social system based on "meritocracy" or the "belief that because the race for social rewards is fair, those who reach the finish line must be faster and thus more meritorious runners than those who came in last" (Oakes et al. 1997:485). This view creates the common-sense notion about difference that people become wealthy and powerful through a "natural" sorting process that is fair and that separates the best from the rest. It also promotes the related notion that those who are not powerful will never acquire power because they lack the ability and that we therefore live in the best of all possible worlds (Oakes et al. 1997). In short, the American Dream ideology provides a powerful explanation for the fundamental contradiction of democratic capitalism. But consider what happens when we look more closely at the premises of this ideology.

1. *Equality of Opportunity.* In his speech Bill Clinton did not say, nor does the American Dream imply, that financial success or even a minimal standard of living should be *guaranteed* to everyone. He says only that people should be given a "chance," *if* they "work hard and play by the rules."

   Does U.S. society give everyone a chance? Does everyone start on a level playing field? Are the rules the same for everyone? Does a student going to school in the South Bronx have the same chance as a student in Beverly Hills? Does Theo have the same chance as an upper-class White girl in his same city?

2. *Reasonable Anticipation of Success.* In the last 20 years, the declining standard of living among the poor and the working and middle classes and the redistribution of wealth to the very rich have made this premise increasingly difficult to sustain, particularly for people of color. Many signs of despair in the population—one outcome of the breakdown of the dream—have risen dramatically, particularly among youth: violent crime rates, school dropout rates, drug abuse, teenage pregnancy. And some argue that the anger of White men and the push to institute repressive social measures, such as the current welfare reform, is the result of the limited opportunities for working- and middle-class White men in the present economy (Newman 1988, 1993).

   Can everyone reasonably anticipate success? Could Theo Wilson have reasonably anticipated success before he reached out to Marie and Bill? Could he now? Can youth today, as many have in the past, reasonably anticipate that they will be more successful than their parents—that they will be better educated, have better jobs, make more money?

3. *Individual Responsibility for Success.* Assigning responsibility for their place in life to individuals rather than to unjust social systems maintains the dominant group's power and position. When people truly believe in the American Dream, it is difficult for them to understand that capitalism is an economic system based on the exploitation of the labor of most people for the benefit of the few. Directing attention to individuals rather than to the system obscures the absolute impossibility that *all* talented and hard-working people will become financially successful in capitalist societies.

   When you believe in the American Dream, the success of some individuals reinforces the belief that success is possible for all and that the unsuccessful must, therefore, be untalented and lazy at best, morally corrupt at worst. Success stories such as that of Lynn Johnson are often construed to be the result of the talent and hard work of the individual. While Lynn Johnson is talented and hard working, other systemic factors worked toward her success:

   - The support of the school principal and teachers.
   - Her placement in a college preparatory track.
   - The involvement of the community in her mobility.
   - The ready availability of college scholarships and loans.
   - The lower cost of higher education in the 1960s.

When Lynn's efforts are seen as the only forces responsible for her success, the urge is strong to blame Theo and other poor and working-class youth if they fail to succeed.

Theo, too, is talented and hard working, but many systemic factors work toward his failure:

- School tracking, which ensures that students like Theo will be placed in vocational or general tracks.
- His mother's drug problems, his father's death.
- Lack of positive role models, both in his community and in his school.
- The rising cost of a college education and the difficulty of moving into the middle class without one.
- Lack of sex education and support for dealing with his developing sexual identity and expressions.

Those like Theo who do everything they can but still fail may come to see that effort and talent are not necessarily the keys to success, but they have trouble convincing others because, after all, why should we listen to losers? As Hochschild (1995:29) notes:

> Because success is so central to Americans' self-image, and because they expect as well as hope to achieve, Americans are not gracious about failure. Others' failure reminds them that the dream may be just that—a dream, to be distinguished from waking reality. Their own failure confirms that fear. As Zora Neale Hurston puts it, "There is something about poverty that smells like death."

Why in our society does poverty "smell like death"? Why do we equate success with money, failure with poverty? What other measures of success do we have? How seriously do we take them? Do you know people who go to high-paying jobs every day even though they hate the jobs and what the jobs are doing to their lives? Why don't they leave these jobs and take ones that are more satisfying? And finally: Was Theo solely responsible for his failure in school? Was Lynn solely responsible for her success?

4. *Success as Virtue, Failure as Sin.* This equation ignores the structures of society that support the success of some and the failure of others. It ignores the fact that in our society many of the major wealth holders inherited their wealth (Conlin et al. 1997; Hacker 1997). It ignores the fact that wealth is achieved for a relative few at the expense of the many—that the seven-figure salaries of top CEOs depend on their ability to increase their companies' earnings and that the increase is frequently the result of "downsizing," of putting people out of work.

Most Americans would find humorous the following description by 19th-century reformers:

> [Prostitutes are] . . . daughters of the ignorant, depraved, and vicious part of our population, trained up without culture of any kind, amidst the contagion of evil example, . . . [they] enter upon a life of prostitution for the gratification of their unbridled passions, and become harlots altogether by choice (cited in Hochschild 1995:30–31).

We certainly would recognize today that unbridled passion amidst the contagions of evil is not the prime reason for prostitution. Economic hardship; sexual and physical abuse by parents, spouses, and partners; and the limited employment options for poor women are the prime reasons. But if we were to substitute "welfare recipient" for "prostitute" and "welfare queen" for "harlot," the quotation would sound quite familiar today.

Humorist Fran Liebowitz describes the paradox of this premise succinctly:

> The misfortune of the fortunate, it seems, always appears as an act of God. In other words, "no fault of their own." The misfortune of the unfortunate is, on the other hand, perceived to be a direct result of the slothful, irresponsible, ill-intended, but not unanticipated bad choice of the embryo that insists upon taking up residence in the body of a 14-year-old crack addict—not, apparently, an act of God (1997:220).

Is the child of a 14-year-old crack addict a sinner? Is the 14-year-old crack addict a sinner? Thinking back to Margaret Welch, is she a sinner? Are Bill Gates, the Mellons, the Rockefellers, the duPonts more virtuous than the rest of the population? Are highly paid CEOs always virtuous people? Are the people who lose their jobs through "downsizing" sinners? Is Lynn Johnson more virtuous than Theo Wilson?

Given all of the evidence that the American Dream is just that—a dream—why do most Americans continue to believe so strongly in it? Why instead of attacking unjust systems of power do they attack each other? Blaming "losers" is critical to preserving the current system. It is the flip side of rewarding the winners, and it encourages everyone—including those near the back of the pack—to distance themselves from losers instead of joining with them in challenging an unfair system.

EDUCATION: THE CORNERSTONE OF THE AMERICAN DREAM

Through its central role in reproducing race, class, gender, and sexuality hierarchies and in justifying those hierarchies, the institution of education is a cornerstone on which the ideology of the American Dream rests. To have an equal opportunity to pursue success, particularly financial success, citizens need equal access to the skills necessary to that pursuit. Schools are charged not only with providing everyone with these basic skills but also with identifying talented and hard-working individuals and providing them with the extra knowledge, skills, and certification to reach the top, to become successful. Given its critical role in reproducing the American Dream ideology, the educational system must be seen as free of bias—not as racist, classist, sexist, or heterosexist. Otherwise, the premise of equal opportunity cannot stand. All people must be seen as having a chance to succeed, or we cannot blame them if they do not.

How does the ideology of the American Dream get reproduced and reinforced in the educational system? Ideologies are believable only if they emerge when ordinary people act out the stories daily. And every day, as people act out the social relations of race, class, gender, and sexuality hierarchies within schools, some do "make it." Lynn Johnson's story, an excellent example of someone living the American Dream, reinforces the Dream. If Theo is successful, the Dream will be reinforced. But individual success stories obscure the "failures" of the vast majority. These exceptions, which prove the possibility of success, justify our sealing the coffin of restricted life chances on most people while opening the door of almost unlimited choice to a few.

Individuals, Education, and the Dream

Every day children drop out of school, are suspended, are tracked into lower classes, and are retained in grade for reasons of discipline, poor performance on standardized tests and teacher bias (Anyon 1997; Brantlinger 1993; Entwisle, Alexander, and Olson 1997; Kozol 1991). The education of thousands of poor and working-class students, students of color, and immigrant students is much like that of Theo Wilson, who until his sophomore year was enrolled in classes that were not preparing him for college, but only for menial jobs.

As these children go through their day—for some, in separate and inferior schools whose entire curricula are less challenging (cf. Spade, Columba, and Vanfossen 1997); for others, sometimes in the same school with upper-track children and with teachers who are middle class and often White—they may come to recognize, as Theo Wilson did, that they are being tracked for a particular place in the world. They may come to see that their educations have cut them off from many desirable options in life. The education that Theo received was inferior by most criteria; he learned less, and what he did learn would be less useful for securing decent employment when he graduated. Whatever employment options students in poor and working-class schools and lower-track students in all schools have after graduation will be severely restricted by the failure of their education to prepare them for college.

As students in tracks similar to Theo's end up unemployed or working in the menial labor jobs they were tracked for, people in positions of greater power (children in higher tracks, middle-class teachers, and employers) will find it easy, logical, and even "natural" to assume that these students lack ability, talent, desire, effort, or all of these. In this way, the American Dream is reinforced in conjunction with race, class, gender, and sexuality hierarchies.

And as a result of the American Dream ideology, Theo Wilson and others are encouraged to believe that they are inferior, and they find trying to resist internalizing their oppression more and more difficult. They increasingly lose motivation—it is difficult to stay motivated when school work appears trivial. They lack skills—an inferior education leaves them less able to compete in the marketplace. Before Theo began taking charge of his own education, he had already internalized limits and the belief in his own inferiority. He said he couldn't dream because "Everything takes good math skills, and I'm not good at math."

Groups, Education, and the Dream

Although the consequences are felt by individual students, the process of reproducing race, class, gender, and sexuality hierarchies by sorting people for different treatment and then of justifying the unequal outcomes of this sorting process by promoting beliefs about group inferiority is fundamentally a group process. These group processes are less apparent than the processes that shape our individual lives, but we are led to consider them by group indicators such as national racial differences in educational outcomes. Race and gender data indicate, for example, that in 1994, 28.1 percent of Hispanic girls and 31.6 percent of Hispanic boys aged 16 to 24 were high school dropouts. These rates were roughly 2.5 times the percentage of high school dropouts among African-American girls (11.3 percent) and boys (14.1 percent) and 3.75 times the percentages for White girls (7.5 percent) and boys (8.0 percent) (U.S. Dept. of Education 1995: Table 101).

Think about these statistics for a moment. Were you surprised to see how high the rates were for Hispanics? How about for girls? Did you realize that girls drop out of school at rates so similar to boys? If you were not aware of these facts, you are not alone. Perhaps the people most discussed in the media as high risk for dropping out are urban African-American males and Latinos. But the dropout rate for Latinas is double the rate of African-American males and similar to that of Latinos.

If the public is uneducated about *who* is dropping out, we tend to be even less knowledgeable about *why* these youth drop out. What comes to mind first if you try to explain the high Latino/a dropout rates? How would you explain these patterns? If you first thought about negative traits that you have come to associate with Hispanic culture—devaluing education, lacking motivation, valuing family over work, or lacking the work ethic, your explanation rests on the notion that the beliefs and values of the group members are to blame, a critical tenet of the American Dream ideology. But if you think of macro system factors, you might consider

- the problems of learning in English-only schools when English is your second language
- the inferior quality of the education in most bilingual classrooms (cf. Valdes 1996; Ortiz 1988)
- the impact of family dislocation on the children of recent immigrants and farm workers
- the lack of community links between educational institutions and families
- the failure of schools to educate youth about sexuality and pregnancy and to provide support for continuing school after childbirth
- the inferior quality of education for the urban and rural poor (Kozol 1991).

Because these kinds of explanations challenge rather than reinforce the American Dream tenet that everyone is given an equal opportunity to succeed, they are not promoted or encouraged. To the contrary, people offering these kinds of explanations are often disparaged. For example, in 1999 the newly installed governor of South Carolina, Jim Hodges, put forth his plan to the legislature to improve public schools in the state. School improvement, particularly early childhood education and school readiness, had been the major focus of his election campaign since South Carolina schools consistently rate among the lowest two or three states on almost every standard indicator of educational performance—ranging from ACT and SAT scores to dropout rates, where some estimates are that as many as 57 percent of eighth graders don't complete high school ("Figures show" 1999). The rates of poverty among the largely rural, African-American population in South Carolina are among the nation's highest while indicators of children's health (e.g., infant mortality, low birth-weight babies) are among the poorest (Stroud 1999b). With strong backing from the business community and on the heels of a resounding upset victory over an incumbent conservative governor, Hodges proposed legislation called First Steps, modeled after Smart Steps, a similar program in North Carolina targeted to improve the health and educational performance of the state's children. First Steps included provisions for school construction, class size reduction, and other changes within schools as well as state grants to underwrite grassroots efforts to provide day care, immunization and other health services, parenting classes, and transportation—resources needed to address related problems associated with poverty that also impede children in school (Robinson 1999; Stroud 1999a).

Despite its eventual adoption and widespread support in the state, Hodges's proposal faced stiff opposition when it reached the legislature. House Majority Leader Bobby Harrell said committee members balked at funding First Steps because it "looks more like a social program than an education proposal." He and others later called the proposal "a disguised attempt to expand the welfare state" (Stroud 1999a). Representative Dan Tripp repeatedly called it "creeping socialism" (Robinson 1999), insinuating that addressing sources and consequences of inequality outside the individual efforts and abilities of the oppressed is somehow anticapitalist and thus anti-American.

This process of denying structural sources for oppression—and thus structural change as a solution—is reinforced not only by promoting images of inferiority of some groups but also by promoting equally damaging constructions that others are superior. Just as Lynn Johnson may be cited as proof that success is possible for all Americans if they work hard enough, entire groups are identified as "model minorities." The educational attainment levels of these groups, especially of Asian Americans—higher than that of other racial groups, including Whites—are cited as proof that the educational system is not racially biased (see Table 2.2a and Table 2.2b). As a result, the dominant ideology—that the lower educational attainment and higher poverty rates of African Americans, Native Americans, and Latinos/as are evidence of these groups' lack of motivation, of ability, or of both, not as evidence of racial bias—is reinforced.

This argument obscures not only racial bias in the schools but also

- the discrimination that Asian Americans have faced in U.S. higher education, including quotas limiting their numbers (Takagi 1993)
- the fact that many Asian people with advanced education were not educated in the United States—over two-thirds of Asians with doctorates in the United States were educated abroad or were allowed to immigrate only *because* of their professional status and high education (Woo 1995)
- the fact that when people believe the dream is attainable, as immigrants are more inclined to do, they work harder to achieve and are willing to tolerate less humane treatment because they believe it will end.

And as long as we focus on these "model minorities," we can ignore the daily reality of students like Theo Wilson. These students, for whom the schools predict failure and who see generations of dropouts in their neighborhoods, are less able to hold out hope for their own success and thus are less able to sustain the same work ethic of students who see success as possible.

SUMMARY

The American Dream ideology is used to justify the extensive social inequality in U.S. society. And it does so by promoting four basic tenets:

- Equality of opportunity.
- A reasonable chance of success.
- Individual responsibility for success.
- Success as virtue, failure as sin.

In the end, belief in the American Dream supports the current race, class, gender, and sexuality hierarchy. And education is key to promoting the ideology because it is the cornerstone on which is built the belief that all citizens have an equal chance of success. Thus, the promise of education in the United States is that it will be the great equalizer. That it produces race, class, gender, and sexuality oppression is a contradiction that demands explanation.

CHAPTER 8

Themes: Historically and Geographically/Globally Contextual, Socially Constructed

This chapter focuses on the first two themes of the framework: the historical and globally contextual and socially constructed nature of race, class, gender, and sexuality hierarchies. Race, class, gender, and sexuality intersections must be understood in their historical context, in specific places, with careful attention to how these relationships are socially constructed—generated, preserved, challenged, and transformed through social contests. Understanding the ways that these hierarchies are socially constructed in education must begin with an examination of the historical roots of the U.S. education system, how the modern patterns of these hierarchies were established, and how they have changed as a result of resistance by subordinate groups. How did the ideology of the American Dream shape and how was it reinforced by the social organization of education in the 20th-century United States?

Rather than try to explicate the entire history of a single group or of all race, class, gender, and sexuality struggles in the United States, this chapter will illustrate the ways that hierarchies are socially constructed in time and place by focusing the discussion around a particular theme, segregation, that weaves its way through the history of and contemporary struggles between those who control the institution of education and those who have sought unfettered access to knowledge despite their lack of control over the dominant culture institution.

The term *segregation* is most often associated with racial residential segregation, and its deleterious effects on poor communities of color have been well documented. As Douglas Massey and Nancy Denton (1993), Jean Anyon (1997), William J. Wilson (1987), Patricia Hill Collins (1998) and others point out, segregation isolates communities and sets up the conditions of control over the poor by concentrating poverty to build a set of mutually reinforcing and self-feeding processes of decline. When communities are poor and people lack work, skills, education, and other resources, businesses leave and are less inclined to locate there, schools lack a tax base and have fewer resources, many good teachers choose not to teach there. So residential segregation is a structural process that produces and increases inequality. As Douglas Massey and Nancy Denton state in their study of Black residential segregation:

> The effect of segregation on black well-being is structural, not individual. Residential segregation lies beyond the ability of any individual to change: it constrains black life chances irrespective of personal traits, individual motivations, or private achievements (1993:2–3).

Since schools are differentiated by class and neighborhood, understanding segregation processes is critical to understanding race, class, gender, and sexuality inequalities produced in and by schooling.

When groups have different educational experiences, a host of other aspects of life are affected: income, occupation, employment status, job security, health status, life expectancy, and life satisfaction. And when entire groups have low incomes, low-status occupations, poor health, and high mortality, the American Dream ideology along with other dominant culture influences encourages people to explain and understand these facts by referring to notions of group inferiority, not to systemwide practices that segregate and exclude, discriminate against, and harm less powerful race, class, gender, and sexuality groups.

Once groups are segregated and educated differently, ideologies of group inferiority are rather easily generated and maintained. The historian Barbara Fields (1990), for example, pointed out in her study of slavery and racial ideology that African people were enslaved in America *before* the notion of racial inferiority was developed by slave owners to "explain" the inhumane treatment of their slaves. And underfunded systems such as the reservation schools for Native Americans and the segregated schools for African Americans that prevailed until the 1960s also isolated these groups, enhancing the dominant ideology of racial inferiority and facilitating differential treatment in other realms such as the labor market.

The "war of maneuvers," the processes of resistance that take place when a group lacks full citizenship, economic resources, and other bases of power, took place in the racially homogeneous communities created by the pervasive residential segregation before the 1960s—in Black communities of the urban North and the South, on reservations, in barrios, and Chinatowns (Omi and Winant 1994). And although not residentially segregated, women's education for most of the last century, particularly higher education, typically took place in separate schools. When groups are physically segregated and isolated from one another, the type of control described above is possible, but so are the close conditions among the oppressed that foster group identity, awareness of the oppression and the common plight of others, and collective action for survival.

There are also other forms of segregation—when physical proximity is much closer—when oppressor and oppressed occupy the same physical space. One example is school ability group tracking, a process highly organized by race, class, and gender, where students attend different classes in the same school. In tracking, where the texts and curricula differ, and even in situations where dominant and subordinate groups sit next to each other in the same class, there is a kind of segregation of ideas into different intellectual spaces. Women, people of color, gays, and lesbians, for example, are often either excluded from classroom texts or are segregated into certain parts of a text where they are presented in stereotyped ways that serve to reinforce the dominant ideologies: women in family roles, not as workers;

internationals as immigrants, not as families; men of color in sports or as criminals, not as leaders in business or industry (Feree and Hall 1990; AAUW 1999).

Dominant groups have employed new mechanisms of social control in the race, class, and gender desegregated spaces of the recent past (e.g., residential, workplace) where select members of subordinate groups have attained access to centers of power not open before. "Surveillance" represents a politics of control—in plain view—reminiscent of the mechanisms of racial control in the South during slavery and over domestic workers even up to the present (Collins 1998). In this situation, subordinate group members are present in the same space—they are seen and watched, even on display—but they lack the institutional power to change the race, class, gender, or sexuality balance of power. Surveillance methods of control have perhaps always been the prevalent method in the control of women, who have not been segregated as a group into different communities.

Surveillance control methods range from violence—the violence women experience in households and in public spaces—to fairly elaborate rules of social interaction. For example, the South takes pride in being a place that is polite, hospitable, genteel. In large part this self-definition derives from the rules of social interaction that accompanied the close living and working conditions of slaves and masters in a plantation economy. These rules included, for example, prescriptions that people be addressed by title as a way of acknowledging different statuses and signaling the kind of treatment that they should receive. Even today, these rules have a different significance in the South than in other parts of the country. As legislators across the country address the problems of poor performance in schools, particularly in poor, rural, inner-city, and minority school districts, southern states—Kentucky, Louisiana, Alabama, South Carolina—have passed "character education" legislation that requires school children to address their teachers as "Sir" or "Ma'am." Failure to do so results in punishment (Chadwell 2000; Kirkpatrick 2000).

Given the centrality of the segregation process for developing and challenging race, class, gender, and sexuality hierarchies, it is not surprising that a fundamental struggle of some groups for equality has centered on eliminating segregation in schools. If we think of the process of segregation as broader than its typical referent to racially segregated schools, especially in the South before the civil rights movement, we can use the concept to identify critical social processes that generate and maintain race, class, gender, and sexuality hierarchies in society, not just as conflict between poor Whites and African Americans in the South. These processes of segregation and surveillance, isolation and control, resonate throughout the following overview of the historical and contemporary social constructions of race, class, gender, and sexuality in education.

HISTORICAL CONSTRUCTION OF RACE, CLASS, GENDER, AND SEXUALITY IN EDUCATION

The foundation for the current political, economic, and ideological domains of oppression within our education system was laid during the rapid industrialization of the late 19th and early 20th centuries. At that time, particularly in urban centers, an unprecedented population explosion occurred, primarily of poor, uneducated, unskilled immigrants from Eastern Europe as well as of rural migrants from the United States who sought the promise of a better life through industrial labor. From 1880 to 1918 student enrollment across the nation increased from 200,000 to 1.5 million; by 1909, 58 percent of students in 37 of the largest U.S. cities were foreign born (Oakes 1985:19–20). As a result of these changes, secondary schools came under increasing pressure to do more to meet many conflicting social needs.

> Colleges and universities wanted a more standardized pre-collegiate education. Many of the middle class called for free public education available to all youth. Poor and immigrant families were eager for the economic benefits they believed schooling would provide their children. Businessmen were interested in acquiring a more productive and literate work force. Organized labor was concerned about who should control the training of workers. Progressive reformers sought humane solutions to the immense social problems confronting the burgeoning population of poor and immigrant youth. But most of the population increasingly feared the potential dangers that could result from what was seen as unrestrained hordes of urban immigrants, and a perception of a need for the exercise of greater social control was widespread (Oakes 1985:20).

The Educational Model

The public comprehensive high school was envisioned as the answer to these demands. And its particular form was shaped largely by three dominant themes (as discussed in Oakes 1985):

- *Social Darwinism.* The application of Charles Darwin's theories of evolution to human social life, suggesting that those holding power in the competitive social world survived because of their superior moral and biological fitness (p. 20). This theory provided scientific justification for the social dominance of Anglo-Saxon White men and the inferior makeup (lower evolutionary stage) and subordinate status of the rest of the population (e.g., immigrants, the poor, people of color, and women). At the same time, its proponents argued that human intervention could exert some positive influence on the evolutionary process, thus justifying the education of "others."
- *Americanization Movement.* The movement to preserve the dominance of White, Anglo-Saxon Protestant (WASP) culture in the face of mass immigration by eliminating the "depraved lifestyles" of immigrants and making cities safe by teaching immigrants the "American values of hard work, frugality, modesty, cleanliness, truthfulness, and purity of thought and deed" (p. 25).
- *Belief in the Unlimited Potential of Science and Industry.* The factory model of industrial efficiency, based on the division of labor and principles of scientific management, was hailed as the solution to all problems of human organization. It became popular to think of schools as factories turning the raw material of children into a finished product—educated, productive, Americanized adults.

From these principles, the modern, comprehensive public high school was forged:

- Students were grouped according to ability. Theories of human evolution, which postulated superior and inferior groups, justified separation of the curriculum into vocational education and academic education (Anyon 1997).
- Anglo-Saxon culture was valued and promoted as superior to all others. To develop common American ideals and modes of thought, school curricula unabashedly promoted Anglo-Saxon culture and excluded other cultures, values, and histories.
- Schools were organized along the scientific management principles of the factory. Schools were structured on the industrial model of bureaucratic organization—with authority and central decision making at the top, specialization, division of labor, established rules and regulations, and an impersonal attitude toward the individual (Oakes 1985; Katznelson and Weir 1985).

This stratified model of public education was justified by referring to democratic ideals and to the American Dream ideology. In 1908 the superintendent of the Boston public schools espoused this "new view" of equal opportunity, taking individual needs, interests, and abilities into account:

> Until very recently (the schools) have offered equal opportunity for all to receive *one kind* of education, but what will make them democratic is to provide opportunity for all to receive education as will fit them *equally well* for their particular life work (cited in Oakes 1985:34).

Writing in *Scientific Monthly* in 1921, another educator stated:

> We can picture the educational system as having a very important function as a selecting agency, a means of selecting the men of best intelligence from the deficient and mediocre. All are poured into the system at the bottom; the incapable are soon rejected or drop out after repeating various grades and pass into the ranks of unskilled labor. . . . The more intelligent who are to be clerical workers pass into the high school; the most intelligent enter the universities whence they are selected for the professions (cited in Oakes 1985: 35).[1]

By 1918 the National Education Association recommended that the following nonacademic vocational programs begin in junior high school: agriculture, clerical, industrial, fine arts, and household arts. Students were openly classified by race, ethnicity, economic background, and gender into different programs.

Testing

Also at this time, the burgeoning field of psychology and testing entered the political educational arena when the group intelligence test, the IQ test, became the "scientific" means to separate the rich from the poor within a common school.

---

[1]At the time, clerical workers were mostly male and represented the lowest level of the white-collar/managerial track. Clerical jobs were not the female-dominated, highly technical, and low-authority jobs they have come to be today.

Initially developed by a group of psychologists, including Alfred Binet, H.H. Goddard, Lewis Terman, Robert Yerkes, and Edward Thorndike, the tests reflected their belief that intelligence was a single, general attribute that was innate, stable, and inherited (Oakes et al. 1997). The IQ test was first administered on a mass scale during World War I to army recruits and to immigrants entering Ellis Island, as a mechanism for ranking and sorting individuals in terms of their perceived mental abilities. The determination by the test that 80 percent of immigrants were "feeble-minded" merely reinforced the prevailing theories of social evolution—and raised no concerns of test bias—in part because the use of scientific and sophisticated statistical techniques lent an air of objectivity to the tests.

What Thorndike and other test developers actually accomplished was a self-fulfilling prophecy:

- They based intelligence tests on knowledge common to Anglo-Saxon, middle-class culture, which they deemed the superior culture.
- Because prediction of future school success was based on test performance, test results were used to sort students into different tracks—academic or vocational—to train students for future work roles.
- Students ended up in occupations and earning incomes commensurate with their IQ and the educations they received, with Anglo-Saxon, middle-class men in the top professions and immigrants and the poor in the trades and on the bottom.
- These educational "results," which had been predicted from the test scores, thus reinforced belief in the "scientific merit" of the test.

Educating "Others"

While the White working class and poor and Eastern European immigrants were being tracked for different educations and different places in the social order, "other groups" (e.g., people of color, women, and gays and lesbians) faced multiple forms of discrimination in the educational system. The histories that follow are selected highlights that illustrate the kinds of treatment different oppressed groups have historically faced in the United States.

African Americans

In the early 19th century, African Americans were prohibited from attaining an education. Not until the Reconstruction period, 1865–1877, did private missionary groups and the War Department's Freedmen's Bureau establish separate private and public schools for African Americans. By 1900 one-third of African-American children 5 to 19 years old were enrolled in school—a dramatic increase from 10 percent in 1870 (Meier, Stewart, and England 1989:41). Yet the distribution of government resources to African-American and White schools was grossly unequal. Legal challenges to the constitutionality of this inequality culminated in the Supreme Court ruling in the case of *Plessy v. Ferguson* (1896) that affirmed the "separate but equal" doctrine and legally slammed the door shut on any hope for equal opportunity for nearly 60 years.

Schools remained separate and unequal until the decision was overturned by the Court's *Brown v. Board of Education* (1954) decision, which concluded that over a half-century of evidence proved that separate facilities were inherently unequal in education. Widespread implementation of *Brown,* which called for desegregation of schools with "all deliberate speed," didn't take place until after the Civil Rights Act of 1964 when, under pressure from the civil rights movement, the federal government began to withhold funds and to bring lawsuits against recalcitrant school districts. By the 1970–1971 school year, 79 percent of Black students in the South were attending school with Whites, and enforcement efforts began to focus on the urban centers of the North (Meier, Stewart, and England 1989:48).

Meier, Stewart, and England called the exclusion of African Americans from education and education in separate and grossly unequal schools that occurred before the *Brown* decision "first generation discrimination." While segregation in unequal schools still exists, what they call "second generation discrimination" also occurs now within desegregated schools to deny equal educational opportunity to African Americans. This type of segregation represents a consistent pattern of actions that actually increased after 1954, including discrimination in ability group tracking and use of discipline to track and to encourage dropouts, with resulting differentials in educational outcomes (Meier, Stewart, and England 1989). Second generation discrimination was possible in part because African Americans entered into a system already well organized and functioning to sort the powerful from the undesirables—a system originally designed to discriminate against White immigrant, poor, and working-class men at the beginning of the 20th century.

Native Americans

Also at the turn of the last century, many Native-American children were removed from reservations and sent to a system of boarding schools, day schools, or schools in converted Army posts for as many as 10 years. These schools were developed by missionaries to "save" Indians who were facing extermination by settlers, prospectors, and the U.S. Army. The missionaries proposed to educate Indians to work as farmhands, laborers, and chambermaids. In the midst of the Americanization movement, obliterating Indian culture and replacing it with European culture were deemed both economically productive and humane. Mary Crow Dog, for example, attended the same mission school in the 1960s that her grandfather had attended earlier in the century. The missionaries gave this poster to her grandfather to post in his room:

1. Let Jesus save you.
2. Come out of your blanket, cut your hair, and dress like a white man.
3. Have a Christian family with one wife for life only.
4. Live in a house like your white brother. Work hard and wash often.
5. Learn the value of a hard-earned dollar. Do not waste your money on giveaways. Be punctual.
6. Believe that property and wealth are signs of divine approval.
7. Keep away from saloons and strong spirits.
8. Speak the language of your white brother. Send your children to school to do likewise.

9. Go to church often and regularly.
10. Do not go to Indian dances or to the medicine men (Crow Dog and Erdoes 1996:511).

The educational goal of "Americanizing" Indians and preparing them for menial labor (e.g., be punctual, work hard, wash often) and promoting the American Dream ideology (e.g., property and wealth are signs of divine approval) could not be more clearly stated.

Women

From the inception of vocational education, working-class White girls were tracked for home economics and garment work while Black, Native-American, and Chicana girls were trained to be servants, laundry workers, and farm laborers (Wrigley 1992; Amott and Matthaei 1996). Although middle-class Anglo-Saxon women were not denigrated with the same biological referents as people of color, most White immigrants, and the poor, they were deemed to be biologically suited for different social locations than men—in the private sphere of the home and in occupational roles that became associated with that sphere. From the late 19th and early 20th Century, some middle-and upper-class White women were supported in pursuing higher education, yet college curricula for these women were designed to

- prepare women for sex-segregated occupational roles (e.g., teacher, nurse, librarian)
- prepare women for the social roles of homemaking, marriage, and mother-hood and to impart cultural capital—key for status maintenance (Ostrander 1984; Streitmatter 1999).

Gays, Bisexuals, and Lesbians

Although gays, bisexuals, and lesbians were not segregated into different schools, since its beginnings U.S. culture has sanctioned only heterosexual sex within marriage and has relegated other sexual practices, even some heterosexual ones, to the darkness of the closet. And the people who engage in anything other than heterosexual sex within marriage are defined as sinful, sick, and morally depraved. Silence, judgment, and punishment have thus been the primary modes of addressing homosexuality. Throughout this century, homosexuals have been marginalized in education by

- exclusion from the curriculum
- the closeting and witch-hunting of gay and lesbian teachers
- verbal and physical assaults (Carlson 1997).

Early in the 20th century, Freudian psychoanalytic theory validated heterosexual development as healthy and homosexuality as immature and psychologically un-healthy, thus providing scientific justification and legitimation for the prevailing moral and religiously based discriminatory treatment. Throughout the first half of the century, dismissing gay and lesbian teachers was justified on the grounds that it kept young people from exposure to improper role models, lechery, and child molestation. In a pervasive disease metaphor, homosexuality was viewed as contagious, and homosexuals were presumed to be lecherous and immature—to desire sexual relations with their young students (Carlson 1997). While witch-hunts no longer prevail, the "contagion theory" is still prevalent and the "don't ask, don't tell" policy of most school districts effectively silences gay and lesbian teachers and students, leaving them alone in their "otherness."

Higher Education and Credentials

At the same time that the modern comprehensive high school forged its place in the social order, U.S. higher education established its relationship to these high schools and to the new economic order—as the credentialing institutions for the new middle class of professionals, managers, and administrators. From the early 20th century, certain occupations (e.g., medical doctor, lawyer, and teacher) became accessible only to people with college degrees.

Interestingly, the social learning necessary to perform these middle-class occupations is obtained incidental to the pursuit of a college degree. It is not the focus of the curriculum. Not surprisingly, from early in the century, athletics and sororities and fraternities were incorporated into higher education as places where social class capital was explicitly developed in highly gendered and racialized ways (Brown 1995; Messner 1992). As David Larabee (1995) notes, it is this corporate structure of student life—not the curricular content—that most prepares students for middle-class occupations. The process of getting admitted to and completing a college education gives students an enhanced sense of social superiority and qualification for leadership.

In sum, since the late 19th century, the American system of education has served a key role in creating, reinforcing, and justifying race, class, gender, and sexuality hierarchies and in creating and reinforcing the American Dream ideology. A system of mass public education was structured to support the mobility and social dominance of middle- and upper-class, heterosexual Anglo-Saxon males. It segregated and excluded people of color and ranked and educated differently—often within the same schools—Eastern European immigrants, the working class and the poor, and middle-class Anglo-Saxon women. This process of tracking students for different educations and different places in the social order remains as a primary source of social inequality today (Anyon 1997; Brantlinger 1993; Entwisle, Alexander, and Olson 1997; Hallinan 1995; Oakes 1985; Page 1991).

CONTEMPORARY SOCIAL CONSTRUCTIONS OF RACE, CLASS, GENDER, AND SEXUALITY IN EDUCATION

Segregation and isolation processes take place both at the macro level in different schools and different academic tracks and at the micro level in different classroom experiences. Segregation of women and men; heterosexuals and homosexuals; the poor, working, middle, and upper classes; and Whites and people of color into different roles both at work and in the home is a societal process that enables differential distribution of valued societal resources such as income, health care, and housing (Chow 1994; Higginbotham 1994; Ortiz 1994). This societal segregation both reinforces and is reinforced by educational segregation processes that begin very early. To understand why the labor market is so segregated, for example, we must understand how early education begins by segregating people along the lines of race, class, gender, and sexuality. In these processes of segregation, students meet different people, learn different things, and develop different hopes, dreams, and expectations for their futures.

Entire race, class, and gender groups are segregated and educated differently in several macro social processes when they

- follow a curriculum that excludes or includes their experiences and backgrounds
- attend different schools
- attend the same schools in different academic tracks
- drop out of school at different rates.

School Segregation

Although segregation into different schools is much less central to gender hierarchies and plays little or no part in maintaining sexuality hierarchies, it is a central process supporting class and racial hierarchies. From kindergarten through postgraduate education, most poor and working-class students and people of color attend different schools from those of middle- and upper-class students. The U.S. educational system is made up of many different types of schools.

- *Kindergarten–12.* Racially homogeneous schools (including reservation, barrio, and ghetto schools); class homogeneous schools (including many racially homogeneous schools as well as desegregated schools); same gender schools; rural, urban, and suburban schools; public and private schools; college preparatory and vocational schools.
- *Post-High School.* Community colleges, technical schools, four-year colleges, universities; elite private schools, religious schools, state public schools; women's colleges; traditionally Black colleges and universities; and military colleges.

Many processes support this segregation:

- the legacy of a history of de jure (by law) racial school segregation that lasted effectively until the 1960s.
- extensive class and racial residential segregation since the 1960s, including the shift of the White middle-class population and businesses from urban to suburban residences and increased class stratification as deindustrialization and the rise of the service economy have prompted the bifurcation of the labor force into high-paid professionals and low-wage service workers.
- the financial requirements of private school education.
- the knowledge and political clout of White middle-class parents to pressure local school boards to provide their children special schools such as magnet or charter schools within the public school system (Meier, Stewart, and England 1989).
- school voucher plans.

Class Segregation

From preschool programs through 12th grade, public education is fundamentally organized around neighborhoods, reflecting the class and socioeconomic segregation of U.S. housing, and private education is restricted to those who can afford it. Valerie Polakow describes the class segregation of children that begins as early as preschool:

> In contemporary practice a two-tiered system means that poor children go to Head Start and other at-risk public preschools (if they gain access), and middle- and upper-income children attend fee-based child care centers where parents choose the kind and quality of program they wish their children to enroll in. Not only does this two-tiered system create economic and racial segregation, but it also ensures that children, in their earliest developing years, are placed in stratified educational landscapes. Cost-benefit accountability for poor children's early education is demanded, whereas fee-based centers do not have to prove their right to provide a place for children to play and to learn. In the absence of a national child care system, public education becomes a gift bestowed by the haves upon the have-nots. It is not surprising that the two-tiered system is fostering a separate and unequal education—a pedagogy for the poor (1993:128–29).

Kindergarten through high school education is also class stratified. In a classic study of the "hidden curriculum," Jean Anyon (1980) studied fifth-grade classrooms in working-class, middle-class, affluent, and elite elementary schools, documenting the varied kinds of elementary education that students receive to prepare them for different places in the class system. She called it a "hidden curriculum" because the differences she observed occurred even though the fifth grades were similar in many respects: All the schools, for example, used the same math textbook, and all language arts classes included aspects of grammar, punctuation, and capitalization. Similar processes have been observed by other scholars (Brantlinger 1993; Page 1991; Thorne 1993; Spade, Columba, and Vanfossen 1997).

Working-Class Schools

The children of manual laborers and clerical workers were taught to follow orders and to perform routine tasks and mechanical work in the service of others—not to think for themselves, to plan ahead, or to be creative. Teacher priorities included disciplining and controlling the class. Language arts focused on the mechanics of punctuation, capitalization, and the four kinds of sentences. Math focused on rote learning.

> The teacher in one school gave a 4 minute lecture on what the terms are called (i.e., which number is the divisor, dividend, quotient, and remainder). The children were told to copy these names in their notebooks. Then the teacher told them the steps to follow to do the problems, saying, "This is how you do them." The teacher listed the steps on the board, and they appeared several days later as a chart hung in the middle of the front wall: "Divide; Multiply; Subtract; Bring Down." (Anyon 1980:364)

This learning approach was retained by teachers even when students were having difficulty understanding. One teacher said:

> You're confusing yourselves. You're tensing up. Remember, when you do this, it's the same steps over and over again—and that's the way division always is." When some students still had problems several weeks later she said they needed more practice (Anyon 1980:364).

Middle-Class Schools

Students whose parents were low-level bureaucrats (e.g., social service workers or business managers) were prepared for bureaucratic roles where self-expression is denied. In these schools, students were rewarded for knowing the answers *and* how to find them, but not for creativity.

The primary goal in this middle-class school was to "get the right answer." As in working-class schools, students had to follow directions to get the right answer, but the directions usually called for some choice and decision making. The children were often asked to figure out for themselves what the directions asked them to do to find the answer.

Language arts consisted of simple grammar, but also involved writing in forms they would need to know, such as business letters and thank-you letters. Math involved some choice: Two-digit division was taught two ways—the long and the short way. Providing both ways of dividing, the teacher said, "I want to make sure you understand what you're doing—so you get it right." She also asked for students to tell how they solved the problem and what answer they got (Anyon 1980:368).

Elite or Affluent Professional Schools

The children of the producers of culture—artists, intellectuals, legal, scientific, and technical experts and other professionals—are prepared in school for creative roles in society. In these schools, creativity and working independently had priority over maintaining discipline or control, rote task performance, or getting the right answer. Work was evaluated for its interpretation of reality, for the quality of its expression, and for the appropriateness of its conception to the task at hand.

Language arts emphasized individual thought and expressiveness, and students produced written stories, essays, and editorials, as well as murals, graphs, and crafts. A typical math problem asked students to take home a sheet of paper and to have their parents fill in the number of cars, television sets, refrigerators, games, or rooms in the house. Each child then compiled the data from all the students and used the calculators provided in the classroom to compute the class average for each item.

Executive Elite Schools

The children of top executives and owners are prepared to develop their analytical intellectual powers. These students were continuously asked to reason through a problem and to conceptualize the rules that governed a system. This ability to analyze and to plan systems prepares elite students to own and control businesses. Language arts were seen as a complex system to be mastered, and grammar was emphasized in written and oral work for other classes. The math teacher taught area and perimeter by having the children derive the formulas for each:

> First, she helps them through discussion at the board, to arrive at $A = W \times L$ as a formula (not *the* formula) for area. After discussing several, she says, "Can anyone make up a formula for perimeter? Can you figure that out yourselves?"

The teacher discusses two-digit division as a decision-making process. She asks:

> "What's the first kind of decision you'd make if presented with this kind of example? What is the first thing you'd think? Craig?" Craig says, "To find my first partial quotient." She responds, "Yes, that would be your first decision. How would you do that?" Craig explains and then the teacher says, "OK, we'll see how that works for you." The class tries his way. Subsequently, she comments on the merits and shortcomings of several other children's decisions (Anyon, 1980:374).

The teacher made little effort to control students' movements about the class and, in stark contrast to the working-class students, her students never had to wait in lines to go anywhere—to the cafeteria, to the playground, to the bathroom.

Anyon's research documents critical social class differences in how and what—despite many surface similarities—students are taught in different schools. Differences in school resources were also pronounced between two school districts, one with the working-class and middle-class schools and the other with the affluent middle-class and executive elite schools. The affluent and elite schools had

- more variety and abundance of teaching materials
- increased preparation time by teachers
- teachers from higher social class backgrounds and more prestigious schools
- more stringent requirements by the board of education concerning teaching methods
- more frequent and demanding evaluations of teachers
- more teacher support services
- higher expectations for student ability and demands for student achievement
- more positive attitudes by teachers for the future occupations of students
- better student acceptance of classroom assignments (Anyon 1980:377; see also Anyon 1997; Brantlinger 1993; Entwisle, Alexander, and Olson 1997; Kerckhoff 1995; Kozol 1991).

Race Segregation

The segregation of different social classes into different schools, while having less effect on gender or sexuality hierarchies, is greatly implicated in the outcomes of differential education for racially oppressed groups. Despite a history of school busing and court-ordered desegregation, most students still attend schools that remain largely segregated. In a study of race and public school quality, Boozer, Krueger, and Walkon (1992) report that most African-American and Hispanic students (the two largest racial ethnic groups) attend schools in which the majority of students are people of color. But White students, even in the public schools, typically attend schools with few people of color.

In 1989–1990 the average African-American student attended a school that was more than 65 percent non-White; the average Hispanic, a school that was 68 percent African American or Hispanic. Yet the most segregated group was White students: The average White student attended a school that was 83 percent White. In the urban schools of the Northeast, where racial segregation is the greatest in the country, White, Black, and Hispanic students experience extreme degrees of racial isolation. One-half of African-American students and 43 percent of Hispanic students attended schools whose student populations were between 90 percent and 100 percent non-White. The South, once the home of the most segregated public schools in the country, became the least segregated region. These changes resulted largely from government efforts to desegregate schools across the nation, but most significantly in the South (Boozer 1992).

From 1968 to 1972 segregation rates dropped precipitously nationwide, remained roughly constant over the 1970s, and increased slightly in the 1980s. In 1968, for example, 77.8 percent of all Black students in the South attended schools that were at least 90 percent people of color, but by 1972 only 24.7 percent of Black students did so (Boozer 1992).

A report highlighting more recent trends documents the resegregation of public schools, a shift that began to take place between 1988 and 1991 and has continued ever since (Orfield et al. 1997). For example, the percentage of White students in a school attended by the average Black student is as low now—32 percent—as it was before the busing decisions of the early 1970s. The South and the Border States (the six states bordering the Confederacy from Oklahoma to Delaware) are now resegregating faster than other regions of the country, yet they remain the least segregated regions. In every southern and Border State, Whites, on average, go to school with 10 percent or more Black classmates, and for two states, as high as 30 percent Black students (Mississippi and South Carolina). This is not true of a single state in the North, Midwest, or West. These patterns of segregation and resegregation provide the context for the construction of White privilege through methods of segregation and surveillance.

Gender Segregation

Although the United States has a long history of all-women and all-men schools, for the most part they have been private schools and colleges. By the 1960s several forces combined to bring about the beginning of a precipitous decline in enrollments and school closings at all-women secondary and higher education institutions. First, higher education experienced its greatest ever expansion fueled by economic expansion and the societal need to keep the baby-boom population out of the labor force. For the first time, large numbers of working-class women and men could afford to attend college. Furthermore, as a consequence of Title IX in 1972, which prohibited discrimination on the basis of sex in most federally assisted educational programs, and the Civil Rights Act of 1964, women increasingly gained access to all types of colleges and universities as well as the promise of equal treatment once they entered coed institutions. Finally, even before Title IX, all-women schools had already begun to decline because they were too expensive for most people and because the spirit of racial integration following the civil rights movement led most people to believe that "separate could never really be equal" (Streitmatter 1999).

By the 1990s, however, enrollments at all-women colleges began to increase as the failure of Title IX to eliminate gender inequities in a variety of areas, including performance on standardized tests and enrollments in science and math, became increasingly clear (AAUW 1994). Schools began to argue convincingly that all-women environments are generally more supportive for women and that their students have higher self-esteem and self-control, more positive attitudes about the changing roles of women, more willingness to take risks, more confidence in science and math, and greater rates of attaining Ph.D. and M.D. degrees (Baker and Velez 1996; Streitmatter 1999). Still women's college graduates account for less than 4 percent of the college-educated women in the United States (Women's College Coalition 2000).

Same-sex schools have also received increasing attention as military academies (e.g., Virginia Military Institute and the Citadel) have been forced to desegregate and some educational reformers have proposed same-sex middle schools and high schools as a remedy for the educational problems faced by inner-city youth (Streitmatter 1999).

The significance and impact of gender-segregated schools must be examined in light of the historical social relations of power and oppression among groups. For example, girls' schools and Black community calls for segregated education for Black males arise as a response to the negative effects of segregation among oppressed groups: the lack of ideological, political, and economic resources and limited access to power. Military academies, in contrast, were designed as sites for the consolidation of ideological, political, and economic power among privileged White, heterosexual men and thus serve a much different purpose in the production of race, class, gender, and sexuality inequality.

Sexuality Segregation

Although gay and lesbian students have not been historically segregated into different schools, same-sex schools such as men's and women's colleges have provided environments where White middle- and upper-class gay and lesbian communities have developed and thrived. Gay and lesbian communities were more likely to develop in these class-restricted settings primarily because White middle- and upper-class people were better able to sustain a homosexual lifestyle and identity in modern capitalism (D'Emilio 1993). Today, gay and lesbian youth have begun to organize student groups in high schools for many of the same reasons that race- and gender-segregated schools have developed: to serve as sites for self-determination, valuation, and resistance to oppression. According to the

Gay, Lesbian, Straight Education Network, most of the groups are gay-straight alliances and are organized to support gay students and to oppose discrimination and harassment in schools. They increased from 2 organizations in 1991 to over 100 in 1997 (Cloud 1997).

Segregation within Schools: Tracking

In addition to segregating students into different schools, segregating them into different academic tracks in the same schools is another critical process in the production of social hierarchies. In tracking, students are separated into different classes or into different groups within the same class to teach them at different speeds and at different levels of difficulty. Some form of tracking is practiced today in nearly every school in the United States, and it begins as early as the first grade (Entwisle, Alexander, and Olson 1997). Most educators justify tracking by arguing that differentiating students according to "ability group" makes teaching easier and raises student achievement by allowing curricula and instruction to be tailored to the abilities and interests of students.

But research on the effects of school tracking in K–12 education reveals a much more complex reality. The few studies comparing homogeneous and heterogeneous groups suggest that tracking and ability grouping do not seem to raise the average achievement of students any higher than heterogeneous instruction does: The top group does better, the bottom group does much worse, and the middle group remains the same (Entwisle, Alexander, and Olson 1997; Dougherty 1996; Kerckhoff 1995; Page 1991). Later, academic track students score better on math and verbal tests, have higher educational aspirations, and get more education than lower track or vocational track students. But there are so few heterogeneous groups to study that we cannot generalize confidently from these results. These studies also overlook a number of points about tracking:

- Students advantaged to begin with make up most of the top group.
- Students are educated differently in different tracks, increasing the gap between advantaged and disadvantaged children.
- Students live up to the expectations of their teachers, whether positive or negative.

We do know, however, that at the macro group level, tracking

- widens inequalities in academic achievement
- hinders the mixing of students of different social classes and races.

And at the micro level of students' individual lives, tracking

- undercuts the self-esteem and academic self-concept of lower-track students
- lowers educational aspirations of lower-track students
- increases the likelihood of delinquency and dropout rates among lower-track students (Anyon 1997; Dougherty 1996; Entwisle, Alexander, and Olson 1997; Kerkhoff 1995; Page 1993).

Two things are particularly distressing about these negative effects of tracking:

1. Students are supposedly tracked into different groups and provided different educations because they have different academic abilities to begin with. Yet academic aptitude is only one of the factors that actually influence how students are tracked—social class and race also affect placements both directly and indirectly (e.g., teachers' subjective assessments and parent preferences are also typically a part of the assignment process).
2. Academic aptitude is typically measured by scores on tests that measure only one type of intelligence and that are race and class biased.

Studies attempting to predict how students were tracked based solely on their test scores accurately predict for no more than 50 percent of the students' placements (Dougherty 1996). The race and class background of the students affects both teachers' perceptions of student abilities and parental influence on the placement process for their children—two factors that also affect track placement.

Race, Class, Gender, Sexuality and Tracking

Race, class, and gender affect track placement both directly and indirectly. White middle-class students and/or girls are more likely to be placed in higher tracks, particularly in elementary school, than are poor, working-class students, students of color, and/or boys regardless of test scores. Poor and working-class students of color are more likely to be placed in vocational and lower tracks. But most of the difference in the track placement of Whites and people of color, which is considerable and apparent in almost any school setting, is a function both of the lower-class position of students of color, teachers' perceptions of their potential, and parents' involvement and of class and racial bias in the aptitude tests (Brantlinger 1993; Entwisle, Alexander, and Olson 1997; Kerckhoff 1995; Persell 1977). In one recent study, high socioeconomic status students were found to be 46 percent more likely than low socioeconomic status students *with the same test scores* to end up in the academic rather than in the general track (Jones, Vanfossen, and Ensminger 1995).

Girls seem to have a slight advantage in access to the higher track in elementary school, but the advantage is gone by junior high school, when career tracking and gender socialization for different future lives is much more significant and overt (AAUW 1994; Pipher 1994). For example, girls are more likely than boys to be tapped for the gifted and talented programs in elementary school, but they are not retained in these programs to the same extent as boys once they reach middle school. And even though girls have increased their presence in science and math (but not computer science) courses in the 1990s and make higher grades than boys throughout their school years, they still perform lower on high–stakes standardized tests: ACT, SAT, and AP credit. They are also less likely to take advanced placement tests in math, science, and computer science (AAUW 1999).

Gay, bisexual, and lesbian students are not systematically tracked into different classes, because sexual identity does not begin to develop until adolescence. And most gay, bisexual, and lesbian students remain invisible in schools—much as Theo's gender and sexual identity development remains hidden from authorities at school. Gay, bisexual, and lesbian youth do, however, experience isolation and silencing in the curriculum and social life of schools, the negative effects of which inhibit their personal development and school progress. Increasingly gay, bisexual, and lesbian youth are organizing to combat discrimination in schools. For example, the Gay, Lesbian and Straight Education Network has 85 chapters across the nation. Their volunteers educate school officials about the need to pass nondiscrimination policies in schools, train teachers to prevent antigay name-calling, and serve as community resources for teachers, parents, and students grappling with gay, bisexual, lesbian, and transgender issues. In addition, their Student Pride Project provides resources and technical support to over 400 school-based Gay-Straight Alliances (GLSEN 2000).

Bilingual Education and Tracking

Bilingual education has been championed as a mechanism for preserving culture among America's non-English-speaking minorities, primarily Latinas/os. But in her study of bilingual classrooms, Flora Ida Ortiz (1988) found that Hispanic children receive a lower quality of education than their White counterparts whether that education was provided in separate schools or in separate classrooms in the same schools. The bilingual classes segregated Hispanic children from their classmates, were crowded, and were often taught by teachers' aides. In addition, because teachers assumed that the students were less capable of learning, the instruction was remedial. The schools were often in poor districts and received few resources. And even when Hispanic children were in the same classrooms with Anglos, they were often ignored by teachers, spoken to in different tones, and given different (nonverbal) activities to perform.

To illustrate the intimate connection between race, class, gender, and tracking, a story from Reba Page's (1991) study of tracking in two predominantly White (less than 12 percent were students of color), middle-class high schools is instructive. She discovered that the entire tracking system in the school had been established as an administrator's way of dealing with the race, class, and gender dynamics in the school. He described it as follows:

> Well, anyway, on October 26, 1980, there were three incidents in one day, and there had been a series of days with single incidents for over a week. It was a black-white thing. We had these girls who were coming to school, not going to class. Oh, they'd get their free lunch, but no attendance in classes. And, of course, they were bored. So they started fights: girl-girl fights with whites. They'd go around to classrooms, knock on the door, and ask for a kid, the kid would come to the door, and there'd be pushing and shoving. So I gathered them all up in the Commons and said, "Look, you're not getting any credits for all this time you've been putting in here at Southmoor. If you could have a class, what would it have to be like to make you attend?" (Page 1991:116)

Note that the administrator identified the Black "free-lunch" girls as the problem, "gathered them all up," and proposed a resolution to their boredom which in no way required the school that created the alienating environment for those girls to change what it did for White middle-class girls and boys. The subordinate groups were defined as the problem, isolated, and tracked for a different education.

Different School Continuation and Dropout Rates

As the high school dropout rates presented at the beginning of this chapter reveal, race and gender affect the rates at which groups continue in the educational system. Because continuing one's education beyond high school in different types of institutions significantly affects earnings and occupation, the transition to college is a critical juncture in the system of race, class, gender, and sexuality hierarchies (Pallas 1995). Social class is a key determinant of the likelihood that students will continue on. Further, different educational options after high school (e.g., community colleges, technical schools, colleges, universities, graduate schools) also provide different experiences and prepare students for very different life chances.

Colleges are critical institutions in the reproduction of social class and related racial advantage, yet they hide that function under a thin veneer of merit. Even though *tests* and *performance* are foregrounded in higher education, students from middle- and upper-class families have a distinct advantage in admission to and completion of college as well as in securing the best employment with their degrees in an overcredentialed market (Brown 1995).

In a review of research on college access, Therese Baker and William Velez (1996) reported that in 1992:

- Eighty-one percent of high-income students entered college directly from high school, 57 percent of middle-income students did so, while only 41 percent of low-income students continued—one-half the rate of their higher class counterparts.
- The impact of socioeconomic status was greatest for academically weak students: When they are middle class, they attend college anyway; when they are low income, they do not.
- High-income students were *eight times* as likely to attend elite colleges as low-income students, and they were much more likely to graduate from any college they attended.
- Students with a lower socioeconomic status were more likely to attend college part-time, work 33 to 36 hours a week, and have lower educational aspirations and weaker academic credentials.

The data in Table 8.1 show both race and gender differences in SAT and ACT scores, the tests used by most colleges to determine admittance. Average incomes for these groups fall in the same rank order as the test scores below, reinforcing arguments about class advantage and college admission (Brown 1995; Larabee 1995).

In 1994, 42.7 percent of White high school graduates aged 18–24 were enrolled in college while only 35.5 percent of Blacks and 33.2 percent of Hispanics were enrolled in college. In 1990, 21.6 percent of Whites, 36.6 percent of Asians, 9.3 percent of American Indians, 11.3 percent of Blacks, and 9.2 percent of Hispanics aged 25 and older held bachelor's, graduate, or professional degrees (CHE 1996:18).

TABLE 8.1. Average Scores on SAT and ACT by Sex and Race, 1996

	SAT			ACT
	Verbal	**Math**	**Total**	
Men	507	527	1,034	21.0
Women	503	492	995	20.8
Asian	496	558	1,054	21.6
White	526	523	1,049	21.6
Other Hispanic	465	466	931	18.9
American Indian	483	477	960	18.8
Mexican American	455	459	914	18.7
Puerto Rican	452	445	879	
Black	434	422	857	17.0

Source: Chronicle of Higher Education, Almanac Issue, "The Nations," September 2, 1996, p. 14.

SUMMARY

In spite of the ideology of equal opportunity, the gross differences in the kinds of schooling people receive based on race, class, gender, and sexuality persist throughout American history. This happens in part because the American Dream ideology, in offering individual explanations for differential school and group outcomes, detracts attention from systemic processes—segregation by school and within schools—that educate race, class, and gender groups in unequal ways. Those who are disadvantaged in the educational system—poor and working-class students, students of color, girls, and gay, bisexual, and lesbian students—have the fewest economic resources (money), political resources (influence, control over school boards), and ideological resources (expertise, knowledge of the system, control of media) to bring about change. Changing systems that clearly advantage some and disadvantage others requires a shift in the ideological, political, and economic power arrangements of society.

Themes: Power Relationships, Macro Social Structural and Micro Social Psychological Levels, Simultaneously Expressed

This chapter focuses on the last three themes of the framework: that race, class, gender, and sexuality are power relations simultaneously expressed at both macro institutional and micro individual levels. To explore these power relations, I look first at some of the macro institutional arrangements in political, economic, and ideological realms that structure educational inequality today. I then explore micro processes by looking at the various ways that race, class, gender, and sexuality relations are produced and challenged in the face-to-face encounters between teachers and students in the classroom everyday. To give a sense of the way that students actually experience these classroom dynamics, I discuss them in the order that students pass through school: preschool and kindergarten, first to third grades, fourth to sixth grades, junior high and high school.

I briefly highlight the final theme of the framework by returning to the cases of Theo and Lynn to remind us of the simultaneous operation and interlocking nature of these systems—a fact that cannot be ignored when we look at how multiple social locations play out in an individual life. Finally, to assess the significance of the race, class, gender, and sexuality framework for social justice, I review some of the implications that it has for social action to promote social justice in education.

MACRO SOCIAL STRUCTURAL POWER RELATIONS

As the stories of Theo Wilson and Lynn Johnson suggest, schools are not passive mirrors of the race, class, gender, and sexuality hierarchies in society today. Schools actively help to form those hierarchies in political, economic, and ideological domains (McCarthy and Apple 1988). Education is central to producing ideologies that undergird race, class, gender, and sexuality relations of oppression and resistance. It is also central to establishing and reinforcing political and economic power relations of race, class, gender, and sexuality.

Political Power and Education

Educational policy is a political arena where race, class, gender, and sexuality struggles are fought and relations shaped. Schools act as sites of oppression by assessing where people belong in the larger economy, preparing them for their place in it, and promoting ideologies that justify the very race, class, gender, and sexuality hierarchies they helped to create. As Pitirim Sorokin explained in 1927:

> The school, even the most democratic school, open to everybody, if it performs its task properly, is the machinery of the "aristocratization" and stratification of society, not of "leveling" and "democratization" (Sorokin 1927:190).

Kenneth Meier, Joseph Stewart, Jr., and Robert England (1989) contend that the educational policy arena is the single most important site of political struggle against racial discrimination in the United States today. People of color have long emphasized that resistance to oppression must take place in the educational arena, and many of the major racial conflicts of the 20th century have been over educational issues:

- School funding.
- School desegregation and busing.
- Affirmative action in higher education admissions, minority scholarships, and faculty hiring.
- The content of curricula (from sex education to multiculturalism).

Race, Class, Gender, and Sexuality Contests

One of the hotly contested issues in the current educational arena, for example, explicitly addresses the meaning and social construction of race, class, gender, and sexuality—who is to be considered a disadvantaged group for the purposes of hiring and admissions in higher education? In 1996 the University of California Board of Regents decided to change its affirmative action policy, using economic and *social* disadvantage, not race and gender, as criteria for special consideration in hiring and admissions for the state's nine campuses (Kershaw 1996). Under the new guidelines, 50 percent of the applicants would be admitted on the basis of academic achievement alone. But up to 50 percent of the applicants meeting minimum academic requirements would be evaluated based on "special circumstances." Those special circumstances include whether a student shows unusual persistence or determination, needs to work, is from a socially or educationally disadvantaged environment, or has a difficult family situation.

This new policy, deemed to be "race- and gender-blind," recognizes that because they come from economically advantaged, middle- or upper-class families, many women and people of color are not seriously disadvantaged. That is, it recognizes in part the complex intersections of race, class, and gender. Targeting limited slots for admission and hiring to those "truly disadvantaged" along multiple dimensions would seem to be a noble goal and consistent with the intent of affirmative action.

But, because race and gender are replaced with "difficult family situations" as a special circumstance that would account for up to 50 percent of admissions, many proponents of affirmative action questioned the actual intent of the Board of Regents and the likely *effects* of the new policy. As Keith Widaman, a professor of psychology at the University of California, Riverside, who was on the task force that helped the regents develop the guidelines, said, "Most of us thought that was kind of bizarre. What teenager doesn't think they come from a dysfunctional family?" "Difficult family situations" represents a designation that is difficult to define and that is prevalent throughout the economic hierarchy (Kershaw 1996).

Advocates of the current system of affirmative action argue that such a system would most likely reduce the number of people of color, women, and poor and working-class students by equally weighting criteria that advantage *groups* that are already advantaged in the process—men, Whites, and middle-class people. By focusing on individual family pathology instead of on group disadvantage, the inequalities in the social system that systematically operate to the exclusion or disadvantage of *groups* based on race, class, gender, or sexuality will not be challenged and will continue to operate in formal and informal processes (cf. Guinier, Fine, and Balin 1997; Sturm and Guinier 1996).

In recent years, class and economic inequality has also been the basis for political clashes over educational policy. Since the 1980s and 1990s, for example, mostly rural, poor school districts have brought suit against their states to challenge school funding formulas that allocate resources to schools based on the property taxes raised in the school district. Such formulas benefit already rich school districts, particularly well-to-do suburban schools, and disadvantage poor rural and inner-city school districts (Anyon 1997; Burkett 1998; Kozol 1991).

Political conflicts have also arisen over state support for Virginia Military Institute and the Citadel, all-male military academies; male admissions to all female colleges such as Mississippi University for Women, Texas Women's University, and Mills College; gender bias in the curriculum; unequal allocation of resources to women and men in higher education, centered in Title IX gender equity legislation of 1972.

Education is also a critical arena for contests over the institution of compulsory heterosexuality—the political pervasiveness and dominance of heterosexual norms throughout all areas of the culture (cf. Rich 1993). Elected and appointed school board members around the country exert political power when deciding how family life and sexuality will be treated in the schools. These decisions are hotly contested, particularly as they relate to who can teach in the schools and what the curriculum will contain about sexuality—both heterosexuality and homosexuality—and the family. Are female-headed families to be treated as real families? What of gay and lesbian marriages, parents, families? Openly gay men and lesbians, particularly those who teach in elementary school, have also faced harassment and have lost their jobs (Carlson 1997; Sears 1992). Lynn Phillips and Michelle Fine report that many public school teachers are inhibited from discussing issues of sexuality in a critical vein because

> they are evaluated on the basis of "value-free" discourse that privileges and "naturalizes" chastity, marriage, and heterosexuality; that denigrates teen mother-

hood; and that hesitates to discuss abortion lest they be "leading" the young woman (as if *not mentioning* is not "leading") (1992:243).

Perhaps nowhere is the attack on gays and lesbians and its connection with attacks on other oppressed groups more clearly laid out than in the political agendas of right-wing groups such as Phyllis Schlafly's Eagle Forum and Beverly LaHaye's Concerned Women of America (CWA). These groups oppose

- sex education in schools
- female access to all male educational institutions
- national standards
- the "extremist" National Education Association
- bilingual education
- antidrug programs
- multicultural curricula
- gays and lesbians in the classroom.

In her recent study of women's activism on the political right, Susan Marshall (1998) reports that the Eagle Forum told its members that sex education teaches children how to engage in sex and what devices to use and that CWA advised its members that these programs "countenance pedophilia, tell innocent children to indulge in promiscuity, and show eight-year-olds how to use a condom (Phyllis Schlafly Report 1993; CWA, LaHaye letter to membership, October 1995, March 1996).

Marshall summarizes the positions of these movements as follows:

> Homosexuality is the most heinous moral result of the sexual revolution, and the gay movement is perceived as a conspiracy—"a nationwide assault on the Body of Christ and the traditional family"—that is pushing to "take over our culture, step-by-step," infiltrating business, the media, the schools, and even churches. Borrowing an imagery from science fiction, one CWA "expert" advises that gays have devised a plan to breed a counterculture by marrying and having children, and homosexuals who do not participate in this eugenics experiment get revenge by recruiting children inside the schools. Needless to say, these organizations support state antigay constitutional amendments and proposed legislation to bar gay teachers from the classroom as well as the federal Defense of Marriage Act [*which bars states from recognizing gay marriages*] (Family Voice 1994, 1995; CWA, LaHaye letter to membership, August 1995; Marshall 1998:169–70).

In sum, power relations of dominance and subordination in education are exerted and contested in the political arena. Struggles are waged over access to education, the content of curricula, and the treatment of groups in school. The interrelated nature of race, class, gender, and sexuality systems is especially evident as groups seek through political processes to shape education and control dominant ideologies about every aspect of society, from family to sexuality, from religion to business.

Although schools are sites of oppression, they are also key sites of resistance to oppression. The relative isolation of poor and segregated schools often makes them powerful sites for the development of a collective oppositional consciousness and for protest movements. Many student leaders and participants in civil rights activism during the 1950s, 1960s, and 1970s were located in traditionally Black colleges, just as many activists in the American Indian Movement developed a consciousness and resistance strategies from the segregated space of the reservation (Robnett 1997; Carlson 1997).

Many groups have fought against oppression in schools:

- Native Americans against culturally biased and inferior education in reservation schools and state-sponsored boarding schools (Carlson 1997).
- Asian Americans and Jews against quotas in higher education (Takagi 1993).
- Latinos for bilingual education and against inferior education in bilingual classes (Ortiz 1988).
- Women and people of color against exclusion from math and science tracks (AAUW 1992, 1994, 1999; Rosser, 1997).
- Gays and lesbians against the silencing of homosexuality in curricula and the oppression of gay teachers and students (Carlson 1997; Cloud 1997; Sears 1992).

Both European immigrants and African Americans have emphasized education as a primary mechanism for uplifting the ethnic or racial group. Lynn Johnson was clearly selected for mobility by her community and supported in whatever way necessary to see that she succeeded—from demanding that she attend school while pregnant to paying for her SAT tests. Lynn was chosen by her teachers and other community leaders to represent the African-American community in Memphis as one of the first groups to attend a local all-White, private liberal arts college. Her good performance was seen as a way of contradicting negative stereotypes about Black ability as well as of producing a professional who would be expected to give something back to the Black community later. Today Lynn is a successful professional who feels a strong sense of commitment to the African-American community and to supporting others in their quest for fair treatment and upward mobility.

Economic Power and Education

The political struggle over educational policy is, in part, so intense because education is the primary determinant of income, providing access to good jobs, and is the key to upward mobility, to passing on middle-class standing, and to allowing intergenerational escapes from poverty (Meier, Stewart, and England 1989; Duncan 1984). At the same time, however, increasing the educational attainment levels of the population has not eliminated poverty because graduates are dependent on the available jobs for employment. In the last 25 years, as middle-class employment opportunities have declined, employers have responded by raising the educational requirements for the same jobs (Mickelson and Smith 1995; Brown 1995). Jobs that once required a bachelor's degree, such as public school teacher, increasingly require some graduate work, if not a master's degree. And jobs that once required a high school diploma, such as sales representative, now often require a college degree.

Michael Boozer, Alan Krueger, and Shari Walkon (1992) report that racial segregation of schools, still very high for Blacks and Hispanics, has a direct economic impact on wages and jobs. The researchers demonstrated that Blacks and Hispanics who attend racially isolated schools tend to obtain lower-paying jobs than Whites and that those jobs tend to be in racially isolated sectors of the labor force. On the other hand, Marvin Dawkins and Jomills Henry Braddock II demonstrate that desegregated schooling reduces racial differences in educational and occupational attainment and promotes interracial contact. African Americans who attend integrated elementary and high schools are more likely to

- attend and persist in integrated colleges
- enter scientific and business occupations
- work in integrated organizations
- work and socialize with White people
- live in integrated neighborhoods (Dawkins and Braddock 1994).

If anything is clear, it is that social class shapes both students' place in the educational system and their opportunities for employment. Working-class and poor students, educated differently and lacking the economic and social resources of their middle-class counterparts, fare less well in the labor market. It can be argued that gender and racial discrimination have some of their greatest impacts on women and racial ethnic people by blocking their entry into the middle classes and thus relegating them in greater proportions than White men to the working classes, where they will be educated differently and prepared for working-class occupations. Eric Wright (1989) estimated that a majority of the working class was constituted of women and people of color.

The labor market is even more segregated along gender lines than along race lines, and occupational segregation (i.e., of women into low-paying, female-dominated occupations) is the primary explanation for the persistent gap in the earnings of women and men (McGuire and Reskin 1993). One process implicated in the sex-segregation of the labor force is the differing preparation for the workforce that women and men and girls and boys receive in their educations. Feminist scholars and national science organizations such as the National Academy of Sciences and the National Science Foundation have, for example, established initiatives to understand and to reverse the gross underrepresentation of women, especially women of color, in careers in science, mathematics, medicine, and engineering (Chaney and Farris 1991; National Research Council 1993, 1996; National Science Foundation 1992, 1993). The gender gap in these fields contributes not only to a wage gap but also to intellectual bias in the fields.

In the early 1990s, the American Association of University Women first commissioned a review of over 1,000 articles and studies on girls and K–12 education. Published in 1992, *How Schools Shortchange Girls* brought national attention to its extensive findings: that the limited participation of women in these careers is linked to processes that take hold by junior high school, when girls become discouraged in the pursuit of these subjects, come to see themselves as inadequate, and are steered by teachers toward female-dominated occupations. In contrast, both girls and boys who like math and science have higher self-esteem, are more confident about their appearance, worry less about others liking them, aspire to professions, and hold on more strongly to their career goals. Discouraging girls and steering them away from these pursuits have psychological as well as career impacts. The AAUW recommended that girls must be educated and encouraged to understand that mathematics and science are important and relevant to their lives and be supported in pursuing education and employment in these areas.

At the end of the decade, the AAUW commissioned a follow-up study, *Gender Gaps: Where Our Schools Still Fail Our Children* (1999) to assess programs and needs at the beginning of the 21st century. The study found that great progress had been made: Innumerable programs debunked myths and stereotypes about the involvement of girls in math and science, and test scores and course enrollments had risen significantly, with the notable exception of computer science. For example, girls were less likely to take computer science theory, programming, or computer-aided design in high school and only 17 percent of those who took the advanced placement computer science exam in 1996 were girls, unchanged from the previous year. This gap, if it persists, could become enormously significant in promoting economic gaps based on gender, race, and class, because computer technology is one of the most rapidly spreading educational tools and sources of employment. Perhaps more significantly, the work of computer scientists in structuring the Internet is reshaping the way that learning is taking place in and out of schools and the way that the majority of people in the United States conduct their work every day. For women, people of color, and the poor and working classes to be left behind in this most recent technological revolution could have a widespread and long-lasting impact in reinforcing and solidifying race, class, and gender systems of inequality.

As in other realms, the effect of sexuality on jobs is more difficult to assess, in part because so many gays, bisexuals, and lesbians fear discrimination, including the loss of jobs, if their sexual orientation were known. This fear is especially true for people who deal with young children, such as school teachers and child care workers (Button, Rienzo and Wald 1997; Carlson 1997). Still, some research has begun to document the negative effects on wages of sexual orientation discrimination (Badgett 1995).

Ideological Power and Education

The realm of ideas is perhaps most central to the struggle for power in education. As a central institution organized to create and promote the ideas that rationalize, justify, and explain the workings of the dominant social order and to prepare people to function within it, education is a critical locus in the struggle of groups to define themselves and to assert their value and worth. Within schools, these struggles are often critically fought over the content of the curriculum.

The Curriculum

Some of the most bitter struggles have been and continue to be over the content of education—what we teach people, particularly what we teach about race, class, gender, and sexuality. Debates over multicultural and feminist content in curricula have been heated ever since the 1960s when the civil rights, women's rights, and gay rights movements began to push for the revision of basic texts to include the histories and experiences of people of color, women, and gays and lesbians (See, for example, Lerner 1976; Minnich, O'Barr, and Rosenfeld 1988; Schuster and Van Dyne 1984). During the 1980s and 1990s neoconservative politicians and intellectuals such as William Bennett, Allan Bloom (1988), Dinesh D'Souza (1991) and others began to develop an intellectual justification for maintaining the traditional curriculum and for rejecting the new histories and texts as divisive and threatening to the fundamental values of democratic capitalism. They defend the Western philosophical and literary tradition as superior and "universal in scope" and test scores as the "common index for all who seek to improve themselves, regardless of race, sex, or background" (D'Souza 1991:255). Equating test scores with achievement and ignoring the dominant culture biases in standardized tests, D'Souza writes:

> High standards do not discriminate against anyone except those who fail to meet them. Such discrimination is entirely just and ought not to be blamed for our individual differences (1991:250).

In this view of education

- test scores are equated with achievement
- abstract and arbitrary achievement standards are seen as a legitimate basis of discrimination in democratic capitalism
- failure is the fault of the individual who doesn't achieve
- redressing systemic biases that produce group "failures" (e.g., lower test scores of subordinate racial groups, high dropout rates for girls in science and math) violates the tenets of democratic capitalism.

These arguments, often put forth to end affirmative action, recall the Americanization movement of the early 20th century, which proposed a curriculum that would create a unified America out of a diverse immigrant population by teaching immigrants the superior values, interests, and beliefs of middle-class, Anglo-Saxon, patriarchal, heterosexual culture and which justified that curriculum in part with the newly created IQ test.

At stake in these debates is, among other things, what schools teach and students learn about

- dominant and subordinate groups in society
- the American Dream—why some groups get ahead while others lag behind in key societal resources
- their individual abilities and the abilities of others like them in the race, class, gender, and sexuality hierarchies.

The prevalence of these attacks on multicultural, gay-positive, feminist curricula indicates that these curricula pose real challenges to dominant ideologies about who should be included at the center of our curricula and what should be taught about them. The new perspectives have been attacked because they have, in fact, taken hold and are reshaping what students expect and what large segments of the population want in education today. As our population becomes increasingly diverse, we must become increasingly aware of both the extent of diversity and the necessity for citizens to understand diversity and to be able to work with people who have different backgrounds, world views, lifestyles, values, and goals. In an increasingly global economy, major businesses and corporations need workers who can communicate and work with people from very different cultural backgrounds. While the race, class, gender, and sexuality segregation of schools mitigates against this understanding, critical gay, multicultural, and feminist curricula facilitate it.

In sum, macro institutional power relations of oppression and resistance in the political, economic, and ideological domains generate, challenge, and transform race, class, gender, and sexual inequality. Education, as an ideological institution charged with equipping people with the knowledge, skills, and orientation to function as citizens, becomes a key site of political and economic contests over access to quality schooling, the content of the curricula, and the treatment that youth of different race, class, gender, and sexuality groups receive in schools.

MICRO SOCIAL PSYCHOLOGICAL POWER RELATIONS

Political, economic, and ideological domains of oppression are reproduced and transformed when individuals act out and resist race, class, gender, and sexuality hierarchies as they go about their lives every day, everywhere. In schools, these everyday experiences of domination, oppression, and resistance shape the way that students and teachers interact with and what they expect from one another.

What happens in classrooms? How do young people and their teachers interact every day? How do young people's experiences in school influence their self-esteem, aspirations and dreams, self-confidence, identity, their views of and relationships to others?

When we focus on macro systemic processes such as tracking and school segregation that structure different life experiences, it is difficult to imagine that anyone could overcome or challenge such powerful structural forces. Yet these systems, while pervasive, are neither exact nor totally determining—they are social constructions. And individuals face these structures in many different ways, with different personal and social resources. Not all children who are poor, working class, racial ethnic, girls, and/or gay or lesbian fail, drop out of school, get tracked in lower tracks, get pregnant, become drug addicts, or are destined to work in low-paid jobs.

Lynn Johnson grew up in public housing projects with six brothers and sisters and was a teenage mother whose own mother was on welfare. Yet her life was full of love, appreciation, and support both in her family and in her segregated public high school. She also received the academic training and encouragement she needed to succeed in college. Theo Wilson, unlike Lynn, was in a low track at his desegregated high school, his mother is a drug addict, his father just died, and he's now struggling with his sexuality. Theo certainly faces obstacles to developing a positive academic and sexual identity that Lynn didn't face. But, like Lynn, he is seeking out support where he can find it and has developed strong ties with Marie and Bill, who support his healthy development.

How do we experience race, class, gender, and sexuality hierarchies in our everyday lives? Just as there are observable macro systems and trends, there are observable micro patterns of interaction—ways of dealing, expectations, behaviors—that are shaped by race, class, gender, and sexuality and that help to reproduce and challenge those hierarchies. In the educational realm, these patterns of interaction begin as early as preschool and continue throughout all educational levels.

Preschool

Valerie Polakow (1993) documented gross inequities in the way that the poor children of single mothers are treated in public preschool programs. Classrooms can be a place of promise or condemnation, and the children of poor women are often condemned, labeled "at risk," and subjected to exclusion, humiliation, and neglect. Poor children, especially children of color, are more often labeled in one of a growing list of "at risk" labels: language impaired (often used for children speaking nonstandard English), immature, Special Ed, ADD (attention deficit disorder), undisciplined, free lunchers, trailer park kids, low-skilled, LD (learning disabled), and socially maladjusted. Teachers often assign these labels based on their perceptions of the children's parents, act differently toward the children because of the label, and signal to the other children the "otherness" of the selected child.

Like the work of Eleanor Maccoby (1988) who demonstrated children's complex understandings of gender at very early ages, new research by Debra Van Ausdale and Joe Feagin (1996) demonstrates that children as young as three years old use racial ethnic concepts to exclude others, to include others and teach them about racial ethnic identities, to define themselves and others, and to control others.

Conducting observations in preschool and day care programs, they recount the following illustrations of the use of racial ethnic concepts to exclude. In one encounter, Elizabeth, a three-and-a-half-year-old Chinese-American girl, asked if she could play with Rita (3 ½, White/Latina) and Sarah (4, White) who were pretending to bake muffins and had all the tins.

> Rita shakes her head vigorously saying: "No, only people who can speak Spanish can come in."
>
> Elizabeth frowns and says: "I can come in."
>
> Rita counters: "Can you speak Spanish?"
>
> Elizabeth shakes her head no and Rita reports: "Well, then you aren't allowed in" (Van Ausdale and Feagin 1996:781).

In other encounters Van Ausdale and Feagin observed a White girl (4) tell a Chinese-American girl (3) she could not pull a wagon because "Only *White Americans* can pull this wagon." And in a third interaction, a four-year-old White girl tells a four-year-old Black boy that he could not possibly own a White bunny rabbit because "Blacks can't have Whites." (1996:787)

In sum, teachers, parents, and even preschool peers hold different expectations for children and treat them differently depending on their own and their parents' locations in race, class, gender, and sexuality hierarchies. As early as preschool, children have learned that these labels are used to include and exclude, to define themselves, and to control others.

First, Second, and Third Grades

Although social scientists have paid much less attention to the race, class, gender, and sexuality sorting and ranking processes in preschool and the early grades than they have to middle school and high school, Entwisle, Alexander, and Olson (1997) review a growing literature that demonstrates that race, class, and gender power relations are well established in the first grade. When children enter the first grade, parents and teachers tend to see children in the context of their family's social location, not in terms of their potential. For example, when parents are unemployed, teachers hold lower expectations for their children, value their educations less, and begin to view children as having low ability. Positive ratings by teachers of how students "fit in," based on assessments of their classroom behavior in the first grade, lead children to do well in the first year. These ratings also affect the gains students make in the fourth grade more than the ratings of the fourth-grade teacher because the cumulative nature of the curriculum makes it hard for a child to achieve at a high level in the fourth grade without having achieved at a high level in earlier grades. Males, students of color, and/or low socioeconomic status students more often fail or are entered into special education in elementary school, and these same children are later more likely to drop out of high school.

Thus, the first grade is critical for setting the stage for later school performance, for academic self-concept, and self-esteem. When children enter first grade, they continue to learn about and to act upon their understandings of the social placement of children of various race, class, and gender groups.

Polakow (1993), for example, cites the cases of Tim, a nine-year-old White boy from a homeless family, and Heather, a seven-year-old White "trailer park kid." During the school year, Tim lived with his mother and sister in, variously, a truck, a shelter, a trailer, and a welfare motel. Children teased him because of his worn and unkempt clothes, and they picked up on the negative attitude of the teacher. Tim described how he felt:

> They think 'cos I haven't got no home that I haven't got nothing inside of me—they won't play with me—they won't be a buddy when we go on trips either and no kids will be my friends. . . . Also they all think I'm so dumb and I hate this school, and Mrs. Devon keeps saying she got no time when I ask her things (Polakow 1993:145).

Heather also was defined by the teacher as a "problem" second-grader. When Polakow visited, Heather's desk was in the hallway, and other children were not allowed to talk to her nor she to them. When asked what Heather had done, the teacher, Mrs. Mack, replied:

> The child just does not know the difference between right and wrong—she absolutely does not belong in a *normal* classroom with *normal* children. . . . I've given up on this child—she's socially dysfunctional—three times now we've caught her stealing free lunch and storing it in her desk to take home (Polakow 1993:138).

Polakow learned that Heather had been taking lunches home on Fridays to have something to eat over the weekend. Mrs. Mack tried repeatedly to get Heather removed from her classroom, claiming Heather is learning disabled and emotionally impaired. Heather was eventually assigned to special education, which removed her from the classroom several times a day for remedial activities and made it impossible for her to finish her regular classroom assignments, for which she was said to have "poor work habits."

The overall orientation of teachers of poor children in these classrooms was toward containment and regulation: drilling children to produce the correct responses, regulating their imaginations, presenting them with tasks to complete rather than with opportunities to learn. Classrooms were rigidly segregated by ability and gender, with "out-of-order" children, often young Black boys from poor families, becoming classroom "deviants" subjected to disciplinary measures and exclusion and given limited views of their potential.

In an observational study of first- and second-graders in working-class, desegregated classrooms (30–90 percent Black), Linda Grant (1994) documented patterns of race and gender interaction. Focusing on the special roles played by Black girls in desegregated classrooms, Grant reports that teachers encouraged and assessed Black girls more positively in social than in academic roles. Perceived as intellectually average—equal to White boys, below White girls, and above Black boys—most were tracked in the middle or lower tracks. Even though rated equal to White boys, Black girls were seen by teachers as having less promise because White boys were defined as immature while Black girls were regarded as already mature socially and thus not as likely to improve academically.

Grant (1994) identified two social roles, the "helper" and the "enforcer," that were prevalent among Black girls. One social role, the "go-between," was occupied *solely* by Black girls. Although teachers sometimes punished them for assuming these roles, the teachers ultimately reinforced the behavior of these students because they helped to maintain order, peace, and social integration in the classrooms.

Helpers. Black girls sought teacher attention and student respect by acting as helpers (e.g., locating lost materials, comforting emotionally distressed children, and keeping things tidy). One teacher even referred to a helper as "our little housekeeper." As Joyce Ladner (1972) notes, Black girls are often given adult responsibilities in the home and carry these over into the school where they are reinforced, even though the girls are occasionally reprimanded by teachers.

Enforcers. Some Black girls urged peers to follow school rules in the teacher's absence. Grant (1994:47) describes what happened in one situation when the teacher left the room after asking the students to stay seated and be quiet.

> [S]everal students left their seats. When Gerald (White) walked past Pamela (Black), Pamela rose, placed her hands on his shoulders, gently kicked the back of his legs, told him to "move it," and pushed him several feet back to his desk. She then pointed a finger at Steven (Black) and threatened: "You're next." Steven quickly took his seat. She then shook her head sternly at Renee (White), who had started to rise but sat down in response to Pamela's action (1994:47).

The effectiveness of Black girls in this role shows that they have substantial influence with diverse peer groups.

Go-Between. The most complex role, assumed only by Black girls, was as negotiator of deals and relationships between students and teachers and between other students. Consider the following interaction in which a go-between

- identified one student as missing a shoelace, asked a second student for an extra but came up empty
- asked the teacher to send a third student (already on her way out) to another teacher's classroom to ask for a shoelace
- when she returned with the shoelace, thanked her since the teacher hadn't
- asked a fourth student to pick up his coat from the floor
- helped a fifth student with a reading word
- got jellybeans from a sixth student and shared them with a seventh student.

In all, this child interacted with one-third of the class and the teacher in one 10-minute period, with almost all of the interactions beyond the teacher's awareness.

These roles, which require an understanding of the norms in different groups and a willingness to take personal risks for social harmony, begin to prepare Black girls for adult roles in service to others (e.g., as secretaries or teachers' aides, where Black women are overrepresented). Although Black girls had the most diverse and extensive peer ties of any group, teachers responded to these social skills by encouraging them *but* simultaneously failing to encourage the girls' academic interests and pursuits to the same degree that they did with White girls and even with boys. In contrast, Grant notes that Black girls in all-Black schools tend to be academic leaders and to be encouraged in academic pursuits.

As Grant and Polakow document, teachers' expectations for students were shaped by the race and gender of the students and powerfully influenced the students' behaviors. Interestingly, the patterns of race-gender interaction (e.g., Black girls as go-betweens) and teacher expectations (Black girls for social, not academic, achievement) occurred in the classrooms of both Black and White teachers.

Karl Alexander, Doris Entwisle, and Maxine Thompson (1987) explored the impact of teachers' backgrounds on their expectations and examined achievement among first-graders. During this critical period of transition to school, teachers have a tremendous impact—both on how students will adjust and how they will perform. Teacher impressions of students' academic potential at this crucial entry point are often based on superficial and inappropriate cues such as dress, style, language, and deportment. Sorting students into ability groups begins, and "chronic underachievement starts early." And once started, it is difficult to reverse.

Hypothesizing that teachers from low socioeconomic backgrounds would be less likely to read cues such as "different" style of dress and language usage as fundamental failings because these cues would be familiar, the researchers found indeed that both Black and White teachers from high socioeconomic status backgrounds

- perceived African-American and low-status youngsters as relatively lacking in the qualities of personal maturity that make for a good student

- held lower performance expectations for them
- evaluated the school climate less positively (i.e., less pleasant and rewarding, more tense and frustrating) when working primarily with low-status students.

One result of these perceptions is that Black and lower-status students who entered first grade with the same test scores as their White and high-status classmates had fallen well behind by year-end. The researchers also found that boys got worse conduct grades than girls, but their academic grades were no worse. Later in the education process, racial ethnic youth, especially boys, are more often placed in lower tracks for nonacademic reasons of discipline (Meier, Stewart, and England 1989).

Fourth, Fifth, and Sixth Grades

Many of the patterns of interaction begun in early years are reinforced and elaborated as children grow older and other issues (e.g., sexuality) develop and begin to shape race, class, gender, and sexuality dynamics. Barrie Thorne (1993) studied gender interactions in fourth, fifth, and sixth grades in a public working-class school and also found that race and class were related to student placement in ability groupings and that students were segregated by gender for many activities (e.g., seating arrangements, lines, lunch tables, and playgrounds).

Power differences were exhibited, especially in these segregated settings, for example, when boys had 10 times more space on the playground and were more likely to interrupt girls' activities and space and to treat the space as "contaminating." But Thorne also points out that these relationships were fluid: They varied by location and activity, and some students crossed the gender borders. Interactions in schools were more segregated than in neighborhoods and more segregated still on the school playground than in the classrooms. That is, schools are important sites for the reproduction of gender inequality.

Thorne's work is important because she points out that the "different cultures" research[1] exaggerates the differences and thus reinforces the hegemonic view of gender as oppositional dualisms attached to individuals—the belief that boys' groups are large, public, hierarchical, and competitive while girls' groups are small, private, cooperative, and focused on relationships and intimacy. Instead, Thorne contends that gender dynamics are much more fluid than these oppositional images that come from research on White middle-class girls suggest. Thorne observed frequent "borderwork" activities—girls playing with boys, being competitive, and using insults and threats. She also noted that Black girls were marginalized more often than other groups and played the border-crossing role more often.

Jessie, for example, was the only African American in her class and was the most active and adept student at moving between boy and girl groups, even on the playground, where segregation was greatest. Her teacher once observed, "Jessie

---

[1]See Carol Gilligan, Nona Lyons, and Trudy Hanmer, eds., *Making Connections: The Relational Worlds of Adolescent Girls at Emma Willard School* (Cambridge: Harvard University Press, 1990); and Mary Pipher, *Reviving Ophelia: Saving the Selves of Adolescent Girls* (New York: Putnam, 1994).

wants action with both groups," and occasionally someone would remark that the class has a "girls' side" and a "boys' side," "except for Jessie." Of Jessie, Thorne observes:

> During the part of the year when she had a desk with the girls, Jessie often went to the boys' side of the room to join an informal cluster or to find a spelling partner. Only one other girl, Tracy, ever practiced spelling with a boy. Jessie kept a continual eye on happenings in both sides of the room. One day when Miss Bailey was moving from student to student, checking a spelling test, Jessie, who was then sitting with the girls, whispered loudly, "Kevin got his all right; me and him got one hundred." Making eye contact with John from across the room, she added, "I was watching you make mistakes" (Thorne 1994:128).

Jessie's behavior looks very much like that of the go-between identified by Grant and foreshadows the "outsider within" status identified by Patricia Hill Collins (1991b) as the unique social position occupied by adult Black women. A "peculiar marginality," this role provides Black women with a distinct view of the contradictions between the dominant group's actions and ideologies and with a unique standpoint on self and society. This peculiar marginality is created not only in adult work roles such as domestic worker but also in the social roles that Black girls play in early school settings.

As children grow older, Thorne notes that boys have greater sanctions for crossing boundaries than do girls—who have much more latitude to play multiple roles before adolescence. As children approach adolescence, however, the forceful intrusion of the system of compulsory heterosexuality begins to take precedence in gender interactions. The segregation of boys and girls increases, and by the fifth grade terms such as "sissy," "fag," and "faggot" are serious insults used to enforce heterosexual norms. Focusing on girls' bodies and changes, sex education defines girls in terms of sexuality.

Junior High School and High School

As girls enter adolescence (12 to 14 years old), they have already begun to develop

- higher rates of depression
- lower self-esteem
- more negative images of their own bodies
- declining academic performance in science and math
- a social position that is increasingly derived from their relationships to boys.

The "decline" happens for all girls but more so for White and Hispanic girls than for African-American girls, whose self-esteem is higher than that of Whites to begin with (AAUW 1991, 1994).

Extensive research has documented the differential treatment of boys and girls in classrooms. Initially reported by the AAUW in *How Schools Shortchange Girls* (1992) and reiterated in the follow-up study, *Gender Gaps* (1999), girls

- received less teacher attention than boys
- received less complex, challenging interaction with their teachers than boys

- received less constructive feedback from teachers than boys
- received less wait time (time to respond once called upon) than boys.

In addition, gender bias in teacher-student interaction was greater in science and math than in other subject areas (AAUW 1992, 1999).

Young people struggling to understand and come to terms with their sexuality, particularly young people who are bisexual, lesbian, or gay, have few affirming markers about what they feel and think (Carlson 1997). Official school policies across the country on homosexuality are much like that of the military—"don't ask, don't tell"—official silence about the subject and about the sexual orientations of teachers and students. So even gay teachers often studiously avoid discussing homosexuality when it comes up in class, leaving gay youth feeling isolated and devalued. It is estimated that as much as one-third of adolescent suicide victims and one-fourth of homeless youth are gay and that drug abuse and dropout rates among gay youth are high (Gibson 1989). Because the most visible gay people in society—as portrayed in the media and in the public political arena—are White, middle-class men, adolescence is especially hard for gay, working class and racial ethnic youth and for young lesbians (Cloud 1997). Some conservative forces in minority communities have even used this visibility to portray homosexuality as a White issue (West 1993).

In junior high school and high school, ability group tracking is pervasive and is highly correlated with race and class. And although it is possible to change tracks as many students do, racial ethnic and low-socioeconomic status students are most likely to drop to lower tracks, not to jump to higher ones (Hallinan 1995). Think of Theo and Lynn, tracked differently. Theo had tremendous obstacles to overcome even to make it into college: lack of academic credits, lack of readiness for the SATs, and his own sense of having few options. His situation is in stark contrast to Lynn's: Tracked for mobility and encouraged by teachers, she feels she can do almost anything she wants in life.

Comments by high school students in Jeannie Oakes's study reveal these different attitudes and knowledge bases in tracks. Here we can begin to see the longer range effects of the processes described among much younger children (Polakow 1993; Alexander, Entwisle, and Thompson 1987; Grant 1994; and Thorne 1993). When asked about the most important thing they have learned or done so far in class, these students replied:

- I want to be a lawyer and debate has taught me to dig for answers and get involved. I can express myself. (High Track English)
- How to present myself orally and how to listen and to think quick. (High Track English)
- To understand concepts and ideas and experiment with them. Also to work independently. (High Track Science)
- Behave in class. (Low Track English)
- I learned about being quiet when the teacher is talking (Low Track Social Studies)
- I have learned that I should do my questions for the book when he asks me to. (Low Track Science) (Oakes 1985:86–89)

In sum, classrooms are powerful settings where teacher expectations, specific curricula, and student interactions with one another create and reinforce race, class, gender, and sexuality hierarchies every day. In subtle and not so subtle ways, young people are treated differently across race, class, gender, and sexuality, and they are taught to think about and to treat each other unequally as well.

SIMULTANEOUSLY EXPRESSED

Macro systems of race, class, gender, and sexuality operate simultaneously, and individuals experience them in their own lives all at once. Theo Wilson is African American, male, and working class and is unsure about his gender expression and sexual identity. Lynn Johnson is African American, female, middle class but raised in the working class, and heterosexual. All of these dimensions form critical aspects of their lives and identities.

Marie and Bill have been tutoring Theo to help him to develop skills, to get a better education, to have more life options. Marie saw herself as teaching writing to a Black, working-class, teenage boy who was struggling in school in a low track. She never expected the phone call she got from Theo to discuss his gender expression and his sexuality. Yet Theo's world view, the issues he confronts and the sense he develops of himself, are shaped all at once by the many realities of his life that include his sexual orientation and gender expression as well as his race, class, age, and urban home.

Lynn Johnson is older than Theo, and some things are clear to her: She did succeed in the education system and in the working world. She has a strongly positive sense of herself that was shaped in her development as a working-class, African-American girl in a segregated community in the 1960s and 1970s. She was pregnant at age 16, and had she been White or Latina, the community response to her pregnancy might have been different. But because Lynn's gendered heterosexual experience of pregnancy took place in a racial context where the African-American community was focused on racial uplift through education, Lynn was encouraged and supported in continuing in school.

As we look at these lives, it is clear that the intersections of race, class, gender, and sexuality are at play all the time. Yet most of the research and writing about these dimensions addresses only one, or sometimes two, of them but rarely more than two at once. So we must bring our understanding of the complexities of race, class, gender, and sexuality to our reading of others' research and to our own analyses of social life. In any analysis, we should ask the following:

- What was left out?
- What difference does the omission make?
- What would change if it were included?

Think back to the observation about Elizabeth, the Chinese-American girl, who was excluded from baking with her schoolmates because she could not speak Spanish. Van Ausdale and Feagin's analysis (1996) focused on race. But we can ask: What is the significance of the fact that the racial exclusion took place in a gendered activity? The girls were pretending to bake. This dimension was not considered in the study, but the girls were practicing racial exclusion and developing gender identities simultaneously.

Attending to these simultaneous dynamics enables us to address different issues. A common contention in political analyses, for example, is that women, oppressed by gender, are or should be more empathetic to others and more socially active in redressing other oppressions such as racism, classism, or homophobia. But attending to gender in Van Ausdale and Feagin's racial analysis would not lead to that conclusion. Quite the contrary, these young girls are learning racial exclusion while they are learning to play traditional female roles. This coexistence is further born out by Kathleen Blee's research on women in the Ku Klux Klan (1991) and on modern right-wing movements (1998).

Of Van Ausdale and Feagin's analysis, we could also ask:

- What of social class? Would upper-class girls have been pretending to bake?
- What if a White, non-Spanish-speaking boy and not Elizabeth had asked to enter the game? Would he have been excluded? Called a sissy?

As we hypothesize answers to these questions, we can see that all of the dimensions, some foregrounded and some backgrounded, operate in every situation.

IMPLICATIONS FOR ACTIVISM AND SOCIAL JUSTICE

What will it take to seriously challenge the system of education as a primary site for the reproduction of race, class, gender, and sexuality hierarchies? Thinking first of the micro realities of the lives of Lynn Johnson and Theo Wilson, some of the implications for social activism become clear. Both Theo and Lynn came of age in segregated African-American communities, Theo in the Northeast in the 1990s and into 2000, Lynn in the South in the 1960s and 1970s. Poor African-American girls have always needed strong supports to attain an education in a society organized to deny their worth, intelligence, and access to knowledge. Over the last century, African-American civil society resisted this oppression in many ways, perhaps most significantly by emphasizing education as a means of racial uplift and a form of resistance to oppression and by organizing and functioning in ways to make education happen not only for Black but for all oppressed peoples. When Lynn Johnson was growing up, she had access to the full benefit of that African-American tradition; she was valued for her intelligence, not only allowed but encouraged to remain in school after she became pregnant, funded to take the ACT, and guided in the curriculum and grooming she needed to ultimately become one of the people who desegregated institutions of higher education across the country in the late 1960s.

By the 1990s, when Theo and other poor African-American youth across the country entered high school, the Black civil society that supported Lynn had undergone dramatic shifts. As Patricia Hill Collins notes (1998), changes in the global economy, the denial of the deeply entrenched racial practices in the United States, and the ubiquity of the color-blind ideology have fostered major changes.

While the Black middle class has increased dramatically, poor African Americans are increasingly concentrated in racially segregated inner-city neighborhoods, a shift that fostered the breakup of community organization—crumbling family structures, unemployment, gangs, drugs, and other social problems. Consequently, she argues, "the structures and experience of Black poverty have radically changed" (Collins 1998:31). What this meant for Theo was that the resources available to Lynn were not there for Theo. Theo and his father continued to look for supports for Theo, but they could not find them in the traditional places. Instead, Theo found them in an outreach program run by White professors from an urban branch campus.

These stories, taken in combination, point to the kinds of support that poor women and men of color need to succeed, and they caution us that they cannot be met in the same ways today that they were 30 years ago. If the family and community network cannot provide what youth need to succeed, programs must be put in place that can.

Scholars whose works are discussed in this chapter look closely at the harsh truths of life structured by the inequalities of race, class, gender, and sexuality— not at the dream but at the reality. Yet they undertook their research out of a desire for social change, to find ways to make a more humane and egalitarian social order. In the process of examining closely and describing precisely the ways that inequality operates, they develop specific ideas about how to promote inclusive and egalitarian social ideals and specific ideas for educational reform.

These researchers also develop hope, as Dennis Carlson (1997) and Jean Anyon (1997) argue, a hope that arises out of the concrete struggles currently being waged by dispossessed groups for freedom, equity, and social justice over the course of U.S. education. So long as the state remains so heavily influenced by economic elites who benefit from social inequalities, the hope for a serious impetus for reform must come from these social movements of the dispossessed. Most of these authors draw some conclusions about the current condition of education in the United States and recommend educational reforms that their research suggests would reduce inequalities and promote a more inclusive educational system and society. They also look to social movements as necessary to see that the reforms are implemented.

When all other social institutions are structured unequally, we cannot hope to achieve equality in the educational system. Even though Americans believe, for example, in an educational system that gives everyone a fair chance, they want their own children to succeed in the competition for economic and social advantage and thus seek an unequal education to help in that process (Tyack and Cuban 1995). Reformers who are a part of a growing movement for "detracking" in schools have begun to learn just how powerful the forces promoting inequality can be. For example, Jeannie Oakes and her collaborators (1997, 1998) conducted a study of 10 racially and socioeconomically mixed secondary schools across the country that are participating in detracking reform. Attempting to provide access to high standards for all students, the schools implemented reforms based on the latest scholarship reflecting the multidimensional, developmental, and culturally varied nature of intelligence as well as people's unlimited potential for learning. They eliminated the lower track, developed common curricula, put all students on a college preparatory track for some subjects, designed a customized school calendar and after-school programs for students having difficulty, adopted classroom strategies that allowed students to demonstrate knowledge in new ways, developed multicultural curricula, and created a wide range of innovative learning projects to challenge each student.

Yet these projects ran into enormous opposition from teachers and administrators within the schools who continue to believe conventional, normative conceptions that intelligence is

- essentially unchangeable—either for biological or cultural reasons or both
- unidimensional—reflected in the speed of getting right answers on standardized tests
- "normally" distributed—across a bell curve
- readily apparent—associated with the way that students comport themselves, an assessment that overlaps with race, class, and gender as reflected in statements like the following:

"Smart students . . . look like they're paying attention, turn in their homework, help classmates who don't understand something, and are good leaders."

"We're getting fewer honors kids, and that's just demographics" (Oakes et al. 1997:490).

In the final analysis, these educators believe that tracking students is the most effective way to educate a student population that is "naturally, innately" already ranked by intelligence.

The more significant resistance, however, has come from the affluent White parents of high-track students who benefited from the unidimensional view of intelligence and the tracking system that is built on those views. These parents, often working in conjunction with resistant teachers in the schools, employed several strategies to stop the practice: threatening to leave the school, co-opting educational elites who see their roles as serving the elites of the community, buy-ins of not quite elite parents who accept the dominant "common-sense" ideology, and extracting bribes—demanding preferential treatment for their children—smaller classes, the best teachers, the latest technology. What the reformers learned was that while they had focused on the technical aspects of knowledge acquisition and learning, powerful social forces were invested in the role of the school to sort, rank, and reinforce the hierarchy of power that existed outside the school. As Carlson (1997:57) states:

It is naive to believe that public schools can be detracked outside of a broad-based movement for democratic renewal in the culture, including a movement toward a more equitable economy and an improvement in the quality of people's working lives.

And addressing the inequities across and within schools, Jean Anyon similarly concludes:

Attempting to fix inner-city schools without fixing the city in which they are embedded is like trying to clean the air on one side of a screen door (1997:168).

We can't expect schools to be structured around principles of equity as long as they are implicated in preparing students for such unequal futures. Attaining educational equality will thus require improvements in the quality and pay of jobs and macro economic policies to counter the two-tiered economy that has developed over the past 40 years. We cannot expect educational equality alone to reduce larger economic and occupational inequalities because, as we have seen, increasing the educational levels of the population when good jobs are not available merely leads to credential inflation (Brown 1995; Mickelson and Smith 1995).

Recommendations for Educational Reform

Most scholars recommending educational reform to redress inequities emphasize several key bases for true reform.

School Reform and Movements for Social Equity

Reform must be accompanied by and tied to movements for social equity and social justice in society at large. If *all* children are to be educated, society must guarantee that basic human needs can be met. In addition to decent jobs and living wages, all citizens need health care, affordable housing, a child allowance significantly above the $1,000 tax deduction currently in place, and a national child care system (including provision of full services for families in need), a national public system for early childhood education, and reduced funding and resource disparities across schools (Polakow 1993).

Access for All to Programs that Work

Effective reform must include access for all students to programs and opportunities with proven success in improving the learning of oppressed groups such as preschool and full-day kindergarten, reduced class size (in the context of improved pedagogy and teachers' skill in giving individualized attention), bilingual and English as a second language instruction, intensive curricular intervention programs, safe schools programs, school-to-work and school-to-college transition activities, full-service schools [e.g., including health care, general equivalent diploma (GED) classes, job training], support for mainstreamed students and their teachers (Anyon 1997:179).

Desegregation and Detracking

Heterogeneous classroom experiences across race, class, gender, and sexuality are preferable to segregation and school tracking (Carlson 1997; Oakes et al. 1997; Orfield et al. 1996; Thorne 1993). The unequal allocation of resources to schools—human resources such as well-trained teachers and material resources such as physical facilities, curriculum materials, and computers—based on race and class differences in the communities surrounding the schools is a continuing threat to equity in education and in society. Recent trends in the resegregation of schools are exacerbating that threat (Orfield et al. 1996; Orfield et al. 1997). Likewise, recent economic trends have affected school tracking within schools. Primarily because of shifts from a manufacturing to a service economy, vocational education has declined dramatically (50 percent in the last 10 years) and the general education track has expanded to accommodate those students, producing some "detracking." With the development of magnet schools,[2] however, these trends have served to increase, not decrease, the inequality in the schools because general track education receives even lower expenditures and teachers' expectations are lowered further, while magnet schools further separate college track students from the rest of the student population.

We need social policy that eliminates unequal practices, such as funding schools through property taxes and "ability group" tracking within schools, and that guides us in a systematic way to both housing and school integration. Instituting such a policy will require a major shift in the current political trends that focus on dismantling the desegregation plans of the 1970s but do not include

- full discussion of how the new plans for school system structures will not deepen inequality
- research to develop new strategies and to evaluate them
- funding to implement strategies
- oversight to monitor progress toward equity.

Pedagogy of Equity

A new pedagogy of equity is called for. Race, class, gender, and sexuality scholars offer significant promise for what a pedagogy of equity would address. The reforms that Dennis Carlson (1997), for example, demands as a necessary part of a democratic multicultural curriculum and pedagogy reflect the basic themes of race, class, gender, and sexuality scholarship.

Contextual, Socially Constructed. Challenge "essentialist" world views that take categories such as race, class gender and sexuality as "natural categories having a fixed meaning" in all times and places.

Power Relations. Discuss race, class, gender, and sexuality as power relations antithetical to democratic "virtues," including protection of minority rights and individual freedoms, respect for difference, equity, and development of interlocking webs of caring and supportive relations among individuals. Within the context of human rights in a democratic community, teachers can, for example, involve young people in a discussion of gay identity.

---

[2]The U.S. Department of Education established four criteria to define a magnet school: 1) a distinctive school curriculum based on a special theme or method of instruction, 2) a unique district role and purpose for voluntary desegregation, 3) voluntary choice of the school by students and parents, 4) open access to school enrollment beyond a regular attendance zone (Blank et al. 1983:2). Magnet schools were founded primarily to solve the pressing political problem of preventing active, dramatic, and possibly violent resistance by some Whites to the creation of the desegregated schools required by the courts (Metz 1986:15).

Macro and Micro Levels. Discuss these issues at the structural level as well as at the level of personal identity. Emphasize the connections between macro structures and personal experience, always looking for evidence of each in every discussion. Help students see that the success of a few people does not necessarily prove that the American Dream is a reality.

Simultaneously Expressed. Seek to cross or rupture the borders that classify separated individuals into neat categories or camps. One way to rupture these borders is to emphasize the multiple subject positions we all occupy (i.e., race, class, gender, sexuality). A corollary is that all truths are partial, and therefore classroom discussions should seek to clarify agreements and disagreements, not to identify a single truth.

Implications for Social Activism. Help students see the connection between knowledge about race, class, gender, and sexuality and social movements for equity.

The educational system holds promise as a potential site for increasing race, class, gender, and sexuality equity. It will require, however, a major transformation of the system at both the macro and micro levels. That transformation will depend on the success of social movements in providing the impetus for equity and on the establishment of policies that are more likely to produce it, including redistribution of fiscal resources, changes in organizational structures, a pedagogy of equity that emphasizes promoting understanding and collaboration across diversity, and involvement of activists, community people, parents, and teachers in the process of designing reform.

SUMMARY

This section illustrates the conceptual framework by applying it in a comprehensive analysis of a major social institution, education. Education was selected for many reasons, but particularly because it is the first institution with which most people have extensive contact outside their immediate families. This analysis, however, could have been conducted on any social institution—work and economy, religion, family, government/polity—or even applied to the circumstances of an individual life. Furthermore, as the analysis of education should have made apparent, none of these institutions operate in isolation from others. The race, class, gender, and sexuality processes that are generated and reinforced in one institution also affect the others.

CHAPTER 10

Envisioning Social Justice

In 1955, one year after *Brown v. Board of Education of Topeka* removed the legal foundation of segregation, Mamie Mobley sent her 14-year-old son, Emmett Till, to Mississippi to visit his cousins. A few weeks later, her only child returned to Chicago—in a body bag. He had been beaten and shot, a gin-mill fan had been wired to his neck, and he was tossed in the Tallahatchie River. He was unrecognizable, identifiable only by the ring on his finger. Emmett Till was mutilated for allegedly saying "Bye, baby" to a White woman in a country store. The two White men who killed him were quickly acquitted by an all-White male jury. Mamie Mobley was grief stricken: "Death at that time would have been welcome" (Terkel 1992:22).

Newspapers spread pictures of Emmett's corpse across the country. The sight of Emmett Till's body and the enormity of the injustice done mobilized many people to action in the cause of civil rights. In 1985 Toni Morrison wrote *Dreaming Emmett,* a play commissioned by the New York State Writers Institute to commemorate the first national observance of Martin Luther King's birthday.

Nearly 40 years later, Studs Terkel interviewed Mamie Mobley about those events and her life since Emmett's murder.

TERKEL: Don't you harbor any bitterness toward the two men—toward whites, for that matter? It would be unnatural not to—

MOBLEY: It certainly would be unnatural not to, yet I'd have to say I'm unnatural. From the very beginning that's the question that has always been raised: "What would you do to Milam and Bryant if you had the opportunity?" I came to the realization that I would do nothing. What they had done was not for me to punish and it was not for me to go around hugging hate to myself, because hate would destroy me. It wouldn't hurt them . . .

The Lord gave me a shield . . . . If I had to, I could take their four little children—they each had two—and I could raise those children as if they were my own and I could have loved them. Now that's a strange thing to say, but I haven't spent one night hating those people. I have not looked at a white person and seen an enemy. I look at people and I see people (Terkel 1992:21).

After Emmett's death, Mamie Mobley went back to school, became a teacher, and taught for 24 years in the Chicago public schools. She also traveled across the country lecturing for the National Association for the Advancement of Colored People (NAACP) to inspire and mobilize others to work for social justice.

MOBLEY: My burning—the thing that has come out of Emmett's death is to push education to the limit: you must learn all you can. Learn until your head swells. This is what I was able to energize my children with, the desire for learning.

There has been progress without a doubt. We cannot deny that. I see progress within myself and progress for those who will dare reach for it. Sometimes those steps are steep, they're not easy to climb, but as Langston Hughes said, "You have to keep on climbing" (Terkel 1992:22).

Mamie Mobley framed her life in the pursuit of social justice, and her story reveals the factors that can contribute to effective action in that pursuit. First, Mamie Mobley had a vision of justice that emerged from self-valuation, not internalized oppression—"not hugging hate to myself." It was a vision resting on caring, respect, and love for others and fed by spirituality. It was a vision of justice as a collective enterprise of which she was a part, not as a personality characteristic that was hers alone. Second, her vision was based in a deep understanding of the structures of oppression that shaped her life and that of others. Finally, her vision of justice and deep understanding of oppression formed the foundation that motivated and sustained her in social action—to doggedly pursue knowledge and to teach children to do the same—an activist path in which she was joined by many African-American women of her generation (c.f., Gilkes 1994).

Over the last 25 years, I have looked at the lives of people like Mamie Mobley to guide my search for effective ways to promote social justice. Since 1982, when Bonnie Thornton Dill, Elizabeth Higginbotham, and I began our work at the Center for Research on Women at the University of Memphis and into the 1990s, we have wanted to make a difference in the way that women of color and systems of race, class, and gender[1] were conceptualized, produced, and reinforced in higher education. We began almost immediately to host national workshops for faculty in all arenas of higher education to develop our understanding of race, class, and gender for our research and our teaching, so that we could develop a national community of change agents within our institutions to promote social justice. Over those years we worked with large numbers of dedicated people in all kinds of institutions—community colleges, private liberal arts colleges, research universities—to understand what it takes to make an educational experience that promotes social justice. In that dialogue and in the dialogue with our students and our institutions, we learned much about working for justice, including the incorporation of sexuality into our analyses.

We tried to design the process, structure, and curriculum of our workshops to facilitate people's work for progressive social change. The framework that we em-

---

[1]In the early years of our work at the center, we did not incorporate sexuality into our analysis or workshops. Over time, the scholarship and political work of gays, bisexuals, and lesbians increased our awareness of the significance of sexuality in shaping the other dimensions and as a primary system of oppression in American life.

ployed suggests our understanding of what it takes to make change for social justice, and that framework is reiterated in Mamie Mobley's story:

- A *vision,* a dream of a just society—one based in an ethic of caring, respect for others, and love that rings true and powerful enough to move and to motivate not only individuals but communities of people to affirm their self-worth in the face of pervasive devaluation and to choose to struggle together for social change.
- A *deep understanding* of oppression, contextually grounded in time and place, an understanding of the intersections of race, class, gender, and sexuality as socially constructed relationships of power among groups and operating at both the societal and individual levels.
- Strategic *actions*—actions that are motivated by a vision of justice and grounded in a deep understanding of oppression and that are taken in principled group coalitions that understand and respect differences while pursuing common goals.

VISION

What is perhaps clearest in Mamie Mobley's story is that she has a vision of justice, one that sustains her, gives her hope, and motivates her to social action even in the face of pain. What is the vision of social justice that we can glean from activists such as Mamie, who have struggled against injustice their entire lives?

Visions of social justice focus as much on the process of struggle for freedom from oppression as on what some ideal world would look like where honor, equity, and fairness prevail. Justice is more about the way we choose to live our lives every day than it is about what we'll get if we work hard. This emphasis distinguishes it from dominant culture visions such as the American Dream that motivate people to act to achieve the end of economic success and, in their more ruthless versions, valorize economic success no matter what means are used to achieve it. So, for example, a poor person who makes lots of money by becoming a drug dealer can be respected by some people because he or she has achieved economic success against the odds. Or a man like Ross Perot, largely because he has billions of dollars, is held in enough esteem that he was able to start a third political party and wage a viable candidacy for president in 1992. That he paid no taxes for many years and publicly denounced the work of the federal government—even though his own wealth was acquired by selling computer software developed by government researchers—does not tarnish the image because it is the achievement of wealth itself, not how he got it, that is honored in this model.

We are much more apt to wonder why Mamie Mobley continues in her struggle than we are to ask why people continue to pursue economic success. Yet in America, the reality is that although many people pursue vast economic success, most never achieve it. And the pressures in our society to equate money and self-worth also help to reinforce the existing hierarchies of power by devaluing those who do not achieve economic success and valorizing those who do.

But that is clearly not the vision of Mamie Mobley or others seeking social justice. When seeking freedom and self-determination instead of economic success, the means involve caring, respect centered in a deep understanding of differences, and love. Moral authority accrues to the person whose own child is lynched and yet could "raise those children [of her son's killers] as if they were my own and I could have loved them." That kind of moral authority empowers oppressed groups in the struggle for freedom.

The vision is also collective: It has life in the context of communities working together for change. When thinking about the ways in which policy changes in the 1980s made life more difficult for poor people, Mamie Mobley said:

> We can see what's happened to the income tax, the health insurance, and a whole lot of other things. You wonder how these things were allowed to come about. Then you think of dollars and cents, you can see that this is what it's all about: not the love of humanity, but the love of the dollar. *It's just another river we're going to cross* (Terkel 1992:25) (emphasis added).

When she speaks, it is in the plural—"We can see." She is obviously a part of a community that sees these policy changes in the same way. But it is also a community that is acting together for change, and her emphasis is on the process of getting there: She focuses on crossing the river, not on what it looks like on the other side. Perhaps most important for oppressed groups in the struggle for freedom is that the vision contain some hope for positive change. In this, Mamie Mobley's vision is perhaps at its most powerful. Despite the intense difficulty of making change when political, ideological, and economic power rests in the hands of others, she doesn't equivocate: "It's just another river *we're going to cross.*"

UNDERSTANDING/KNOWLEDGE

The real promise of the race, class, gender, and sexuality analysis presented here is that it can deepen our understanding of oppression by opening up new ways of looking at social institutions, raising new questions, and suggesting more effective ways of addressing seemingly intractable systems of social inequality. And just as visions of social justice focus on the path to freedom, what we learn about race, class, gender, and sexuality is determined in large measure by the atmosphere, the context, the environment, and the process through which we learn. For example, in the late 1980s I taught a night class on race, class, and gender at Memphis State University. The composition of the class was typical of the many classes I taught there—about 15 working-class, first-generation college students, two-thirds of whom were women, about one-third African Americans, one or two international students, and the rest White men and women mostly in their 20s and 30s who worked full-time jobs during the day.

About half way through the semester, after the students had gotten to know each other pretty well, Jim[2], a White male student about 25 years old, said:

---

[2]Jim is a pseudonym.

A White man doesn't have a chance anymore. The Blacks and women are getting all the jobs.

In a matter of seconds, the atmosphere in the room went from warm to boiling hot. Several of the students raised up, put their hands on the table. I knew I had to do something fast. I don't know where it came from, but I said to Jim, "Why do you feel that way?" The other students in the room sat back, and Jim looked at me as if I were crazy, as if the answer should have been obvious. He was speechless. So I tried another tack, "What makes you think that is true, where did you get your information?"

Jim then told his story. He said he knew this was true because he worked at Memphis Light, Gas, and Water Division (MLGW), the public utility and one of the largest employers in the city. He had been working there for five years as a meter reader, and he was due to get a promotion to supervisor because "that's the way it usually goes." Then he said, "And they went and hired a Black woman off the street and made her my supervisor." I asked Jim why he thought they had done that. He really didn't know, so he relied on the reverse discrimination arguments so prevalent in public discourse.

But I knew. MLGW was under a court order to hire women and African-American men because it had been successfully sued for discrimination. The settlement required hiring some supervisors and upper-level managers as well as increasing the hiring of women and African Americans at the entry level because the workforce at MLGW was so out of line with the local labor market that simply changing the hiring practices at entry level could not hope to produce a balanced workforce in the foreseeable future.

I asked Jim, "How did it make you feel to lose out on your promotion?" He described in detail how upset he had been, how hard he had worked, how the money was going to contribute to his education. Students in the class were sympathetic with his plight, since they too were working hard to make ends meet while pursuing an education.

We then went back to the question that started us off: "Are Blacks and women getting all the jobs, so White men don't have a chance?" We decided to focus attention on the labor market in Memphis and to get more systematic data. I asked Jim and several other students to gather information about the macro structures of the labor market—where women, African Americans, men, Whites, and other groups were actually employed in Memphis and at MLGW. The data they gathered and our discussions made eminently clear that Jim's impression wasn't true of the city and certainly not of the place he worked. In fact, quite the reverse.

During that class, Jim, the other students, and I developed a deeper understanding of the dynamics of race, class, gender, and sexuality. The understanding we developed was grounded in time and place, not about some abstract category of "the Blacks and women" but about the labor force in Memphis and at MLGW in the late 1980s. We analyzed the power dynamics involved: the power of a group of middle-class White men to maintain control for years over a public utility paying among the highest wages in the city, in the midst of a city whose adults were over 50 percent Black and over 50 percent women. We examined the ideological power of dominant groups to promote the idea that reverse discrimination was a prevalent reality in the presence of a highly race, class, and gender segregated labor market. And we self-consciously reflected on the power that the students— working class, multiracial men and women—collectively took when they investigated the macro systems of inequality in Memphis and grappled with their effects in their individual lives.

My students were able to take that power in part because the class had also developed an atmosphere of respect and trust, a foundation on which to challenge these tough issues. Because oppression has shaped all of our lives, often in harmful ways, and because many forces obscure these systems, seriously interrogating the meaning of race, class, gender, and sexuality—as my class did and as this text asks us to do—may be emotionally upsetting and personally difficult. Facing the ways in which our lives and those of others have been made easier by our privilege or have been harmed by oppression may be difficult. And yet, because our own experiences largely shape what we know and believe about race, class, gender, and sexuality, expanding our knowledge requires that we become clearer about our own social location in these systems and that we remain open to hearing about others' experiences, particularly experiences that are different from our own.

It is especially important when examining our taken-for-granted everyday practices and beliefs connected with these hierarchies that we separate our emotional and intellectual reactions to a person's ideas—which can be quite negative—from our assessment of the person's value or worth as a human being. We can critically assess and vehemently disagree with the ideas, beliefs, and even values of other people without denigrating the people who hold them. Oppressed groups are routinely portrayed in society as different, as less worthy, and as responsible for their devalued status and for their lack of resources and options. In contrast, dominant groups are taken as the invisible norm, the standard, against which we are all asked to judge ourselves. If we are to understand race, class, gender, and sexuality systems, we must be willing to have our stereotypes of subordinate groups challenged and to make the social privilege of dominant groups visible. To do this, we must be open to learning information and ways of thinking that previously may not have been included or validated in our education. We must also be aware that everyone holds stereotypes—we may even have them about our own groups—and that we can challenge and change them. And since all of these dimensions operate in our lives at all times, recognizing the complexity in our own multiple statuses helps us to consider the complexity in the lived experiences of others.

In my teaching, I try to promote a classroom environment that encourages understanding and respect across differences. Jim, other students, and I developed a set of guidelines for classroom discussion that asks us to work to understand what oppression means in people's lives (for a discussion, see Weber 1990; 2000). The guidelines ask us to consider that everyone—both the groups that we study and the people in the class—are always doing the best that they can. In other words, they ask us to assume that everyone and every group does their best to live and to live well and that if they are not living well, are sick or die, just as with the miner's canary, we need to examine the social context in which they are striving, not to blame them for failing to live. When we give each other human respect, learning can take place across the most diverse of groups.

In addition to the classroom, Lani Guinier points out that discussions that move people toward deep understanding can also take place in "intermediate public spaces"—civic associations, churches, and neighborhood associations. In *Lift Every Voice: Turning a Civil Rights Setback into a New Vision of Social Justice,* Guinier (1998) shares the lessons she learned about justice from her life as a civil rights attorney and through the political maelstrom that occurred in 1993 after President Clinton nominated and then withdrew her nomination as Assistant Attorney General for civil rights. She argues that knowledge to promote effective action for social justice is gained in collaborative environments that become safe spaces because differences are respected and trust develops. In these spaces, people can be empowered to solve problems, not just to win arguments.

Guinier contends that these spaces for serious committed conversation should at a minimum involve

- a willingness to include a range of people (as individuals and as members of organized, interested groups such as neighborhood associations and organizations such as the NAACP)
- continued interaction around concrete local challenges, informed by an understanding of the way race links issues of gender, power, and class
- the capacity to deliberate and collaborate again and again because the process of public education, brainstorming, sharing solutions, and experimenting in the field is never totally finished (1998a:310).

And while Guinier was focusing on racial justice, her suggestions are consistent with the kinds of processes envisioned by people working for social justice along different and intersecting dimensions of oppression. For example, in *Community Activism and Feminist Politics: Organizing across Race, Class, and Gender,* Nancy Naples (1998) collected the stories of women community activists working against the abuse of women, against corporate poisoning of their neighborhoods, against homophobia and racism, and for people-centered economic development, immigrants' rights, educational equity, and adequate wages. Naples summarizes the process of change for justice that can be gleaned from the stories of these activists working at the intersections of multiple systems of oppression:

> I remain convinced that progressive social change requires envisioning a "just society" as well as drawing upon contemporary political practices based on participatory democracy, antiracism, and deep understanding of, as well as respect for, our many differences. I believe that women community activists from diverse racial, ethnic, class, and regional backgrounds have much to teach us about achieving such a vision (Naples 1998:346).

From workplaces to neighborhood associations to classrooms, the general contours of a process that generates knowledge that guides effective action for social justice are consistent.

ACTION

Developing a deep understanding of the forces of oppression and acting in the pursuit of social justice are mutually reinforcing parts of the same process. The actions we choose to take in the pursuit of social justice flow from and create the knowledge we have of the forces of oppression around us in specific times and places. The extent to which particular actions will be effective in bringing about a change in the distribution of power in a particular social context will depend on a variety of factors, including the depth of understanding of the forces of oppression, the nature of the coalitions involved, and the strength of the forces of dominance. And as the examples of reform efforts in education suggest, each of these forces is likely to come into play in any effort for social change.

It is by collaborating and cooperating across our differences in respectful environments that meaning accrues and empowerment occurs. This theme appears in the writings of many different groups struggling for change. Awiakta, a Cherokee poet, teaches about justice, wisdom, and native values, through telling the story of the Corn-Mother:

> [T]he Corn-Mother teaches many wisdoms, one of which is cooperation. Just as a single plant cannot bear fruit and it requires a field of corn to bring in a harvest, neither can a person be as strong alone as in connection with one's family and one's people. In developing a new model for American life, each of us alone can do very little. But if we fuse our energies, if we plant together, we can do much. Let us do so. And look for signs of the harvest . . . (1993:166).

The pursuit of social justice gives meaning to people's lives. To derive meaning from the struggle for justice, we don't have to bring about a revolution; we can plant together. By preparing the fields and planting the seeds together, we can live fulfilling lives even as we wait for the harvest.

Appendix: Historical Time Line References

EDUCATION

1896   Jack Salzman, David Lionel Smith, and David West, eds., *Encyclopedia of African American Culture and History,* vol. 4 (New York: Simon & Schuster, 1996), p. 2162.

1944   Victor Bondi, ed., *American Decades: 1940–1949,* vol. 5 (Detroit: Gale Research, 1994), p. 143.

1948   Bondi, *American Decades: 1940–1949,* p. 133.

1954   Jack Salzman, David Lionel Smith, and David West, eds., *Encyclopedia of African American Culture and History,* vol. 2 (New York: Simon & Schuster, 1996), p. 859.

1955   David O'Brien, *Constitutional Law and Politics: Struggles for Power and Government Accountability,* vol. 1 (New York: W.W. Norton, 1997), p. 172.

1964   O'Brien, *Constitutional Law and Politics,* p. 176.

1965   Richard Layman, ed., *American Decades: 1960–1969,* vol. 7 (Detroit: Gale Research, 1994), p. 215.

1966   Layman, *American Decades: 1960–1969,* p. 215.

1968   Layman, *American Decades: 1960–1969,* p. 124.

1969   Judy Galens, Anna J. Sheets, and Robyn V. Young, eds., *Gale Encyclopedia of Multicultural America,* vol. 2 (Detroit: Gale Research, 1995), p. 959.

1970   Layman, *American Decades: 1960–1969,* p. 117.

1971   Victor Bondi, ed., *American Decades: 1970–1979,* vol. 8 (Detroit: Gale Research, 1994), p. 149.

1972   Irene Franck and David Brownstone, *Women's World: A Timeline of Women in History* (New York: HarperCollins, 1995), p. 509; National Women's History Project (NWHP), "A timeline of the women's rights movement, 1848–1998," available from http://www.Legacy98.org/timeline.html, accessed March 19, 2000.

1973   Bondi, *American Decades: 1970–1979,* p. 158.

1975   Bondi, *American Decades: 1970–1979,* p. 158.

1978   NWHP, "A timeline of the women's rights movement, 1848–1998."

—   Bondi, *American Decades: 1970–1979,* p. 166.

1979   Bondi, *American Decades: 1970–1979,* p. 152

1983   National Women's History Project (NWHP), *Living the Legacy: A National Women's History Project Gazette* (Santa Rosa, CA: NWHP, 1998), pp. 13–15.

1988   Franck and Brownstone, *Women's World,* p. 578.

1994   NWHP, "A timeline of the women's rights movement, 1848–1998."

1996   California Secretary of State, "Proposition 209: Prohibition against discrimination or preferential treatment by state and other public entities," available from http://Vote96.ss.ca.gov/Vote96/html/BP/209.htm, accessed March 19, 2000.

—   NWHP, "A timeline of the women's rights movement, 1848–1998."

—   Tarlton Law Library–University of Texas Law School, "Hopwood v. State of Texas Materials," available from http://www.law.utexas.edu/hopwood/hopwood.htm, accessed March 19, 2000.

1997   Ethan Bronner, "Black and Hispanic admissions off sharply at U. of California," *New York Times,* April 1, 1998.

—   Susan Richardson, "Texas educators seek clarification of Hopwood decision: Minority admissions to Texas elite public college in free-fall," *Black Issues in Higher Education* 14, no. 5 (May 1, 1997), pp. 18–22.

—   NWHP, "A timeline of the women's rights movement 1848–1998."

1999   Lynn Weber, e-mail to Suzanne Ozment, Dean of Women Students, The Citadel, February 10, 2000.

—   Tim Simmons and Irwin Speizer, "Busing for balance halted," *Raleigh News and Observer* (North Carolina), September 11, 1999; Irwin Speizer, "Charlotte schools face the future," *Raleigh News and Observer* (North Carolina), November 26, 1999.

—   American Civil Liberties Union, "Utah school discriminated against lesbian high school teacher, court rules," available from http://www.aclu.org/news/n113098a.html, accessed March 19, 2000.

CITIZENSHIP

1778   James Q. Wilson, *American Government: Institutions and Policies* (Lexington, MA: D.C. Heath, 1986), p. 167.

1790   Ronald Takaki, ed., *From Different Shores: Perspective on Race and Ethnicity in America* (New York: Oxford University Press, 1994), p. 26.

1830   Institute for Learning Technologies, "Native American Navigator Project Pages," available from http://www.ilt.columbia.edu/k12/naha/1800s.html, accessed March 19, 2000.

1848   Nicolas Kanellos, ed., *The Hispanic American Almanac: A Reference Work on Hispanics in the United States* (Detroit: Gale Research, 1993), p. 230.

1857   Harold W. Chase, Thomas C. Cochran, Jacob E. Cooke, Robert W. Daly, Wendall Garrett, and Robert P. Multhauf, eds., *Dictionary of American History,* vol. 2 (New York: Scribner, 1976), p. 370; *Encyclopedia of African American Culture and History,* vol. 4, p. 1788.

1866   Franck and Brownstone, *Women's World,* p. 161.

1870   *Encyclopedia of African American Culture and History,* vol. 5 (New York: Simon & Schuster, 1996), p. 2589.

1875   Kathryn Cullen-DuPont, ed., *The Encyclopedia of Women's History in America* (New York: Facts On File, 1996), 77; Franck and Brownstone, *Women's World,* p. 173; Robert J. Dinkin, *Before Equal Suffrage: Women In Partisan Politics from Colonial Times to 1920* (Westport, Conn.: Greenwood Press, 1995).

1882   *Dictionary of American History,* vol. 2, p. 29; Takaki, *From Different Shores,* p. 30.

1887   Institute for Learning Technologies, "Native American Navigator Project Pages"; Britannica Online, "Native American," available from http://www.britannica.com/ bcom/eb/article/0/0,5716,127680+2,00.html, accessed March 20, 2000.

1902   Kanellos, *Hispanic American Almanac,* p. 230.

1920   Sheila Ruth, ed., *Issues in Feminism: An Introduction to Women's Studies* (London: Mayfield, 1990), p. 435.

1924   Kanellos, *Hispanic American Almanac,* p. 232.

—   Judith S. Baughman, ed., *American Decades: 1920–1929,* vol. 3 (Detroit: Gale Research, 1994), p. 234; Britannica Online, "Native American," available from http://www.britannica.com/bcom/eb/article/0/0,5716,127680+3,00.html, accessed March 20, 2000.

1926   Britannica Online, "Eugenics," available from http://www.britannica.com/bcom/ eb/article/5/0,5716,33785+1,00.html, accessed March 19, 2000.

1934   Britannica Online, "Native American."

1942   Wilma P. Mankiller, *Mankiller: A Chief and Her People* (New York: St. Martin's Press, 1993), p. 64; Britannica Online, "Nisei," available from http://www.britannica.com/bcom/eb/article/2/0,5716,57322+1,00.html, accessed March 19, 2000; The Japanese American Network, "A short chronology of Japanese American history," available from http://www.janet.org/janet_history/niiya_chron.html, accessed March 19, 2000.

—   Mankiller, *Mankiller,* p. 63.

1945   Mankiller, *Mankiller,* p. 65.

1948   Galens, Sheets, and Yonng, *Gale Encyclopedia of Multicultural America,* vol. 2, p. 963.

1952   Takaki, *From Different Shores,* p. 26; Kanellos, *The Hispanic American Almanac,* p. 262.

1957   Galens, Sheets, and Yonng, *Gale Encyclopedia of Multicultural America,* vol. 2, p. 963.

1965   Kanellos, *The Hispanic American Almanac,* pp. 232–33.

—   Layman, *American Decades: 1960–1969,* pp. 291–92.

1975   *Encyclopedia of African American Culture and History,* vol. 5, pp. 2753–54; U.S. Code, "Voting Rights Act Amendment (1975)," available from http://www4.law. cornell.edu/uscode/42/1973b.text.html, accessed March 20, 2000; Kanellos, *The Hispanic American Almanac,* p. 236.

1983   Galens, Sheets, and Yonng, *Gale Encyclopedia of Multicultural America,* vol. 2, p. 917.

1985   NWHP, "A timeline of the women's rights movement 1848–1998."

1988   The Japanese American Network, "A short chronology of Japanese American history," Britannica Online, "Nisei."

1990   Kanellos, *The Hispanic American Almanac,* p. 233.

1992   Nicolas Kanellos, *Hispanic Firsts: 500 Years of Extraordinary Achievement* (Detroit: Gale Research, 1997), p. 131.

GOVERNMENT OFFICES

1822   Kanellos, *The Hispanic American Almanac,* p. 257.

1870   Joseph Nathan Kane, *Famous First Facts* (New York: H.W. Wilson, 1981), p. 543, 569.

1892	Sharon Malinowski, *Notable Native Americans* (New York: Gale Research, 1995), pp. 105–07.
1917	Ruth, *Issues in Feminism*, p. 435.
1958	Susan Gall and Irene Natividad, eds., *The Asian American Almanac: A Reference Work on Asians in the United States* (Detroit: Gale Research, 1993), p. 650.
1969	Ruth, *Issues in Feminism*, p. 438.
1970	NWHP, *Living the Legacy*, p. 13.
1974	NWHP, "A timeline of the women's rights movement, 1848–1998."
1976	Gall and Natividad, *Asian American Almanac*, pp. 617–18.
1981	NWHP, "A timeline of the women's rights movement, 1848–1998."
1986	Malinowski, *Notable Native Americans*, pp. 64–65.
—	NWHP, A timeline of the women's rights movement, 1848–1998."
1988	"Our Brightest and Best Advocates," *The Advocate*, available from http://www.advocate.com/html/stories/792/792 frank.html, accessed March 20, 2000; U.S. House of Representatives "Congressman Barney Frank," available from http://www.house.gov/frank/, accessed March 20, 2000.
1989	U.S. House of Representatives, "Representative Ileana Ros-Lehtinen," available from http://www.house.gov/ros-lehtinen/, accessed March 20, 2000.
1992	Gall and Natividad, *Asian American Almanac*, p. 655; U.S. House of Representatives "Congresswoman Lucille Roybal-Allard," available from http://www.house.gov/roybal-allard, accessed March 20, 2000; United States Senate, "Senator Ben Nighthorse Campbell," available from www.senate.gov/~campbell/bio.htm, accessed March 20, 2000. U.S. House of Representatives "Congresswoman Nydia M. Velázquez," available from http://www.house.gov/velazquez, accessed March 20, 2000; NWHP, "A timeline of the women's rights movement, 1848–1998."
1997	Gale Group, "Madeleine Korbel Albright," available from http://www.gale.com/freresrc/womenhst/albrighm.htm, accessed March 20, 2000.
1998	Tammy Baldwin for Congress, "About Tammy," available from http://www.tammy baldwin.com/about/index.html, accessed October 4, 2000.
1999	CIS Congressional Universe 2000, "Member Profile Reports," available from Congressional Universe (Online Service), Bethesda, MD: Congressional Information Service.
2000	Center for American Women and Politics, "Women in State Legislatures 2000," available from http://www.cawp.rutgers.edu/pdf/stleg.pdf, accessed March 20, 2000.

MILITARY

1792	Salzman, Smith, and West, *Encyclopedia of African American Culture and History*, vol. 4, p. 1787.
1812	Salzman, Smith, and West, *Encyclopedia of African American Culture and History*, vol. 4, p. 1788.
1917	Vincent Tompkins, *American Decades: 1910–1919*, vol. 2 (Detroit: Gale Research, 1994), p. 259.
1948	Salzman, Smith, and West, *Encyclopedia of African American Culture and History*, vol. 4, p. 1793.
—	Franck and Brownstone, *Women's World*, p. 423.
1973	NWHP, "A timeline of the women's rights movement, 1848–1998."
1976	NWHP, "A timeline of the women's rights movement, 1848–1998."

1980   Ruth, *Issues in Feminism*, p. 442.

1991   American Women in Uniform, "Operations Desert Shield / Desert Storm," available from http://userpages.aug.com/captbarb/femvetsds.html, accessed March 20, 2000.

1993   U.S. Coast Guard, "Coast Guard Spars," available from http://www.uscg.mil/reserve/magazine/mag1997/nov1997/spars.html, accessed March 20, 2000; RAND, "New opportunities for military women: effects upon readiness, cohesion and morale," available from http://www.rand.org/publications/MR/MR896/, accessed March 20, 2000.

1994   Service Members Legal Defense Network, "The 'don't ask, don't tell' policy," available from http://www.sldn.org/scripts/sldn.ixe?page=article 0003, accessed March 20, 2000.

1999   Women's Research & Education Institute, "Women in the military project," available from http://www.wrei.org/military/tab7-1.pdf, accessed March 20, 2000.

—   Stacey L. Sobel, et al., "Conduct unbecoming: The sixth annual report on 'don't ask, don't tell, don't pursue.' " available from http://www.sldn.org/reports/sixth.htm, accessed March 20, 2000; Office of the Under Secretary of Defense, "Review of the effectiveness of the application and enforcement of the department's policy on homosexual conduct in the military," available from http://www.defenselink.mil/pubs/rpt040798.html, accessed March 20, 2000.

WORK/ECONOMY

1848   Cullen-DuPont, *Encyclopedia of Women's History in America,* pp. 125–26; Ruth, *Issues in Feminism,* p. 433.

1904   Vincent Tompkins, *American Decades: 1910–1919,* vol. 2. (Detroit: Gale Research, 1994), p. 87.

1910   Tompkins, *American Decades: 1910–1919,* p. 267.

1933   Victor Bondi, ed., *American Decades: 1930–1939,* vol. 4 (Detroit: Gale Research, 1994), p. 93.

1935   Bondi, *American Decades: 1930–1939,* p. 229.

—   Britannica Online, "Works Progress Administration," available from http://www.britannica.com/bcom/eb/article/9/0,5716,79559+1,00.html, accessed March 20, 2000.

1938   Bondi, *American Decades: 1930–1939,* p. 96; Tompkins, *American Decades 1910–1919,* p. 269.

1939   Bondi, *American Decades: 1930–1939,* p. 96.

1941   Bondi, *American Decades: 1940–1949,* p. 95; Worldbook, "A. Philip Randolph," available from http://www.worldbook.com/fun/aajourny/html/bh073.html, accessed July 19, 2000.

1947   Rick Fantasia, *Cultures of Solidarity: Consciousness, Action, and Contemporary American Workers.* (Berkeley: University of California Press, 1988).

1962   Ruth, *Issues in Feminism,* p. 436.

1963   Cullen-DuPont, *Encyclopedia of Women's History in America,* p. 65; Franck and Brownstone, *Women's World,* p. 475.

1964   Cullen-DuPont, *Encyclopedia of Women's History in America,* p. 37; Franck and Brownstone, *Women's World,* p. 478; NWHP, "A timeline of the women's rights movement, 1848–1898."

1968   Fair Housing Act, *Statutes at Large* 82, sec. 804–805 (1968); Ruth, *Issues in Feminism,* p. 440.

1969   Donald L. Barlett and James B. Steele, *America: Who Really Pays the Taxes?* (New York: Simon and Schuster, 1994), p. 44.

1970   Bondi, *American Decades: 1970–1979,* p. 132.

1972   Cullen-DuPont, *Encyclopedia of Women's History in America,* p. 65; Franck and Brownstone, *Women's World,* p. 475.

—   Deb Price, "Gays make state-by-state progress" *Detroit News,* January 10, 2000.

1974   NWHP, "A timeline of the women's rights movement, 1848–1998"; Ruth, *Issues in Feminism,* p. 440.

1975   U.S. Census Bureau, "Historical income tables—People," available from http://www.census.gov/hhes/income/histinc/incperdet.html, accessed March 20, 2000.

1986   NWHP, "A timeline of the women's rights movement, 1848–1998."

1988   *Encyclopedia of American History,* (New York: HarperCollins, 1996), p. 545.

—   Fair Housing Amendments Act of 1988, *Statutes at Large* 102, sec. 5 (1988); Ruth, *Issues in Feminism,* p. 440.

1994   *Encyclopedia of American History,* p. 545.

1995   U.S. Census Bureau, "Historical income tables—People."

1996   State of California Department of Consumer Affairs, "Implementing the Federal Personal Responsibility and Work Opportunity Reconciliation Act," available from http://www.dca.ca.gov/legal/wor_act.htm, accessed March 20, 2000; State of West Virginia, "Executive summary," available from http://www.legis.state.wv.us/joint/perd/workssum1.html, accessed March 20, 2000.

MARRIAGE/REPRODUCTION

1873   Cullen-DuPont, *Encyclopedia of Women's History in America,* p. 41; NWHP, "A timeline of the women's rights movement, 1848–1998."

1921   Cullen-DuPont, *Encyclopedia of Women's History in America,* p. 43; Britannica Online, "Margaret Sanger," available from http://www.britannica.com/bcom/eb/article/7/0,5716,67197+1,00.html, accessed March 20, 2000.

1922   Franklin Ng, ed., *The Asian American Encyclopedia,* (New York: Marshall Cavendish, 1995), p. 156.

1931   Ruth, *Issues in Feminism,* p. 436.

1936   Ng, *Asian American Encyclopedia,* p. 156.

1965   Franck and Brownstone, *Women's World,* p. 482.

1966   Angela Evans, "What's color got to do with it?" available from http://cctr.umkc.edu/wicc/Inter1.html, accessed March 20, 2000.

1967   FindLaw, "U.S. Supreme Court Loving v. Virginia," available from http://laws.findlaw.com/US/388/1.html, accessed March 20, 2000.

1972   Cullen-DuPont, *Encyclopedia of Women's History in America,* p. 43.

1973   NWHP, "A timeline of the women's rights movement, 1848–1998"; Ruth, *Issues in Feminism,* p. 440.

1977   NWHP, "A timeline of the women's rights movement, 1848–1998."

1978   Franck and Brownstone, *Women's World,* p. 539; NWHP, "A timeline of the women's rights movement, 1848–1998."

1981   Britannica Online, "AIDS," available from http://www.britannica.com, accessed March 20, 2000.

1987   AEGIS, "So little time: An AIDS history," available from http://www.aegis.com, accessed March 20, 2000.

1988   AEGIS, "So little time: An AIDS history."

1990   Yggdrasil, "Statistics on interracial marriage," available from http://www.ddc.net/ygg/ms/ms-05.htm, accessed March 20, 2000.

—   Franck and Brownstone, *Women's World,* p. 583.

1992   Franck and Brownstone, *Women's World,* p. 590; Rock For Choice: A Project of the Feminist Majority and the Feminist Majority Foundation, "History of Abortion Rights in the U.S.: January 22, 1973 to Present," available from http://www.feminist.org./rock4c/book/hist.html, accessed March 20, 2000.

1993   Franck and Brownstone, *Women's World,* p. 595; NWHP, "A timeline of the women's rights movement, 1848–1998."

—   NWHP, "A timeline of the women's rights movement, 1848–1998."

1994   Rock for Choice, "History of Abortion Rights."

1996   American Civil Liberties Union (ACLU), "Gay marriage: Should lesbian and gay couples be allowed to marry?" available from http://www.aclu.org/library/aagay marriage.html, accessed March 20, 2000.

—   ACLU, "ACLU blasts senate passage of anti-gay marriage ban; Calls vote a 'deplorable act' and vows legal challenge," available from http://www.aclu.org/news/n091096a.html, accessed March 20, 2000.

1998   ACLU, "ACLU vows to continue fight as Hawaii, Alaska voters rejects same-sex marriage," available from www.aclu.org/news/n110498a.html, accessed March 20, 2000.

1999   Human Rights Campaign, "States denying equal marriage rights to lesbian and gay Americans," available from http://www.hrc.org/issues/marriage/marstate.html, accessed March 20, 2000.

—   National Freedom to Marry Coalition, "Baker v. State," available from http://www.qrd.org/usa/vermont/baker-v-state, accessed March 20, 2000.

—   National Abortion and Reproductive Rights Action League, "Analysis of key findings: Women's rights at risk," available from http://www.naral.org/media resources/publications/2000/2000_analysis.html, accessed October 4, 2000.

—   Britannica Online, "AIDS"; UNAIDS, "AIDS Epidemic Update: December 1999," available from http://www.unaids.org/publications/documents/epidemiology/index.html, accessed March 20, 2000.

2000   Carey Goldberg, "Vermont's house backs wide rights for gay couples," *New York Times,* March 17, 2000.

—   National Abortion and Reproductive Rights Action League, "Who decides? A state-by-state review of abortion and reproductive rights," available from http://www.naral.org/mediaresources/publications/2000/charts_report.html, accessed March 20, 2000.

References

Abramovitz, Mimi. 1996. *Under Attack, Fighting Back: Women and Welfare in the United States.* New York: Monthly Review Press.

Alexander, Karl; Doris Entwisle; and Maxine Thompson. 1987. "School performance, status relations, and the structure of sentiment: Bringing the teacher back in." *American Sociological Review* 52(October): 665–82.

Almaguer, Tomás. 1993. "Chicano men: A cartography of homosexual identity and behavior." In *The Lesbian and Gay Studies Reader.* Henry Abelove, Michèle Aina Barale, and David M. Halperin, eds., New York: Routledge.

American Association of University Women (AAUW). 1991, 1994. *Shortchanging Girls, Shortchanging America: Executive Summary.* Washington, DC: American Association of University Women Educational Foundation.

———. 1992. *How Schools Shortchange Girls: The AAUW Report: A Study of Major Findings on Girls and Education.* Washington, DC: American Association of University Women Educational Foundation.

———. 1999. *Gender Gaps: Where Our Schools Still Fail Our Children.* New York: Marlowe & Co.

Amott, Teresa, and Julie Matthaei. 1996. *Race, Gender, and Work: A Multi-Cultural Economic History of Women in the United States.* Rev. ed. Boston: South End Press.

Anyon, Jean. 1980. "Social class and the hidden curriculum of work." *Journal of Education* 162: 67–92.

———. 1997. *Ghetto Schooling: A Political Economy of Urban Educational Reform.* New York: Teachers College Press, Columbia University.

Anzaldua, Gloria. 1987a. *Borderlands/La Frontera: The New Mestiza.* San Francisco: AuntLute Books.

———, ed. 1987b. *Making Faces, Making Soul/Haciendo Caras: Creative and Critical Perspectives by Women of Color.* San Francisco: AuntLute Books.

Appell, Annette. 1998. "On fixing 'bad' mothers and saving their children." In *Bad Mothers: The Politics of Blame in Twentieth-Century America.* Molly Ladd-Taylor and Lauri Umansky, eds. New York: New York University Press.

Awiakta, Marilou. 1993. *Selu: Seeking the Corn-Mother's Wisdom.* Golden, CO: Fulcrum.

Baca Zinn, Maxine; Lynn Weber Cannon; Elizabeth Higginbotham; and Bonnie Thornton Dill. 1986. "The costs of exclusionary practices in women's studies." *SIGNS: Journal of Women in Culture and Society* 11 (Winter): 290–303.

Baca Zinn, Maxine, and Bonnie Thornton Dill, eds. 1994. *Women of Color in U.S. Society.* Philadelphia: Temple University Press.

———. 1996. "Theorizing difference from multiracial feminism." *Feminist Studies* 22(2): 321–31.

Badgett, M. V. Lee. 1995. "The wage effects of sexual orientation discrimination." *Industrial and Labor Relations Review* 48(4):726–39.

Baker, Therese, and William Velez. 1996. "Access to and opportunity in postsecondary education in the United States: A review." *Sociology of Education* [*Extra Issue*]: 82–101.

Barlett, Donald, and James Steele. 1994. *America: Who Really Pays the Taxes?* New York: Touchstone.

Benkov, Laura. 1994. *Reinventing the Family: The Emerging Story of Lesbian and Gay Parents.* New York: Crown.

Blank, R.K., Dentler, R.A., Baltzell, C.E., & Chabotar, K. (1983). *Survey of magnet schools: Analyzing a model for quality integrated education.* Final Report of a National Study for the U.S. Department of Education, No. 300-81-0420. Chicago, IL: Lowry Associates. (ERIC Document Reproduction Service No. ED 236–304)

Blasius, Mark, and Shane Phelan. 1997. *We Are Everywhere: A Historical Sourcebook of Gay and Lesbian Politics.* New York: Routledge.

Blee, Kathleen. 1991. *Women of the Klan: Racism and Gender in the 1920s.* Berkeley: University of California Press.

———, ed. 1998. *No Middle Ground: Women and Radical Protest.* New York: New York University Press.

Bloom, Allan. 1988. *The Closing of the American Mind.* New York: Touchstone Books.

Bookman, Ann, and Sandra Morgen, eds. 1988. *Women and the Politics of Empowerment: Perspectives from the Workplace and the Community.* Philadelphia: Temple University Press.

Boozer, Michael; Alan Krueger; and Shari Wolkon. 1992. "Race and school quality since Brown v. Board of Education." *Brookings Papers on Economic Activity: Microeconomics:* 269–338.

Brantlinger, Ellen A. 1993. *The Politics of Social Class in Secondary School: Views of Affluent and Impoverished Youth.* New York: Teachers College Press, Columbia University.

Brod, Harry, and Michael Kaufman, eds. 1994. *Theorizing Masculinities.* Thousand Oaks, CA: Sage.

Brown, David. 1995. *Degrees of Control: A Sociology of Educational Expansion and Occupational Credentialism.* New York: Teachers College Press, Columbia University.

Bruner, Jim. 2000. "ACLU slams city, police in WTO report; Officials accused of overreacting." *The Seattle Times.* July 5.

Burkett, Elinor. 1998. "Don't tread on my tax rate." *New York Times Magazine,* April 26:42.

Button, James W.; Barbara A. Rienzo; and Kenneth Wald. 1997. *Private Lives, Public Conflicts: Battles over Gay Rights in American Communities.* Washington, DC: Congressional Quarterly.

Carlson, Dennis. 1997. *Making Progress: Education and Culture in New Times.* New York: Teachers College Press, Columbia University.

Carrier, Paul. 1999. "Education panel OKs state-aid formula," *Portland Press Herald.* May 6.

Centers for Disease Control and Prevention. "United States suicide deaths and rates per 100,000: 1997." Available from http://webapp.cdc.gov/sasweb/ncipc/mortrate.html, accessed March 20, 2000.

Chaney, Bradford, and Elizabeth Farris. 1991. *Survey on Retention at Higher Education Institutions.* Rockville, MD: Westat, Inc. Washington DC: U.S. Department of Education, Office of Educational Research and Improvement, Educational Resources Information Center.

Chesler, Phyllis. 1986. *Mothers on Trial: The Battle for Children and Custody.* New York: McGraw-Hill.

Chiswick, Barry R, and Teresa Sullivan. 1995. "The new immigrants." In *State of the Union: America in the 1990s.* Volume Two. *Social Trends.* Reynolds Farley, ed. New York: Russell Sage Foundation

Chow, Esther Ngan-Ling. 1994. "Asian American women at work." In *Women of Color in U.S. Society.* Maxine Baca Zinn and Bonnie Thornton Dill, eds. Philadelphia: Temple University Press.

Chronicle of Higher Education. Almanac Issue. "The Nation," September 2, 1996:14.

Ciscel, David. 1999. "What is a living wage for Memphis?" Research paper. Center for Research on Women, University of Memphis.

CIS Congressional Universe. 2000. Member Profile Reports. Congressional Universe. Bethesda, MD: Congressional Information Service. Online Service.

Clark, Terry N., and Seymour M. Lipset. 1991. "Are social classes dying?" *International Sociology* 6 (4):397–410.

Cloud, John. 1997. "Out, proud, and very young." *Time,* December 8.

Collins, Patricia Hill. 1991a. *Black Feminist Thought: Knowledge, Consciousness and the Politics of Empowerment.* New York: Routledge.

———. 1991b. "Learning from the outsider within: The sociological significance of black feminist thought." In *Beyond Methodology: Feminist Scholarship as Lived Research.* Mary Margaret Fonow and Judith A. Cook, eds. Bloomington: Indiana University Press.

———. 1998. *Fighting Words: Black Women and the Search for Justice.* Minneapolis: University of Minnesota Press.

Collins, Sharon. 1983. "The making of the black middle class." *Social Problems* 30 (April):369–82.

Comas-Diaz, Lillian, and Beverly Greene. 1994. *Women of Color: Integrating Ethnic and Gender Identities in Psychotherapy.* New York: Guilford.

Concerned Women for America (CWA). 1995–1996. Miscellaneous correspondence in Susan Marshall's possession.

Conlin, Michelle; Carleen Hawn; Peter Newcomb; and Daniel Roth. 1997. "The global power Elite." *Forbes,* July 28:134–38.

Connell, R. W. 1987. *Gender and Power: Society, the Person, and Sexual Politics.* Stanford, CA: Stanford University Press.

———. 1995. *Masculinities.* Berkeley: University of California Press.

Cook, Timothy. 1999. "The empirical study of lesbian, gay, and bisexual politics: Assessing the first wave of research." *American Political Science Review* 93(3):679–92.

Coontz, Stephanie. 1992. *The Way We Never Were: American Families and the Nostalgia Trap.* New York: Basic Books.

Crosby, Faye, and Fletcher A. Blanchard, eds. 1989. *Affirmative Action in Perspective.* New York: Springer.

Crow Dog, Mary, and Richard Erdoes. 1996. "Civilize them with a stick: Education as an institution for social control." In *Mapping the Social Landscape: Readings in Sociology.* Susan J. Ferguson, ed. Mountain View, CA: Mayfield.

Dawkins, Marvin P., and Jomills Henry Braddock, II. 1994. "The continuing significance of desegregation: School racial composition and African American inclusion in American society." *Journal of Negro Education* 63:394–405.

D'Emilio, John. 1983. *Sexual Politics, Sexual Communities: The Making of a Homosexual Minority in the United States, 1940–1970.* Chicago: University of Chicago Press.

———. 1993. "Capitalism and gay identity." In *The Lesbian and Gay Studies Reader.* Henry Abelove, Michele Barale, and David M. Halperin, eds. New York: Routledge.

D'Emilio, John, and Estelle Freedman. 1988. *Intimate Matters: A History of Sexuality in America.* New York: Harper and Row.

Degler, C. N. 1971. *Neither Black nor White: Slavery and Race Relations in Brazil and the United States.* New York: Macmillan.

DeParle, Jason. 1998. "What welfare-to-work really means." *New York Times Magazine,* December 20.

DeVault, Marjorie L. 1991. *Feeding the Family: The Social Organization of Caring as Gendered Work.* Chicago: University of Chicago Press.

Dill, Bonnie Thornton. 1979. "The dialectics of black womanhood." *SIGNS: Journal of Women in Culture and Society* 4:543–55.

———. 1983. "Race, class and gender: Prospects for an all-inclusive sisterhood." *Feminist Studies* 9 (Spring):131–50.

———. 1988. "Our mother's grief: Racial ethnic women and the maintenance of families." *Journal of Family History* 13(4):415–31.

Dolan, Kerry, ed. 1999. "200 global billionaires." *Forbes,* July 5:153–228.

Dougherty, Kevin. 1996. "Opportunity-to-learn standards: A sociological critique." *Sociology of Education [Extra Issue]:*40–65.

D'Souza, Dinesh. 1991. *Illiberal Education: The Politics of Race and Sex on Campus.* New York: Free Press.

Duberman, Martin; Martha Vicinus; and George Chauncey, Jr., eds. 1989. *Hidden from History: Reclaiming the Gay and Lesbian Past.* New York: New American Library.

Duncan, Greg. 1984. *Years of Poverty, Years of Plenty: The Changing Economic Fortunes of American Workers and Families.* Ann Arbor: Survey Reasearch Center, Institute for Social Research, University of Michigan.

Edin, Kathryn, and Laura Lein. 1997. *Making Ends Meet: How Single Mothers Survive Welfare and Low-Wage Work.* New York: Russell Sage Foundation.

Ehrenreich, Barbara. 1999. "Nickel-and-dimed: On (not) getting by in America." *Harpers Magazine,* January: 37–52.

Enloe, Cynthia. 1997. "The globetrotting sneaker." In *Women's Lives: Multicultural Perspective.* Gwyn Kirk and Margo Okazawa-Rey, eds. Mountain View, CA: Mayfield.

Entwisle, Doris R.; Karl L. Alexander; and Linda Steffel Olson. 1997. *Children, Schools, and Inequality.* Boulder, CO: Westview Press.

Family Voice. 1994. "The mainstreaming of homosexuality." May 4–15.

—1995. "Boston youth parade a first in homosexual pride." July 26–27.

Farley, Reynolds. 1996. *The New American Reality: Who We Are, How We Got Here, Where We Are Going.* New York: Russell Sage Foundation.

Feagin, Joe R., and Melvin Sykes. 1994. *Living with Racism: The Black Middle–Class Experience.* Boston: Beacon Press.

Feagin, Joe R., and Hernan Vera. 1995. *White Racism: The Basics.* New York: Routledge.

Feinberg, Leslie. 1996. *Transgender Warriors: Making History from Joan of Arc to Dennis Rodman.* Boston: Beacon Press.

Ferree, Myra Marx, and Elaine J. Hall. 1990. "Visual images of American society: Gender and race in introductory sociology textbooks." *Gender and Society* 4(4):500–33.

Fields, Barbara. 1990. "Slavery, race, and ideology in the United States of America." *New Left Review* (181):95–118.

"Figures show state drop out problem bigger than educators say." *The State* (Columbia, SC). February 28, 1999.

Frankenberg, Ruth. 1993. *White Women, Race Matters: The Social Construction of Whiteness.* Minneapolis: University of Minnesota Press.

Freeman, Richard, ed. 1994. *Working Under Different Rules.* New York: Russell Sage Foundation.

Garnets, Linda, and Douglas Kimmel. 1991. "Lesbian and gay male dimensions in the psychological study of human diversity." In *Psychological Perspectives on Human Diversity in America.* J. Goodchilds, ed. Washington, DC: American Psychological Asociation.

Gay, Lesbian and Straight Education Network (GLSEN). Available from http://www.glsen.org, accessed March 19, 2000.

Gaylin, Willard. 1992. *The Male Ego.* New York: Viking.

Gibson, P. 1989. Gay Male and Lesbian Youth Suicide. U.S. Department of Health and Human Services. *Report of the Secretary's Task Force on Youth Suicide.* Rockville, MD.

Gilkes, Cheryl. 1994. " 'If it wasn't for the women . . . .': African American women, community work, and social change." In *Women of Color in U.S. Society.* Maxine Baca Zinn and Bonnie Thornton Dill, eds. Philadelphia: Temple University Press.

Gilligan, Carol; Nona Lyons; and Trudy Hanmer, eds. 1990. *Making Connections: The Relational Worlds of Adolescent Girls at Emma Willard School.* Cambridge: Harvard University Press.

Giuffre, Patti A., and Christine L. Williams. 1994. "Boundary lines: Labeling sexual harassment in restaurants." *Gender and Society* 8(3):378–401.

Glenn, Evelyn Nakano. 1992. "From servitude to service work: Historical continuities in the racial division of paid reproductive labor." *Signs* 18 (Autumn):1–43.

Goings, Ken. 1994. *Mammy and Uncle Mose: Black Collectibles and American Stereotyping.* Bloomington: Indiana University Press.

Gramsci, Antonio. 1971. *Selections from the Prison Notebooks.* New York: International.

Granfield, Robert, and Thomas Koenig. 1992. "Pathways into elite law firms: Professional stratification and social networks." *Research in Politics and Society* 4:325–51.

Grant, Linda. 1994. "Helpers, enforcers, and go-betweens: Black females in elementary school classrooms." In *Women of Color in U.S. Society.* Maxine Baca Zinn and Bonnie Thornton Dill, eds. Philadelphia: Temple University Press.

Greene, Maxine. 1978. *Landscapes of Learning.* New York: Teachers College Press.

Griscom, Joan L. 1992. "Women and power: Definition, dualism, and difference." *Psychology of Women Quarterly* 16(4):389–414.

Guinier, Lani. 1998a. *Lift Every Voice: Turning a Civil Rights Setback into a New Vision of Social Justice.* New York: Simon & Schuster.

———. 1998b. "Reframing the affirmative action debate." Speech, University of South Carolina, February 26.

Guinier, Lani; Michelle Fine; and Jane Balin. 1997. *Becoming Gentlemen: Women, Law School, and Institutional Change.* Boston: Beacon Press.

Hacker, Andrew. 1997. *Money: Who Has How Much and Why.* New York: Scribner.

Hallinan, Maureen. 1996. "Tracking and detracking practices." In *Transforming Schools.* Peter Cookson and Barbara Schneider, eds. New York: Garland.

Harrison, Roderick, and Claudette Bennett. 1995. "Racial and ethnic diversity." In *State of the Union in the 1990s,* Volume Two: *Social Trends.* Reynolds Farley, ed. New York: Russell Sage Foundation.

Hartmann, Heidi. 1997. "The unhappy marriage of Marxism and feminism." In *The Second Wave: A Reader in Feminist Theory.* Linda Nicholson, ed. New York: Routledge.

Harvard Law Review, eds. 1990. *Sexual Orientation and the Law.* Cambridge: Harvard University Press.

Herek, Gregory. 1987. "On heterosexual masculinity." In *Changing Men: New Directions in Research on Men and Masculinity.* Michael Kimmel, ed. Newbury Park, CA: Sage.

Herman, Judith. 1992. *Trauma and Recovery: The Aftermath of Violence from Domestic Abuse to Political Terror.* New York: Basic Books.

Herrnstein, Richard J., and Charles A. Murray. 1994. *The Bell Curve: Intelligence and Class Structure in American Life.* New York: Free Press.

Higginbotham, Elizabeth. 1994. "Black professional women: Job ceilings and employment sectors." In *Women of Color in U.S. Society,* Maxine Baca Zinn and Bonnie Thornton Dill, eds. Philadelphia: Temple University Press.

Higginbotham, Elizabeth, and Lynn Weber. 1992. "Moving up with kin and community: Upward social mobility for black and white women," *Gender & Society* 6 (September):416–40.

Hochschild, Jennifer. 1995. *Facing Up to the American Dream: Race, Class, and the Soul of the Nation.* Princeton, NJ: Princeton University Press.

Hogan, Dennis P., and Daniel T. Lichter. 1995. "Children and youth: Living arrangements and welfare." In *State of the Union: America in the 1990s.* Volume Two. *Social Trends.* Reynolds Farley, ed. New York: Russell Sage Foundation.

Holland, Dorothy, and Margaret Eisenhart. 1990. *Educated in Romance: Women, Achievement, and College Culture.* Chicago: University of Chicago Press.

hooks, bell. 1981. *Ain't I a Woman.* Boston: South End Press.

Hughes, Langston. 2000. "Dream Variations." In *The Compact Bedford Introduction to Literature: Reading, Thinking, Writing.* Meyer, Michael, ed. Boston: Bedford/St. Martins.

Hull, Gloria; Patricia Bell Scott; and Barbara Smith, eds. 1982. *All the Women Are White, All the Blacks Are Men, But Some of Us Are Brave: Black Women's Studies.* Old Westbury, NY: Feminist Press.

Humphries, Ann C. 2000. "Business etiquette column." *The State* (Columbia, SC). July 3.

Jackson, Shirley. 1998. "Something about the word: African American women and feminism." In *No Middle Ground: Women and Radical Protest.* Kathleen Blee, ed. New York: New York University Press.

Jones, James; Beth Vanfossen; and Margaret Ensminger. 1995. "Individual and organizational predictors of high school track placement." *Sociology of Education* 68(October):287–300.

Katznelson, Ira, and Margaret Weir. 1985. *Schooling for All: Class, Race, and the Decline of the Democratic Ideal.* New York: Basic Books.

Kaufman, Michael. 1994. "Men, feminism, and men's contradictory experiences of power." In *Theorizing Masculinities.* Harry Brod and Michael Kaufman, eds. Thousand Oaks, CA: Sage Publications.

Kennickell, Arthur B.; Martha Starr-McCluer; and Brian J. Surette. 2000. "Recent changes in U.S. family finances: Results from the 1998 survey of consumer finances." Federal Reserve Board. *Federal Reserve Bulletin,* January.

Kerckhoff, Alan. 1995. "Institutional arrangements and stratification processes in industrial societies." *Annual Review of Sociology* 21:323–47.

Kershaw, Sarah. 1996. *New York Times.* January 22:A10.

King, James. 1981. *The Biology of Race.* Berkeley: University of California Press.

Kirkpatrick, Christopher. 2000. "Lawmaker strives for respect in schools." *The Herald-Sun* (Durham, NC). May 10.

Kotlowitz, Alex. 1991. *There Are No Children Here.* New York: Doubleday.

Kozol, Jonathan. 1991. *Savage Inequalities: Children in America's Schools.* New York: Crown.

Ladner, Joyce. 1972. *Tomorrow's Tomorrow.* Garden City, New York: Doubleday.

Larabee, David. 1995. Foreward to *Degrees of Control: A Sociology of Educational Expansion and Occupational Credentialism,* by David Brown. New York: Teachers College Press, Columbia University.

Lambda Legal Defense and Education Fund. 2000. *Cases: Nabozny v. Podlesny.* Available online at http://lambdalegal.org/cgi-bin/pages/cases/record?record=54, accessed March 20, 2000.

LaVeist, Thomas A. 1992. "The political empowerment and health status of African-Americans: Mapping a new territory." *American Journal of Sociology* 97(January):1080–95.

Leibowitz, Fran. 1997. "Fran Leibowitz on race." *Vanity Fair,* October:220–23.

Lerner, Gerda. 1976. "Placing women in history: A 1975 perspective." In *Liberating Women's History: Theoretical and Critical Essays.* Bernice Caroll, ed. Urbana: University of Illinois Press.

Lorber, Judith. 1994. *Paradoxes of Gender.* New Haven: Yale University Press.

Lovell, Peggy A. 1994. "Race, gender, and development in Brazil." *Latin American Research Review* 29(3):7–36.

Lucal, Betsy. 1994. "Class stratification in introductory textbooks: Relational or distributional models?" *Teaching Sociology* 22(April):139–50.

———. 1996. "Oppression and Privilege: Toward a Relational Conceptualization of Race." *Teaching Sociology* 24 (July):245–55.

Maccoby, Eleanor. 1988. "Gender as a social category." *Developmental Psychology* 24:755–65.

Manalansan, Martin IV. 1995. "In the shadows of Stonewall: Examining gay transnational politics and the diasporic dilemma." *Gay and Lesbian Quarterly* 2:425–38.

Margolis, Eric, and Mary Romero. 1998. " 'The department is very male, very white, very old, and very conservative': The functioning of the hidden curriculum in graduate sociology departments." *Harvard Educational Review* 68(1):1–32.

Marshall, Susan. 1998. "Rattle on the right: Bridge labor in antifeminist organizations." In *No Middle Ground: Women and Radical Protest.* Kathleen Blee, ed. New York: New York University Press.

Massey, Douglas, and Nancy Denton. 1993. *American Apartheid: Segregation and the Making of the Underclass.* Cambridge: Harvard University Press.

McCarthy, Cameron, and Michael W. Apple. 1988. "Race, class, and gender in American educational research: Toward a nonsynchronous parallelist position." *Class, Race, and Gender in American Education.* Lois Weis, ed. Albany: State University of New York Press.

McGuire, Gail M., and Barbara Reskin. 1993. "Authority hierarchies at work: The impacts of race and sex." *Gender and Society* 7:487–506.

McIntosh, Peggy. 1998. "White privilege and male privilege: A personal account of coming to see correspondences through work in women's studies." In *Race, Class, and Gender: An Anthology.* 3rd ed. Margaret Andersen and Patricia Hill Collins, eds. Belmont, CA: Wadsworth.

Meier, Kenneth J.; Joseph Stewart, Jr.; and Robert England. 1989. *Race, Class, and Education: The Politics of Second-Generation Discrimination.* Madison: University of Wisconsin Press.

Messner, Michael. 1992. *Power at Play: Sports and the Problem of Masculinity.* Boston: Beacon.

Metz, Mary Haywood. 1986. *Different by Design: The Context and Character of Three Magnet Schools.* New York: Routledge & Kegan Paul.

Mickelson, Roslyn, and Stephen Smith. 1995. "Education and struggle against race, class, and gender inequality." In *Race, Class, and Gender: An Anthology.* 2nd ed. Margaret Andersen and Patricia Hill Collins, eds. Belmont, CA: Wadsworth.

Minnich, Elizabeth Kamarck; Jean O'Barr; and Rachel Rosenfeld, eds. 1988. *Reconstructing the Academy: Women's Education and Women's Studies.* Chicago: University of Chicago Press.

Mishel, Lawrence, and Jared Bernstein. 1994. *The State of Working America 1994–95.* Economic Policy Institute Series, 1994–1995 ed. Armonk, NY: M. E. Sharpe.

Morgen, Sandra, and Ann Bookman. 1988. "Rethinking women and politics: An introductory essay." In *Women and the Politics of Empowerment.* Sandra Morgen and Ann Bookman, eds. Philadelphia: Temple University Press.

Mullings, Leith. 1994. "Images, ideology, and women of color." In *Women of Color in U.S. Society.* Maxine Baca Zinn and Bonnie Thornton Dill, eds. Philadelphia: Temple University Press.

Naples, Nancy. 1998. *Community Activism and Feminist Politics: Organizing Across Race, Class and Gender.* New York: Routledge.

National Center for Health Statistics. 1998. *National Vital Statistics Reports* 47(19): Hyattsville, MD: National Center for Health Statistics.

National Research Council. 1993. *National Science Education Standards Working Papers: An Enhanced Sampler (Progress Report).* National Committee on Science Education Standards and Assesssments. Washington, DC: National Research Council: February and July.

———. 1996. *National Science Education Standards.* Washington, DC: National Academy Press.

———. 1992. *Women and Minorities in Science and Engineering: An Update.* NSF 92-303. Washington, D.C.: National Science Foundation.

———. 1993. *Education and Human Resources Program for Women and Girls Program Announcement.* NSF-93-126. Arlington, VA: National Science Foundation.

Navarette, Ruben, Jr. 1997. "A darker shade of crimson: Odyssey of a Harvard Chicano." In *Race, Class, and Gender in a Diverse Society.* Diana Kendall, ed. Boston: Allyn and Bacon.

Newman, Katherine S. 1988. *Falling from Grace: The Experience of Downward Mobility in the American Middle Class.* New York: Free Press.

———. 1993. *Declining Fortunes: The Withering of the American Dream.* New York: Basic Books.

Oakes, Jeannie. 1985. *Keeping Track: How Schools Structure Inequality.* New Haven: Yale University Press.

Oakes, Jeannie, and Amy Stuart Wells. 1998. "Detracking for high student achievement." *Educational Leadership* 55(6): 38–41.

Oakes, Jeannie; Amy Stuart Wells; Makeba Jones; and Amanda Datnow. 1997. "Detracking: The social construction of ability, cultural politics, and resistance to reform." *Teachers College Record* 98(3):482–510.

Office of the Under Secretary of Defense. 1998. "Review of the effectiveness of the application and enforcement of the Department's policy on homosexual conduct in the military." Washington, DC: Available online from http://www.defenselink.mil/pubs/rpt040798.html, accessed March 19, 2000.

O'Hare, William P. 1992. "America's minorities: The demographics of diversity." *Population Bulletin* 47(4): S2(44).

Oliver, Melvin, and Thomas Shapiro. 1995. *Black Wealth/White Wealth: A New Perspective on Racial Inequality.* New York: Routledge.

Omi, Michael, and Howard Winant. 1994. *Racial Formation in the United States from the 1960s to the 1990s.* New York: Routledge.

Orfield, Gary; Mark D. Bachmeier; David R. James; and Tamela Eitle. 1997. "Deepening segregation in American public schools: A special report from the Harvard Project on School Desegregation." *Equity & Excellence in Education* 30 (September):5–24.

Orfield, Gary; Susan Eaton; and the Harvard Project on School Desegregation. 1996. *Dismantling Desegregation: The Quiet Reversal of Brown v. Board of Education.* New York: New Press.

Ornstein, Allan C., and Daniel U. Levine. 1989. "Social class, race, and school achievement: Problems and prospects." *Journal of Teacher Education* 40(5):17–23.

Ortiz, Flora Ida. 1988. "Hispanic-American children's experiences in classrooms: A comparison between Hispanic and non-Hispanic children." In *Class, Race, and Gender in American Education.* Lois Weis, ed. Albany: State University of New York Press.

Ortiz, Vilma. 1994. "Women of color: A demographic overview." In *Women of Color in U.S. Society.* Maxine Baca Zinn and Bonnie Thornton Dill, eds. Philadelphia: Temple University Press.

Ostrander, Susan. 1984. *Women of the Upper Class.* Philadelphia: Temple University Press.

Page, Reba. 1991. *Lower-Track Classrooms: A Curricula and Cultural Perspective.* New York: Teachers College Press, Columbia University.

Pallas, Aaron. 1995. "Schooling, achievement, and mobility." In *Transforming Schools.* Peter Cookson and Barbara Schneider, eds. New York: Garland.

Persell, Caroline. 1977. *Education and Inequality: A Theoretical and Empirical Synthesis.* New York: Free Press.

Phillips, Lynn, and Michelle Fine. 1992. "What's 'left' in sexuality education?" In *Sexuality and the Curriculum: The Politics and Practices of Sexuality Education.* James Sears, ed. New York: Teachers College Press, Columbia University.

Phyllis Schlafly Report. 1993. "NEA steps up anti-parent policies." September.

Pipher, Mary. 1994. *Reviving Ophelia: Saving the Selves of Adolescent Girls.* New York: Putnam.

Polakow, Valerie. 1993. *Lives on the Edge: Single Mothers and Their Children in the Other America.* Chicago: University of Chicago Press.

Postman, David, Jack Broom, and Warren King. 1999. "Clashes, protests wrack WTO—Police try to break up protesters; Clash delays opening Event." *The Seattle Times.* November 30.

Rich, Adrienne. 1993. "Compulsory heterosexuality and lesbian existence." In *The Lesbian and Gay Studies Reader.* Henry Abelove, Michèle Aina Barale, and David M. Halperin, eds. New York: Routledge.

Roberts, Sam. 1995. *Who We Are: A Portrait of America Based on the Latest U.S. Census.* Rev. ed. New York: Times Books.

Robinson, Bill. 1999. "S.C. house endorses First Steps: Hodges, lawmakers share power in plan." *The State,* (Columbia, S.C.) April 29.

Robnett, Belinda. 1997. *How Long? How Long?: African–American Women in the Struggle for Civil Rights.* New York: Oxford University Press.

Roediger, David. 1991. *The Wages of Whiteness: Race and the Making of the American Working Class.* London: Verso.

Rollins, Judith. 1985. *Between Women: Domestics and Their Employers.* Philadelphia: Temple University Press.

Root, Maria P. 1992. *Racially Mixed People in America.* Newbury Park, CA: Sage.

Rosser, Sue. 1997. *Re-Engineering Female Friendly Science.* New York: Teachers College Press, Columbia University.

Scanzoni, J.; K. Polonko; J. Teachman; and L. Thompson. 1989. *The Sexual Bond.* Newbury Park, CA: Sage.

Schmitt, Eric. 2000. "Minimum wage rise of $1 is approved." *New York Times,* March 10: A1.

Schuster, Marilyn, and Susan Van Dyne. 1984. "Placing women in the liberal arts: Stages of curriculum transformation." *Harvard Educational Review* 54(4):413–28.

Sears, James. 1989. "The impact of gender and race on growing up lesbian and gay in the South." *NWSA Journal* 1(3):422–57.

———, ed. 1992. *Sexuality and the Curriculum: The Politics and Practices of Sexuality Education.* New York: Teachers College Press, Columbia University.

Sidel, Ruth. 1996. *Keeping Women and Children Last: America's War on the Poor.* New York: Penguin.

Skidmore, Thomas E. 1993a. *Black into White: Race and Nationality in Brazilian Thought.* Durham, NC: Duke University Press.

———. 1993b. "Bi-racial U.S.A. vs. multi-racial Brazil: Is the contrast still valid?" *Journal of Latin American Studies* 25(2):373–86.

Smith, Barbara. 1993. "Homophobia: Why bring it up?" In *The Lesbian and Gay Studies Reader.* Henry Abelove; Michele Barale; and David M. Halperin, eds. New York: Routledge.

Smith, Lillian. 1949. *Killers of the Dream.* New York: Norton.

Sobel, Stacey L.; Kathi S. Westcott; Michelle M. Benecke; and C. Dixon Osburn (with Jeffrey M. Cleghorn). 2000. "Conduct unbecoming: Sixth annual report on 'don't ask, don't tell, don't pursue.' " Washington, DC: Servicemembers Legal Defense Network. Available from http://www.sldn.org/reports/sixth.htm, accessed March 19, 2000.

Solinger, Rickie. 1998. "Poisonous Choice." In *Bad Mothers: The Politics of Blame in Twentieth-Century America.* Molly Ladd-Taylor and Lauri Umansky, eds. New York: New York University Press.

———. 1992. *Wake up Little Susie: Single Pregnancy and Race Before Roe v. Wade.* New York: Routledge.

Sorokin, Pitirim. 1927. *Social Mobility.* New York: Harper.

Spade, Joan; Lynn Columba; and Beth Vanfossen. 1997. "Tracking in mathematics and science: Courses and course-selection procedures." *Sociology of Education* 70 (April):108–27.

Spickard, Paul R. 1992. "The illogic of American racial categories." In *Racially Mixed People in America.* Maria Root, ed. Newbury Park, CA: Sage.

Streitmatter, Janice. 1999. *For Girls Only: Making the Case for Single-Sex Schooling.* Albany: State University of New York Press.

Stroud, Joseph. 1999a. "Education policy draws fire: Hodges, GOP split over budget plans." *The State.* (Columbia, SC) February 28.

———. 1999b. "First Steps proposal 'welfare' in disguise, Republicans charge." *The State.* (Columbia, SC) March 3.

Sturm, Susan, and Lani Guinier. 1996. "The future of affirmative action: Reclaiming the innovative ideal." *California Law Review* 84(4): 953–1036.

Takagi, Dana. 1993. *The Retreat from Race: Asian-American Admissions and Racial Politics.* New Brunswick, NJ: Rutgers University Press.

Tavris, Carol. 1992. *The Mismeasure of Woman.* New York: Touchstone.

Terkel, Studs. 1992. *Race: How Blacks and Whites Think and Feel about the American Obsession.* New York: New Press.

Thorne, Barrie. 1993. *Gender Play: Girls and Boys in School.* New Brunswick, NJ: Rutgers University Press.

Timmer, Doug; Stanley Eitzen; and Kathryn Talley. 1994. *Paths to Homelessness: Extreme Poverty and the Urban Housing Crisis.* Boulder, CO: Westview Press.

Twine, France Winndance. 1998. *Racism in a Racial Democracy: The Maintenance of White Supremacy in Brazil.* New Brunswick, NJ: Rutgers University Press.

Tyack, David, and Larry Cuban. 1995. *Tinkering Toward Utopia: A Century of Public School Reform.* Cambridge: Harvard University Press.

U.S. Bureau of the Census. 1998a. *Statistical Abstract of the United States: 1998.* 119th ed. Washington, DC: U.S. Government Printing Office.

———. 1998b. *United States Census 2000 Dress Rehearsal.* Washington, DC: U.S. Department of Commerce, Bureau of the Census.

———. 1999. *Statistical Abstract of the United States.* 120th ed. Washington, DC. U.S. Government Printing Office.

———. 1999. *Income 1998: Historical Income Tables.* Available online from http://www.census.gov/hhes/income/histinc/incperdet.html, accessed March 19, 2000.

———. 1999. *Poverty 1998: Poverty by Selected Characteristics.* Available online from http://www.census.gov/hhes/poverty/poverty98/pv98est1.html, accessed March 19, 2000.

———. 1999. *Resident Population Estimates of the United States by Sex, Race, and Hispanic Origin: April 1, 1990 to July 1, 1999.* Available online from http://www.census.gov/population/estimates/nation/intfile3-1.txt, accessed March 19, 2000.

———. 2000. *National Estimates Quarterly Population Estimates, 1980–1990.* Washington, DC: Available online from http://www.census.gov/population/www/estimates/nat_805_detail.html, accessed March 20, 2000.

———. 2000. U.S. Bureau of the Census. *Projections of the Resident Population by Race, Hispanic Origin, and Nativity: Middle Series, 1999 and 2000 (Table NP-T5-A), 2050-2070 (Table NP-T5-G), and 2075-2100 (Table NP-T5-H),* Available online from http://www.census.gov/population/projections/nation/summary/, accessed, March 19, 2000.

U.S. Bureau of Labor Statistics. 1995. *Employment and Earnings.* 45 (1) Washington, D.C. U.S. Government Printing Office.

———. 1995. 1999. *Highlights of Women's Earnings in 1998.* Report 926 (April). Washington, D.C. U.S. Government Printing Office.

U.S. Department of Education. 1994a. "Distribution of college-bound senior and average verbal and mathematics SAT scores by selected characteristics." In *The Condition of Education.* Washington, DC: U. S. Government Printing Office: Table 19-4:227.

———. 1994b. "Percent of high school seniors who plan to go to college after graduation by student characteristics: 1982 and 1992." *Digest of Education Statistics.* Washington, DC: National Center for Educational Statistics: Table 144:138.

Valdes, Guadalupe. 1996. *Con Respeto: Bridging the Distances Between Culturally Diverse Families and Schools: An Ethnographic Portrait.* New York: Teachers College Press, Columbia University.

Van Ausdale, Debra, and Joe Feagin. 1996. "Using racial and ethnic concepts: The critical case of very young children." *American Sociological Review* 61(October):779–93

Van den Berg, Axel. 1993. "Creeping embourgeoisement? Some comments on the Marxist discovery of the new middle class." In *Research in Social Stratification and Mobility,* 12, Robert Althauser and Michael Wallace, eds. Greenwich, CT: JAI Press.

Vanneman, Reeve, and Lynn Weber Cannon. 1987. *The American Perception of Class.* Philadelphia: Temple University Press.

Weber, Lynn. 1990. "Fostering positive race, class, and gender dynamics in the classroom." *Women's Studies Quarterly* 18 (Spring/Summer, 1990):126–134.

———. 1995. "On West and Ferstermaker's 'doing difference.' " *Gender & Society* 9(4):499–503.

———. 2000. "Empowering Students Through Classroom Discussion Guidelines." In *Teaching Sociological Concepts and the Sociology of Gender,* Marybeth C. Stalp and Julie Childers, eds. Washington, D.C.: American Sociological Association Teaching Resources Center.

Weber, Lynn, and Elizabeth Higginbotham. 1992. "Moving up with kin and community: Upward social mobility for black and white women," *Gender and Society* 6 (September):416–40.

———. 1997. "Black and white professional-managerial women's perceptions of racism and sexism in the workplace." In *Women and Work: Exploring Race, Ethnicity, and Class* 6. Elizabeth Higginbotham and Mary Romero, eds. Thousand Oaks, CA: Sage.

Weber, Lynn; Tina Hancock; and Elizabeth Higginbotham. 1997. "Women, power, and mental Health." In *Women's Health: Complexities and Differences.* Sheryl Ruzek, Virginia Olesen, and Adele Clark, eds. Columbus: Ohio State University Press.

Weber, Lynn; Elizabeth Higginbotham; and Bonnie Thornton Dill. 1997. "Sisterhood as collaboration: Building the Center for Research on Women at the University of Memphis." In *Feminist Sociology: Life Histories of a Movement.* Barbara Laslett and Barrie Thorne, eds. New Brunswick, NJ: Rutgers University Press.

Weber Cannon, Lynn; Elizabeth Higginbotham; and Marianne Leung. 1988. "Race and class bias in qualitative research on women." *Gender & Society* 2(Winter):449–62.

Weis, Lois, ed. 1988. *Class, Race, and Gender in American Education.* Albany: State University of New York Press.

Weis, Lois, and Michelle Fine, eds. 1993. *Beyond Silenced Voices: Class, Race, and Gender in United States Schools.* Albany: State University of New York Press.

Weiss, Daniel Evan. 1991. *The Great Divide: How Females and Males Really Differ.* New York: Poseidon Press.

Wells, Amy S., and Jeannie Oakes. 1996. "Potential pitfalls of systemic reform: Early lessons from research on detracking." *Sociology of Education* [*Extra Issue*]: 135–43.

West, Candace, and Sarah Fenstermaker. 1995. "Doing difference." *Gender and Society* 9(1):8–37.

West, Cornel. 1993. *Race Matters.* Boston: Beacon Press.

Western, Mark, and Erik Olin Wright. 1994. "The permeability of class boundaries to intergenerational mobility among men in the United States, Canada, Norway, Sweden." *American Sociological Review* 59(August):606–29.

"Why choose a women's College?" Women's College Coalition, available from http://www.scrippscol.edu/~dept/admission/wmnscol.htm, accessed March 2000.

Williams, Rhonda. 1997. "Living at the crossroads: Explorations in race, nationality, sexuality and gender." In *The House that Race Built: Black Americans, U.S. Terrain.* Wahneema Lubiano, ed. New York: Random House.

Wilson, William J. 1987. *The Truly Disadvantaged: The Inner City, the Underclass, and Public Policy.* Chicago: University of Chicago Press.

Woliver, Laura. 1998. "Social movements and abortion law." In *Social Movements and American Political Institutions.* A. N. Costain and A. S. McFarland, eds. Lanham, MD: Rowman and Littlefield.

Woo, Deborah. 1995. "The gap between striving and achieving: The case of Asian American women." In *Race, Class, and Gender: An Anthology*. Margaret Andersen, and Patricia Hill Collins, eds. Belmont, CA: Wadsworth.

Wright, Erik Olin. 1989. *The Debate on Classes*. New York: Verso.

———. 1997. *Class Counts: Comparative Studies in Class Analysis*. NY, NY: Cambridge University Press.

Wrigley, Julia, ed. 1992. *Education and Gender Equality*. Washington, DC: Falmer Press.

Wyche, Karen Fraser, and Sherryl Browne Graves. 1992. "Minority women in academia: Access and barriers to professional participation." *Psychology of Women Quarterly* 16(4):429–37.

Yoder, Janice D., and Arnold S. Kahn. 1992. "Toward a feminist understanding of women and power." *Psychology of Women Quarterly* 16(4):381–88.

Young, Susan. 1999. "School funding fails to close gap." *Bangor Daily News*. 20 February.

Permission Acknowledgments

CHAPTER 2

Lani Guinier, excerpt from "Reframing the affirmative action debate" (Speech, University of South Carolina, February 26, 1998). Reprinted with the permission of Lani Guinier.

Figure 2.1: "Immigration Trends by Region of Birth and Period of Immigration: 1990" based on Barry R. Chiswick and Teresa Sullivan, "The new immigrants" in Reynolds Farley (ed.), *State of the Union: America in the 1990's, Volume Two: Social Trends.* Copyright © 1995 by Russell Sage Foundation. Reprinted with the permission of Russell Sage Foundation.

Table 2.4: "Share of National Income: Ratio of Rich to Poor" from Andrew Hacker, *Money: Who Has How Much and Why.* Copyright © 1997 by Andrew Hacker. Reprinted with the permission of Scribner, a division of Simon & Schuster, Inc. and the Robin Straus Agency, Inc.

CHAPTERS 3, 4, AND 10

Studs Terkel, excerpts from "Margaret Welch," "Albert Hourani," and "Mamie Mobley" from *Race: How Blacks and Whites Think and Feel About the American Obsession* (New York: The New Press, 1992). Copyright © 1992 by Studs Terkel. Reprinted with the permission of Donadio & Olson, Inc.

CHAPTER 4

Martin Manalansan IV, excerpts from "In the shadows of Stonewall: Examining gay transnational politics and the diasporic dilemma" from *Gay and Lesbian Quarterly 2* (1995). Copyright © 1995. All rights reserved. Reprinted with the permission of Duke University Press.

Barbara Ehrenreich, excerpt from "Nickel-and dimed: On (not) getting by in America" from *Harper's* (January 1999). Copyright © 1999 by Barbara Ehrenreich. Reprinted with the permission of International Creative Management, Inc.

CHAPTERS 6 AND 7

Langston Hughes, "Dream Variations" and "Harlem (A Dream Deferred)" from *Collected Poems.* Copyright © 1994 by the Estate of Langston Hughes. Reprinted with the permission of Alfred A. Knopf, a division of Random House, Inc. and Harold Ober Associates, Incorporated.

CHAPTER 7

Fran Lebowitz, excerpt from "Fran Liebowitz on race" in *Vanity Fair* (October 1997). Copyright © 1997 by Fran Lebowitz. Reprinted with the permission of William Morris Agency.

CHAPTER 8

Jeannie Oakes, excerpts from *Keeping Track: How Schools Structure Inequality.* Copyright © 1985. Reprinted with the permission of Yale University Press.

Jean Anyon, excerpts from "Social class and the hidden curriculum of work" from *Transforming Curriculum for a Culturally Diverse Society,* edited by Etta R. Hollins. Copyright © 1996. Reprinted with the permission of Lawrence Erlbaum Associates.

Table 8.1: "Average scores on SAT and ACT by sex and race, 1996" from *The Chronicle of Higher Education* (September 2, 1996). Copyright © 1996. Reprinted with the permission of *The Chronicle of Higher Education.*

CHAPTERS 8 AND 9

Valerie Polakow, excerpts from *Lives on the Edge: Single Mothers and Their Children in the Other America.* Copyright © 1993. Reprinted with the permission of The University of Chicago Press.

CHAPTER 9

Van Ausdale and Joe Feagin, excerpts from "The use of racial and ethnic concepts by very young children" in *American Sociological Review 61* (1996). Copyright © 1996 by the American Sociological Association. Reprinted with the permission of the publishers.

Name Index

Subject Index